LOCALIZING FOREIGN POLICY

Also by Brian Hocking

AUSTRALIA TOWARDS 2000 (*editor*)

WORLD POLITICS: An Introduction to International Relations (*with Michael Smith*)

Localizing Foreign Policy

Non-Central Governments and Multilayered Diplomacy

Brian Hocking

Principal Lecturer in International Relations
Coventry University

150th YEAR
M

St. Martin's Press

Softcover reprint of the hardcover 1st edition 1993

First published in Great Britain 1993 by
THE MACMILLAN PRESS LTD
Houndmills, Basingstoke, Hampshire RG21 2XS
and London
Companies and representatives
throughout the world

A catalogue record for this book is available
from the British Library.

ISBN 978-1-349-22965-9 ISBN 978-1-349-22963-5 (eBook)
DOI 10.1007/978-1-349-22963-5

First published in the United States of America 1993 by
Scholarly and Reference Division,
ST. MARTIN'S PRESS, INC.,
175 Fifth Avenue,
New York, N.Y. 10010

ISBN 978-0-312-09720-2

Library of Congress Cataloging-in-Publication Data
Hocking, Brian.
Localizing foreign policy : non-central governments and multilayered diplomacy / Brian Hocking.
p. cm.
Includes bibliographical references and index.
ISBN 978-0-312-09720-2
1. International relations. 2. Federal government.
3. International law. I. Title.
K3201.H63 1993
327.1'1—dc20 93–18910
CIP

Contents

Introduction

Understanding the complexities of international politics increasingly demands an awareness of domestic politics and their institutional frameworks. Similarly, political processes within national boundaries are hard to disentangle without reference to the international environment in which they occur. This applies as much to the policy practitioner as to the analyst, since appreciating the actual – and the potential – linkages, between what have been regarded traditionally as relatively discrete levels of political activity impinges on the achievement of policy objectives.

One consequence of the growing interrelatedness of the domestic and international arenas has been to highlight the significance of political and societal structures to the conduct of foreign policy: the need for policy makers both to control, where they can, those elements of their own social and political systems which affect the attainment of goals within the broader international environment whilst, at the same time, alerting themselves to the relevant features of other states' internal structures. Domestic political institutions and the processes of which they are a part have become, in short, indices on the inventory of national power. Considerable attention has been paid to some manifestations of the trend: intra- and inter-bureaucratic relations being one of them. To take another instance, those who wish to understand – and to influence – the formulation of foreign policy in Washington are continually reminded of the significant role played by Congress.

The same appears increasingly to be true of the territorial distribution of power within the state as non-central governments (NCGs), often acting as the mouthpiece of local economic interests, seek both to influence national external policies and, moreover, to operate in the international arena on their own behalf. Whilst this trend is present even in highly centralized states such as France, it has become particularly notable in federal systems. Despite the fact that federal constitutions emphasize the primacy of the central government in the conduct of foreign relations and, indeed, that this has been regarded as a characteristic of federal systems, it became evident during the 1970s and 1980s that local and regional authorities were demonstrating an enhanced interest in the international environment, motivated in particular by the impact of external economic forces.

Seen by some as a dangerous aberration from central control over foreign policy prescribed by constitutional law, it has become increasingly clear that the growing international interest demonstrated by NCGs is but part of a broader process whereby foreign policy is becoming 'localized'. That is to say, an ever-growing range of local groups and governmental agencies perceive themselves to be affected by events outside their national settings, and have the motivation, resources and opportunities to respond by projecting their interests at both the national and international level. Whether it be local governments in the US passing resolutions on nuclear weapons, hoping thereby to nudge the Reagan Administration towards engaging in Strategic Arms Reduction Talks, city administrations adopting disinvestment policies towards South Africa or NCGs seeking to influence the content of foreign economic policy and to be involved in the processes through which it is shaped, the stimulus to action reflects the intermingling of local interests and the patterns of national foreign relations. The complex relationships that this can create is thrown into sharp relief in the case of the triangular relationship between the German *Länder*, Bonn and the European Community, particularly in the case of the *Länders'* threat not to ratify the Maastricht treaty.

A key problem when confronting these developments is to make some sense of them, however. As Chapter 2 demonstrates, the growth of international interests and activity at the local level is subject to differing interpretations. For some it represents a highly desirable democratization of the foreign policy processes, traditionally the preserve of the executive; even, perhaps, an opportunity to restructure the international order towards more just and peaceful goals. For others, localization is a dangerous derogation from governments' power to conduct a coherent foreign policy, providing the opportunity for other state and non-state actors to profit from internal divisions. Furthermore, on the surface there appears to be a contradiction between the forces of globalization and enhanced economic interdependence between national communities on one side and development of localization on the other.

What appears to confront us are not so much well-defined developments marking the predominance of any one political arena, but a bewildering network of linkages between those arenas through which actors relate to each other in a variety of ways. In other words, policy-makers are required to operate to an increasing extent in a 'multilevel' political environment spanning subnational, national and international arenas where the achievement of goals at one level of political activity demands an ability to operate in the others.

Partly because of this, the traditional distinctions between domestic and foreign policy are becoming harder to sustain. Strategies for accomplishing external policy goals often require, therefore, that negotiators conduct diplomacy in several environments simultaneously, weaving into a tapestry threads of international and domestic negotiation. In this sense, what was regarded traditionally as a phenomenon of international politics – diplomacy – has assumed a domestic dimension which, as trade negotiations demonstrate, are crucial to its success.

Put another way, governments and non-state actors are constrained to pursue a 'multilayered' diplomacy in a variety of political theatres. Such a task poses daunting challenges; not only are there more pieces on the diplomatic chessboard, negotiators are required to play several games on different boards simultaneously. At the same time, however, strategic manipulation of domestic interests, one's own or those of negotiating partners, can become a weapon in the attainment of policy goals.

The central purpose of this study is to cast some light on this phenomenon by examing the international interests and activities of NCGs in federal states. In doing so, it starts with assumptions which set it apart from some of the literature on NCG international activities which began to proliferate in the 1970s and 1980s, a good deal of which has tended to focus on the significance of NCGs in terms of their uniqueness as international actors and their separateness from traditional modes of diplomatic intercourse. Such a tendency has been reinforced by those who have seen in the growth of transborder linkages between regions of different nation-states (such as the US states and the Canadian provinces) indications of a new international order suggestive of the demise of national governments.

As a consequence, rather than attempting to locate NCGs within the foreign policy processes alongside their national governments, there has been a strong presumption that each have incompatible interests and stand in opposition to one another. Such a belief ignores the processes which are rendering the boundaries demarcating state and non-state actors far more permeable than hitherto and creating ambiguities about the status and characteristics of each.

The picture has been clouded further by the emphasis in the literature of international interdependence on change at the systemic level and the relative inattention to the changing character of the foreign policy processes which is accompanying it. Consequently, the impact of the image of NCG international activity thus created has been to set it apart from the patterns of traditional diplomacy, to seek new terms to describe it (such as 'paradiplomacy' and 'protodiplomacy') which serve to reinforce the distinction, and to emphasize the elements of conflict between national and subnational governments which have accompanied its growth. Furthermore, and somewhat ironically, given the desire of some observers to use this phenomenon as a means of rejecting the distortions of state-centric interpretations of world politics, NCGs themselves have tended to be treated as unitary actors, whereas, in reality, they represent quite complex patterns of relationships both inside and outside their national settings, and embrace a diversity of interests.

In contrast to these images, and building on the picture of multilevel politics with its associated multilayered diplomacy outlined above, the interpretation of NCG international involvement developed here is somewhat different. Far from being viewed as unique diplomatic players, NCGs become integrated into a densely-textured web of multilayered diplomacy, in which they are capable of performing a variety of roles at different points in the policy process. In so doing, they may become opponents of national objectives; but, equally, they can serve as allies and agents in the pursuit of those objectives. Thus whereas conflict between central and non-central authorities over the latters' international activities is certainly a part of the picture, it is only a part of a complex pattern of changing attitudes and relationships. The nature of contemporary public policy with its dual domestic-international features, creates a mutual dependency between the levels of government and an interest in devising cooperative mechanisms and strategies to promote the interests of each level.

ORGANIZATION AND STRUCTURE

In pursuing this theme, the first two chapters set the scene for the ensuing examination of multilayered diplomacy and the role of NCGs within it by considering the factors underpinning the localization of foreign policy, its impact on the conduct of foreign relations generally and, more specifically, in federal systems. Having surveyed the broad characteristics of the existing literature on the international activities of the constituent governments in federations, an alternative perspective is offered which seeks to locate NCGs within the complex processes of multilayered diplomacy. The emphasis of this perspective is on the variety of roles that they can assume and the points in the policy cycle where those roles are performed.

Clearly, however, generalizations regarding these roles can be misleading. Not only do federal systems differ in terms of the extent to which, and the ways in which, they reflect the phenomenon of foreign policy localization, but NCGs within the same system are likely to have varying levels of international interests. Hence Chapter 2 examines the factors that determine the scope and intensity of NCG international activity. One of these, not unexpectedly, will be the characteristics of a given issue. It is argued, however, that the assumption that NCGs are involved only in 'low' foreign policy is erroneous. In terms of the significance to national governments of the issues in which NCGs can become involved, these often acquire the status of 'high' policy. Furthermore, as the nuclear ships issue in Australia demonstrates, foreign policy localization can touch the core of traditional high policy, namely military security. This theme is pursued in Chapter 3. In examining the trade and investment interests of NCGs, and their growing desire to gain a voice in the shaping of foreign economic policy, it becomes clear that localities are developing international trade policies which may complement, or cut across, those of national governments.

Chapters 4, 5 and 6 pursue these ideas in the context of three examples of multilayered diplomacy in which NCGs have assumed key roles: the Canada–US free trade negotiations; the dispute between British firms and certain US state governments over the latters' 'unitary taxation' policies, and the conflict between Ottawa and Washington over acid rain. In each case, the objective is to examine why and how NCGs become involved, their roles and the consequences of their involvement at the local, national and international levels.

Chapter 7 is concerned primarily with the management of foreign policy in federal states and the bureaucratic processes that foreign policy localization, and its attendant multilayered diplomacy, have produced. The assumption here is that both central and constituent governments in federal states have a mutual interest in developing linkages and cooperative practices in pursuit of their respective international interests. In other words, patterns of intergovernmental relations so characteristic of contemporary federalism have been extended to the conduct of foreign relations. Not only does this qualify the image of irreconcilable conflict as central government seeks to deny NCGs an international 'voice', it also offers a useful corrective to the assumption that the intermeshing of domestic and foreign policy leads inevitably to a diminished role for foreign ministries. Like many bureaucratic structures, they are capable of developing strategies to contain the challenges that confront them from within the political system.

Chapter 8 attempts to weave together these threads by considering the impact of foreign policy localization and multilayered diplomacy on both national policy makers and the pattern of international relations. Traditionally, federations have been regarded as deficient in key qualities when it comes to the conduct of foreign policy. One question that underpins this study, however, is that of the qualities appropriate to the conduct of contemporary foreign relations, and the extent to which NCG international involvement may be as much a positive as a negative factor in the achievement of foreign policy goals.

Whilst this is intended as a study in the conduct of foreign policy, by its very nature it is also an essay on contemporary federalism. Given the linkages between domestic and international policy, it could hardly be anything else. But it is apparent that, just as the conduct of foreign relations can no longer be understood without reference to domestic politics, so an understanding of the character of modern federalism has to embrace the international dimension. With the globalization and regionalization of the international economy, the relationships between national governments, the regions that constitute the communities over which they preside and the international arena are in a state of flux. The creation of the Single European Market in Europe has, for example, alerted both national and subnational policy makers in Canada, Australia and the US to the fact that, despite the 'federal' status of these countries, their constituent units are divided by a range of non-tariff barriers to trade which create economic inefficiencies.

Thus it is not only the case that the interplay of politics within federal states – as with other political systems – helps to determine the choices and strategies of foreign policy managers; processes and events within the international arena pose problems for the workings of federal systems and challenge assumptions regarding the roles of, and relationships between, their constituent elements.

ACKNOWLEDGEMENTS

Most of the fieldwork on which this study is based was conducted between 1984 and 1990 in Australia, Canada and the US. During this period, some one hundred and fifty interviews with officials, politicians and representatives of the private sector at both central and non-central levels were conducted. These, together with academic colleagues in each of the three countries, were generous with their help and the source of considerable documentation. It would be invidious to single out individuals but my thanks is due to them all. As is always the case, responsibility for errors of fact and eccentricities of interpretation is solely my own.

Conducting research in federal states given their size – and, of course, in the case of this study, the distances involved in reaching the countries under investigation – is expensive. The project could not have been undertaken without the financial support of the Economic and Social Research Council who funded the main body of the research. Thanks are also due to the British Academy and the Central Research Fund of Coventry University for assistance with particular aspects of the project.

1 Localizing Foreign Policy

A leading article in a 1983 issue of the *Wall Street Journal* headed 'George v. Maggie', concerned a dilemma then facing President Reagan: in the long-running dispute over the practice, employed by some US state governments, whereby they taxed foreign corporations on the basis of their worldwide earnings (the 'unitary taxation' controversy examined later in this book) how should the president balance the pressures flowing from the international environment on the one hand – epitomized by the intervention of the British Prime Minister, Margaret Thatcher – and domestic sensitivities, particularly those of California, presided over by Governor George Deukmejian, on the other? Foreign policy or domestic politics? Both – or more precisely an intricate blend of the two which has become increasingly familiar in the conduct of contemporary foreign policy.

What has long been apparent in the world of the policy maker has more lately been reflected in academic analysis. Writes Robert Putnam:

> The most portentous development in the fields of comparative politics and international relations in recent years is the dawning recognition among practitioners in each field of the need to take into account entanglements between the two.[1]

Some might wish to insert 'potentially' before 'portentous' bearing in mind the disparity between assertions of the importance of domestic-international linkages and the analysis of their nature and consequences. Nevertheless, we are confronted daily with obvious manifestations of the interconnectedness of 'domestic' and 'international' politics and at least one neologism, 'intermestic' has been coined to celebrate this trend.[2]

One consequence of this for those engaged in contemporary diplomacy is the need to be sensitive not only to their own domestic political structures and processes but those of negotiating partners. Knowledge of one's own social and political system and that of others becomes, in short, a critical factor in the equation of national power, a major element in the often shadowy processes in the 'conversion process' through which power capabilities are transformed into actual influence. As one of the several studies of the GATT Tokyo Round negotiations has noted, interdependence subsumes interactions between the whole fabric of national and international legal and constitutional systems.[3] Trade policy (in common with other issues on the agenda) is thus conducted in a highly complex environment wherein domestic and international issues and actors jostle one another as they seek to gain the attention of those charged with policy management.

Because of this, domestic political structures, access to them and control over that access, have become critical factors in the achievement of policy goals. Consequently, governments are frequently concerned to control (where this is possible) linkages created by transnational interactions just as foreign governments have come to recognize that their own objectives may demand influence over social groupings within other countries alongside the traditional patterns of intergovernmental diplomacy.

These nationally related concerns merge imperceptibly, of course, into the broader concerns of the international community as a whole. The very fact that domestic political and non-political actors together with the interests they represent are affected by events outside local and national settings enhances the degree to which they are impelled to influence events at the international level. Where this is reinforced by considerable power over a policy area (for example, the role of Congress in the conduct of US trade policy), then the tendency is all the more notable.[4] This, in turn, makes the creation and maintenance of regimes to manage international problems measurably harder. As Chapter 6 suggests, the environmental agenda offers an illuminating example of the problem. Controlling transboundary air pollution is as much a domestic problem as it is an international one. In part, this is because environmental control measures in this, as in other areas, involve sensitive economic and political choices. But beyond this, their development and implementation require the active cooperation of subnational political authorities whose powers and responsibilities make them significant players in the formulation of national environmental policies and, thereby, important to the politics surrounding the negotiation of international agreements.

INTERNATIONALIZATION AND LOCALIZATION

Contemporary diplomacy is therefore characterized by apparently paradoxical trends: on one side, a growing internationalization as national governments respond to an expanding range of international linkages, economic interdependence and the demands of policy issues which can no longer be managed within the framework of individual political systems. On the other, a growing alertness on the part of subnational interests, both governmental and non-governmental, to these pressures as their effects become evident to a wide range of domestic constituencies and those who represent them at the local level.

Indeed, there is a tendency to regard the relationship between these processes of internationalization and localization of the foreign policy milieu in 'zero-sum' terms rather than as complementary to each other. Hence Evan Luard has argued that the 'globalization' of politics has created a situation in which national political arenas have become redundant and 'the only type of political action which is significant is international action'.[5] In the context of the environmental agenda for example, the argument stresses the importance of the international over the national:

> effective political activity relating to the environment today can only take place at the global level. Because it is there, not in the relatively insignificant decisions of national states, that the important steps for safeguarding the world's threatened natural heritage must be taken, it is there too that in the future the significant political struggles will occur.[6]

Whilst there is an apparent logic to such arguments, given the nature of these and other problems which require collective action at the international level, there are several reasons why they are misleading and ultimately unhelpful in dealing with the problems to which they are directed.

First of all, the international processes and institutions which are seen as symbolic of the need and capacity to 'act internationally' are not remote from national governments, unrelated to their interests and policies or removed from the patterns of domestic politics over which they preside. It is not simply that international institutions are part of national governments' foreign policy framework – influencing actions on the one hand; to be used where possible as a means of achieving goals on the other – but that the success of such institutions is often dependent on the willingness and capacity of states to implement their decisions. Neither level of political action can ignore the other. Consequently, internal political structures, the nature of the distribution of power within domestic settings, even the character of political cultures within communities, become relevant to the construction and maintenance of international regimes.[7]

In the case of the environmental agenda, the national-international linkage is reinforced by the very character of the issues involved. Underneath the scientific debates that characterize this policy area there lie difficult economic and political choices. It is one thing to argue that 'something must be done' to combat the problems of air and water pollution, for example; quite another to obtain the necessary agreement to act where corporate profits and the livelihood of employees are involved. Thus limiting emissions of sulphur dioxide will almost certainly create interregional tensions between industrial and non-industrial regions and those localities blessed with 'clean' and those with 'dirty' coal. Because solutions to problems of this kind involve issues of such sensitivity, the patterns of domestic and international politics can easily become enmeshed. It also has to be remembered that the stimulus to national action on the international plane often comes from pressure groups whose membership is organized at the local level. For many activists in the environmental as in other areas, the locality offers a route to political participation represented in the maxim 'think globally, act locally'.

In other words, it is unhelpful to suggest that the challenges that the contemporary international agenda present to decision makers can be perceived as demanding the acceptance of a hierarchy of political arenas and that, in particular, domestic politics, including the politics of the locality, have been rendered irrelevant by the emergence of problems requiring action at other levels. Rather, it appears to be more helpful to an understanding of the complexities of contemporary diplomacy to recognize that much of it is conducted within the framework of complex 'multilevel' political structures and processes that embrace all levels of political activity from the local, through the national to the international. Moreover, these levels intersect with one another in a variety of ways; that is to say, relationships are not ordered in any predictable fashion and a variety of linkage patterns between the levels may develop.

As the following chapter suggests, the realities of multilevel politics demands that decision makers operate in a number of political arenas simultaneously. In particular, they are frequently required to negotiate with local interests in the pursuit of international objectives. It is the nature of these processes, to which we shall assign the term 'multilayered diplomacy', that the following chapter examines. For the moment, the focus of discussion turns to the phenomenon of localization of foreign policy, its nature, the implications for the management of foreign relations and, in particular, the experience of federal states in this regard.

THE NATURE AND CAUSES OF FOREIGN POLICY LOCALIZATION

The growing literature on the role of localities in foreign relations is stimulated by a number of normative orientations and methodological persuasions in the study of international relations, combined with developments in policy processes at both the domestic and international levels. Consequently, explanations of the causes of a growing interest in international issues on the part of subnational actors and their representatives at the local level may vary depending on the perspective being brought to bear on the phenomenon. At the same time, it is possible to identify two key causal factors: the changing nature of the environment in which public policy is conducted and the growing capacity of a range of interest and pressure groups to use the local political arena as a means of achieving objectives at the international level (and vice versa).

The Changing Policy Environment

High on the list of factors to be considered here, of course, are the well-rehearsed consequences of economic interdependence, technological change and enhanced communications. These have at once created the opportunity, desire and the need for localities to adopt an international perspective and for central governments to encourage the controlled involvement of regions in specific areas of external relations. The broad dimensions of Keohane and Nye's 'complex interdependence' are familiar and emphasise the decreasing capacity of the state to act as a coherent entity whose collective interests can be represented and expressed by a central authority.[8]

On the one hand, the expanding agenda of world politics has resulted in a diversification of the channels through which governments conduct their business as reflected in the proliferation of international contacts between departments traditionally regarded as 'domestic' elements of the bureaucratic structure: on the other, a broad spectrum of groupings, governmental and non-governmental, interact across national boundaries producing, thereby, a complex web of relationships which embraces sub-national actors.

Underpinning these trends are two developments which both reflect and help to explain them: the expanding agenda of foreign policy and the diminishing distinctions between domestic and foreign policy. Not only have economic and technological changes broadened the spectrum of issues on which international politics turn, but traditional distinctions between 'high' and 'low' politics and the assumption that the former is represented solely by issues relating to military security, appear far removed from reality. Where economic interests are affected by the international environment and where issues (such as ethnic and human rights matters) stimulate an enhanced interest on the part of domestic groups in influencing events outside and across national boundaries as well as within them, so traditional distinctions between the realms of domestic and foreign policy become hazier.[9] Moreover, some foreign policy issue areas begin to acquire the political characteristics more usually associated with domestic policy with its emphasis on bargaining and compromise.

These processes have helped to produce the major structural changes which Daniel Bell equates with post-industrialism, for there is an obvious link between economic and political structures. As Greer has noted, in the beginning foreign policy was the policy of cities.[10] The emergence of the nation-state and industrialization witnessed a growing centralization which, in turn, is being reversed with the decline of industrial societies: information societies, like agricultural societies, tend to be decentralized. At one level, therefore, the international economy is becoming increasingly integrated whilst many individual polities are becoming more and more fragmented. In turn, this relates to another causal factor in the foreign policy localization picture, namely the frequent inability of modern governments to manage the political systems over which they preside and to satisfy the demands generated within them.

This problem has a general, and a more specific, foreign policy dimension. Taking the more general first, a growing desire by localities to become involved in ever larger sectors of public policy reflects the fact that national governments often find it impossible to serve community interests from a single centre of power. Frequently, complex problems simply do not respond to master-plans devised at the centre; attention has to be paid to the specific needs generated by local conditions and interests. Large central bureaucratic structures lack the knowledge and flexibility to do this. Responding to the problem by decentralization however, whilst it may resolve specific issues, is likely to reinforce demands for more autonomy and greater freedom for local jurisdictions to operate internationally where this is perceived to be necessary. This linkage between central government ineffectiveness and local international involvement has been well-summarized by Seyom Brown:

> In some countries where the national government is ineffective in dealing with the concerns of subnational communities and especially where such communities are concentrated in particular provinces or localities, provincial or local governments have been asserting themselves, not only as agencies of advocacy for the cultural and human rights of the aggrieved communities, but increasingly as their economic agents in the global market place, negotiating trade and investment arrangements with similar subunits of government in other countries.[11]

On the more specific, foreign policy level, confidence in central government management has also declined. Shuman, in his survey of local foreign policies in the US points to growing disenchantment with the Reagan administration's policies on arms control in Central America and towards South Africa as major factors in the development of what he terms 'citizen diplomacy' in the 1980s. Given the oft-asserted requirements for the conduct of foreign policy – coherence, continuity and bipartisanship – this is not infrequently regarded as a particularly serious dimension of the diminution of control exercised by national governments. Yet it can also be perceived as another indication of the growing intricacy of the processes by which public policy is managed. 'The last thing an overworked, underfunded executive branch needs is direct micromanagement of thousands of local investment, cultural exchange and border coordination activities'.[12]

The fact that these issues are identified as falling within traditional definitions of 'foreign policy' and hence within the constitutional preserve of national governments, may well be less significant than are the advantages accruing from a degree of decentralization in the management of external relations. In any case, given the intricate web of relationships that span the globe, trying to prevent local/international involvement developing may well be a fruitless task.

In sum, foreign policy localization is a result of the growing concern on the part of NCGs, localities and their administrative apparatuses to cope with the impact of forces and events that lie outside the national domain. Two obvious dimensions to this process can be detected. Firstly, at the level of non-central governments there is a recognition that the needs of the locality cannot be satisfied without greater involvement in the international system. Hence the proliferation of attempts by NCGs to attract international investment and promote exports from their regions, a phenomenon examined in Chapter 3.

Second, national governments, confronted by an ever more complex policy environment, struggling to manage their foreign relations in the face of multiple external pressures, may seek to divert these by delegating their responsibilities. This may occur in specific functional areas: actively encouraging local export promotions programmes, for example; or in the case of difficult and sensitive bilateral relations, especially where transboundary relations are involved. Here, the combination of local domestic issues and broader international relationships can create significant problems for foreign policy managers and underscores the advantages of devolving the management of regional cross-border issues to the localities involved.

At a broader level, growing internationalization is demanding that governments reevaluate the strategies by which they can manage the problems that this creates. Japan, for example, appears to be conscious of a need, despite its economic success, to develop means by which Japanese society can relate more closely to the international community. Hence the desire of Tokyo to develop a programme intended to 'internationalize' the regions and to produce a multipolar, decentralized country more open to international exchanges. In a different context, Beijing has found it convenient for the accomplishment of foreign economic policy goals to allow the provinces greater scope in developing external economic relationships.[13]

In short, the changing context in which public policy is managed is helping to endow localities with an international profile. To the localist–internationalist pressures of social activism, examined below, which can involve non-central governments in foreign policy, often to their discomfiture, are added governmental responses to the difficulties of policy management. Alongside the growth in linkages between national communities, interdependence is also helping to change the relationships between levels of government within them.

Localization and Social Activism

Another element in the growing localization of foreign policy is closely related to the problem of policy manageability – namely the consequences of a growing disillusion with and alienation from modern politics which often underlies the growing desire of a wide range of groupings to engage in political activities which cut across national boundaries. Here, however, the emphasis is not on adapting political structures to the needs of societies but on bypassing legal and territorial definitions of politics by involving new constituencies in the political processes and redefining the agenda of politics.

According to Sheth, for example, the institutions of conventional politics have 'run their course' and should be replaced by a 'more participative and humane politics'.[14] The stimulus towards internationalization comes from two directions: firstly, action groups recognize that local power structures gain much of their power from the national and international power structures to which they are linked, thus requiring them to involve themselves in politics at the global level. Secondly, national governments, as the representatives of traditional political structures and the guardians of the international order of which they are part, are aware of the transnational processes through which both might be undermined. Especially within the states of the Third World, activist groups are challenging the élites in their own societies and, thereby, threatening to project domestic political stresses and strains onto the international stage. From both directions, a rejection of the basic features and structures of modern politics is turning the local into the international.

Underpinning each of these forces for foreign policy localization is to be found a growing capacity for individuals to operate internationally.[15] Decentralization encourages individual involvement in international issues whilst the pressures that stem from individual demands produce an inclination on the part of central administrations to respond to and involve people at the local level. It should not be assumed, as Rosenau points out, that all individual involvement in international issues is mediated through groups. The phenomenon of what he terms 'leaderless publics' whose opinions and interests are aggregated by such means as newspaper reports and public opinion polls can influence the character and content of public policy in the absence of mediating group actors.[16]

Nor, of course, should it be assumed that there is an automatic linkage between enhanced public awareness of global issues and the desire to act internationally. Apart from the obvious point that individual capacities vary, so do attitudes and beliefs regarding the appropriateness of local involvement in international affairs. Both Alger and Shuman point out that local administrative bodies vary in their attitudes towards involvement in international issues. Thus whilst many local government bodies around the world have been active in declaring themselves nuclear-free zones, some have consciously rejected such moves on the grounds that they relate to issues outside their area of responsibility.[17] Futhermore, it is not necessarily the case that individuals who have international concerns choose to achieve their goals by linking the micro and macro levels of politics. This is but one strategy and stands alongside those which involve individuals working at the international and national levels and for whom the involvement of the locality is peripheral to their concerns.[18]

Pressures for foreign policy localization often come from groups whose interests are related to specific causes. Greenpeace, Friends of the Earth, the Campaign for Nuclear Disarmament are each issue-specific groupings whose strategies involve the internationalization of the domestic and the domestication of the international. Social activism need not, however, as already noted, be organized but can be articulated through unstructured mechanisms such as those provided by the media.

Whatever forms it assumes, localization as activism is directed towards affecting policy at both home and abroad and rests on the perception that people 'are growing in their comprehension of how the foreign policy of states affect their local community and are attempting to mobilize local action in response to those policies'.[19]

It should be emphasized that Alger and others see such developments as qualitatively different from mere pressure group politics directed towards issues that transcend national political communities. Whereas they might embrace traditional populist forms, there is – to use a phrase employed by Walker and Mendlovitz – 'a sense of something new'. The newly emerging social movements possess a 'willingness to articulate alternative ways of knowing and acting that puts the claim to politics as usual into serious question'.[20] A number of writers see the rise of social activism at the local level as symptomatic of a new form of politics which challenges old assumptions and practices. Social activists, whether in the peace, environmental or women's movements have, according to Sheth, succeeded in 'bypassing legal and territorial definitions and bringing new constituencies into the political arena around new definitions of the issues and content of politics'.[21]

Local political units are often the channels for social activism, being both the instruments and the targets of local groups with international policy objectives. Non-central authorities may find certain policies possessing an international dimension the subject of attack and hence required to respond in ways which embroil them in broader national and international policy debates. In other cases they may be in a position, by virtue of their powers and responsibilities, to respond to the goals and interests of pressure groups. An instance in which both situations are clearly demonstrated can be found in policies towards firms investing in South Africa. US state governments, for example, have been active in using their control of pension funds to place pressure on companies to divest themselves of their South African interests, at least partly as a result of local group pressures.[22]

The sources, manifestations and goals of foreign policy localization are diverse. On the one hand, it can be seen as a form of adaptive behaviour by governmental structures to a changing policy milieu, and is marked by differing patterns of conflict and cooperation between central and non-central governments. At the other extreme, it can assume the form of local nationalist groupings whose aim may be – as in the case of the Basque separatist movement, ETA, the Parti Quebecois in Quebec or the Scottish Nationalist Party – the detachment of the region from its existing national setting – or at least a major redefinition of its relationship with that setting. In the process, asserting an international presence may be both an affirmation of local identity through linkages with similar groups in the international system and a strategy for building international support directed towards central government.

THE LOCALIZATION OF FOREIGN POLICY IN FEDERAL STATES

These forms of foreign policy localization can be seen, to a greater or lesser extent, in most political settings. Federal states, however, are likely to exhibit them to a degree and in forms which make them interesting case studies of the phenomenon. In part this relates to opportunity: those federations which are more than decentralized unitary states comprise component units with a significant degree of autonomy vis-à-vis the central government. As Simeon has put it: 'Neither central nor unit governments have hierarchical controls over one another. Except where authority is allocated unambiguously, one cannot dictate to the other'.[23] In terms of powers and responsibilities, then, NCGs have a policy sphere which, given the expansion of the international agenda noted earlier, defines for them areas of international interest. More than this, however, the component units in federal systems such as those of Canada, Australia and the US are, as Elazar has noted, 'polities'.[24] In other words, they are not mere administrative sub-divisions of central government: they are political arenas in their own right, possessing decision-making capacities certainly but, additionally, a sense of collective identity related to a territorial base which provides them with certain qualities attaching to sovereign states.

Furthermore, federal systems offer interesting examples of constitutional and institutional adaptation in the face of pressures related to foreign policy localization. Almost without exception, federal constitutions assign the conduct of foreign policy to the central government. Where some residual capacity is vested in the subnational level – as in the case of the Swiss Cantons and German *Länder* – this is carefully delimited and subject to central control.[25] The US Constitution is clear on this point: 'No state shall, without the consent of Congress . . . enter into any agreement or compact with another State, or with a foreign Power . . .'[26] Indeed, the assumption that foreign policy is an area reserved to national governments permits Duchacek to cite this as one of his ten 'yardsticks' of federalism.[27] Elazar suggests that a key motivating force in the emergence of what he terms 'modern' federalism was the desire to emulate the nation state whilst maintaining the constitutionalized diffusion of power that was considered to be necessary and vital for the preservation of individual liberty.[28] Given the fact that one stimulus to federation has been perceived threat from the international environment, it is not surprising that federal constitutions should seek to establish rules by which the federation's external relations were to be conducted and to ensure that it was the central government to which responsibility for foreign policy be assigned.

Since foreign policy could be equated with the 'high' politics of defence and military security and thus separated to a far greater extent than is now possible from domestic politics, such constitutional provisions appeared logical and sustainable. Thus although the concept of watertight vertical allocations of responsibility between levels of government soon appeared hard to maintain in spheres of domestic policy, it was to endure in the conduct of external policy. That is not to say that contact with the external environment was an undisputed issue in central–regional relations. From the very beginning, a distinction was drawn by non-central governments between essential and non-essential central control of foreign relations. Soon after federation in Australia, the Commonwealth government and the states found themselves locked in conflict on the question of communication with London on matters relating to imperial and foreign relations, the most notable instance being the dispute which developed over the actions of the South Australian government with regard to the Dutch vessel, *Vondel*, in 1902–3.[29] Furthermore, the Australian states and Canadian provinces chose to maintain separate representation in London despite the establishment of Australian and Canadian High Commissions. This reflected a continuing interest in trade and commerce which, as later chapters indicate, has increased markedly in recent years.

As federal systems developed, constitutional disputes turning on issues of access to the international system were to grow, reinforced by the intermeshing of domestic and external elements of public policy. Nevertheless, in general terms, such disputes were sporadic, limited in scope and often reflected power struggles related to domestic politics rather than serious challenges to the centre's conduct of foreign policy. Certainly, it was not unrealistic to view the federal government as 'gatekeeper' between the domestic and international environments. And given the frequently hostile nature of the external environment marked by the depression years, the Second World War and the Cold War era, central control of external relations possessed obvious virtues. However, by the 1970s, it was increasingly clear from the experience of the US, Canadian and Australian federal systems amongst others, that the twin forces of internationalization and foreign policy localization were challenging, to a degree hitherto unseen, the predominance of national governments in terms of their control over relations with the international community.

These were the product of the forces already described developing within the framework of relatively decentralized political systems. In particular, the impact of interdependence, notably in the economic sphere, has encouraged regional governments to extend their interests beyond the confines of local and national boundaries. Similarly, enhanced transnational relations combined with a growing sensitivity on the part of individuals and interest groups to the linkages between local, national and international issues and politics, have helped to reinforce the international involvement of NCGs. These responses interacted with the complex patterns of intergovernmental relations characteristic of federal systems to produce a situation in which non-central governments were to challenge some of the assumptions regarding their legitimate external policy interests and roles together with the rules which gave expression to them.

High on the list of factors accompanying these developments has been a transformation in the character of federalism itself. On the one hand, the post 1945 era has seen the emergence of federal systems whose aim has been to accommodate the stresses and strains within nation states resulting particularly from ethnic tensions.[30] These states (together with older federal systems such as Canada and a variety of unitary states adopting quasi-federal solutions to internal demands for autonomy) have been noticeably prone to the intermingling of domestic and international politics. Partly, this is because human rights and collective liberties have assumed a position high on the international agenda: partly it reflects the linkages between ethnic groups in different states – especially where these assume a transborder dimension. Also, it is a consequence of the fact that regions characterized by ethnic distinctiveness (Quebec is an obvious example) will regard a presence on the international stage as both symbolic of their aspirations and a strategy whereby these might be realised.

Alongside these developments, the component units of the older federations have also raised their sights beyond national horizons. In the case of the US, John Kline traces a connection between the growth of federal–state linkages together with a growing state involvement in the Washington policy-making processes and the development of the Great Society programmes beginning in the 1960s.[31] This, he suggests, created a base from which influence over foreign economic policy could be projected. The 'new federalism' of the Nixon and Reagan eras, although characterized by different philosophies, were both accompanied by the assumption of greater responsibilities on the part of state and local officials.[32] To this was added a growing concern with modes of linkage between regional and central governments represented by the expansion of existing links and the establishment of new ones, often in the shape of ministries of intergovernmental relations at the local level and, in the case of the US, the creation of intergovernmental affairs divisions in departments of the federal bureaucracy.

A recognition of the impact of external economic forces on local economies helped to reinforce these trends and to produce a more general concern with the international environment and national policies directed towards it. Characteristically, ministries of intergovernmental relations – such as those in Ontario and Alberta – extended their responsibilities to relations with foreign governments whilst government departments and agencies concerned with economic development assumed a greater role in trade promotion and the attraction of foreign investment.[33] In the US, the National Association of State Development Agencies (NASDA) created in 1946, established an international division in 1969 to assist state officials concerned with foreign trade promotion and investment attraction.[34]

Changes in the international agenda helped to reinforce such developments. From a predominant concern with East–West relations in the early postwar era, new threats in the shape of inflation and unemployment were emerging in the late 1960s and the 1970s. Whilst the 'high politics' of the Cold War agenda had reinforced the perception of foreign relations as the responsibility of the centre, the international realities of the 1970s seemed to cast doubt on the possibility and wisdom of centrally contrived solutions.[35] The politics of scarcity epitomized in the energy crisis which dominated the 1970s were part of a new scenario in which both the impact of international events on domestic interests and the incapacity of national governments to respond to them were emphasized.

Change in the security agenda also affected the spatial context in which security could be achieved. Alongside a proliferation of political actors mobilized by events in the energy sector, non-central governments, whether as producers or conservers of energy, were impelled to take a close interest in this vital policy sector, 'creating new energy councils, communities and task forces to deal with energy issues and to coordinate policy'.[36] Just as national governments became increasingly engaged in 'resources diplomacy', so did sub-national levels of government, creating situations in which external and internal political factors became more closely entwined. This was to extend beyond the energy sector to other areas, notably food, as 'food power' and 'food security' became prime concerns with the dramatic changes in food markets seen in the 1970s and 1980s.[37]

As manifestations of growing sub-national concern with the international environment increased so its consequences became more marked. Elazar has suggested that the growth of scarcity was instrumental in reinforcing the role of sub-national governments as polities. In the case of the US, the Reagan 'new federalism' enhanced the standing of the states by reinforcing externally generated scarcity with its own internally generated scarcities which demanded policy responses at the state level.[38] Significantly, policy vacuums at the federal level were often as much reflections of international as domestic events. Apart from the need to establish footholds in overseas markets and to attract foreign investment, state governments were required to respond to the problems posed by oil prices and petrol shortages and, in another area, the lack of a federal policy to deal with growing numbers of South-east Asian refugees.

The consequences of these developments, however, were more complex than a mere strengthening of the role of the constituent units in federal systems. First, they helped to reinforce long-standing differences of interest towards foreign economic policy. On the one hand, differences between resource-owning federal units, such as Alberta in Canada, and resource consumers, such as Ontario, reinforced more traditional, but no less significant, differences between those regions favouring free trade and those favouring protection. Federal policy responses – for example, those of the Trudeau government in the energy area – often served to reinforce inter-regional differences as well as to enhance tensions between the national government and those non-central governments who believed that their interests were being sacrificed to the benefit of other constituent units in the federation.[39]

Alongside these developments, other dimensions of foreign policy localization identified earlier began to affect the foreign policy environment, domestic and international, of the federal state. Partly, this was due to the broadening of the international agenda which meant that NCG interests and responsibilities moved out of a purely domestic political setting and on to the international stage. This is, of course, a process whose origins can be traced back several decades, but one which has noticeably increased during the last twenty-five years as issues such as those relating to the environment have featured more and more as problems at the international level. This has not simply provided a scenario for potential conflict between central and regional governments, but also created a backdrop against which the 'social activism' dimension of foreign policy localization could flourish.

On the one hand, as we have seen, the local polity offers interest groups a stepping stone to influence foreign policy at the centre. On the other, an NCG may find itself the target of social activism as its policies become the concern of the international community. Indeed, one official in the International Relations Division of the Ontario Ministry of Intergovernmental Affairs interviewed in the course of this study, regarded the large number of non-government organizations with international interests located in Toronto as a major factor determining the character of provincial international involvement. A clear example of the phenomenon is provided by the human rights agenda discussed in the following chapter. The Australian state governments of Queensland and Western Australia have, partly as a result of activism at the local and national level, found their policies towards the Aboriginal population the target of international concern and criticism. At one and the same time, therefore, the subnational political setting can provide a route through which interests can move from the local to the national and international levels of political activity, whilst also, by virtue of their policies, NCGs may be dragged on to the world stage as the unwilling victims of international opprobrium.

INTERNAL AND EXTERNAL INTERDEPENDENCE

It can be argued that these trends added, during the 1970s, a further dimension to a familiar process within federal states: the growing interdependence between levels of political activity and responsibility. The difference was that this interdependence now extended beyond national boundaries to include the international environment and, in the process, reduced the capacity of foreign policy managers to maintain their claim to regulate the points of contact between domestic and international societies.

The history of intergovernmental relations within federal systems has been one of adaptation to changing political realities.[40] The notion of federalism involving a vertical allocation of responsibility between power centres has been replaced by various images which emphasize powersharing and the evolution of cooperative relationships between levels of government characterized by bargaining processes. Interdependence between levels of government in federal polities has, argues Vile, always been indispensible to their workings and is a recognition of the fluidity of politics.[41] This interdependence has, however, been identified in terms of relationships between national and sub-national levels of political activity: there has been a tendency to assume that the international level of political activity remains a distinct area closely allied to central government.

In fact, for the reasons outlined earlier, the contemporary conditions of world politics recognize no such hierarchical ordering in the patterns of political activity: each level is influenced by processes and events occurring in the other. Moving outside the context of federal systems for a moment, Richard Samuels, in examining the politics of regional policy in Japan, has argued the need to relax accepted assumptions concerning local–national relations and to acknowledge the diversity of relationships that determine local politics:

> If we accept the idea that localities are often linked to international as well as to national decisions, actors and structures, then we must be prepared to assess the impact of *all* that is extra local.[42]

Two related changes in the way that foreign relations are viewed are involved here. First, that foreign policy is not a distinct issue area: it is about 'something' and that 'something' has come to embrace an increasingly large number of issues once assumed to be the preserve of domestic politics. Second, international politics is no longer (if it ever was) a discrete level of political activity but one which increasingly touches national and local political arenas, producing a complex web of interactions which has rendered the claims of central governments to exclusive control of foreign relations increasingly hollow.

The implications of these developments bear as much on the conduct of domestic policy as on foreign relations: the two, indeed, are inseparable. Bringing the 'outside' 'in' has, as suggested earlier, tempered the relations between subnational governments in federal states as well as the patterns of interaction between subnational and central governments. Whereas the intermeshing of domestic and foreign policy has, in some contexts, strengthened the role and powers of subnational governments, in others it has weakened it. Disputes regarding the implications of the central government's powers over foreign relations are characteristic of federal states and, as we have seen, are by no means new. However, the expanding agenda of international relations has offered the opportunity for central governments to extend their powers into areas of local responsibility claiming that these are now legitimate dimensions of external policy.

During the 1980s Australia witnessed two significant instances of this process in which the High Court took a 'maximalist' view of Canberra's external affairs power.[43] In a different context, Bulmer has pointed to the expansion of Bonn's power vis-à-vis the *Länder* which has resulted from the Federal Republic of Germany's membership of the European Community.[44] Usually, disputes about a central government's constitutional powers are more concerned with domestic politics than the conduct of foreign policy: that they have expanded to include the latter is one reflection of fluctuating relations between region and centre produced by the internationalization of domestic politics. The tensions that this can produce were clearly stated in the report of the Myer Committee appointed to consider the management of Australia's relations with Japan. Considering the involvement of the states in Australia–Japan relations, the committee observed:

> As Australia's relations with Japan have grown in extent and importance so has rivalry between the states in seeking to attract Japanese expertise, investment trade and tourists . . . [this] has helped to sharpen the conflict between the powers which the constitution reserves to the Commonwealth, such as external affairs, external trade and export licensing powers and those which lie with the states such as the right of tenement and the right of each state to promote its own development.[45]

CONSEQUENCES FOR THE CONDUCT OF EXTERNAL POLICY

Not surprisingly, the consequences of foreign policy localization both in the general context of international relations and, more specifically, in the conduct of national foreign policies are interpreted in different ways, reflecting varying analytical perspectives and the beliefs and prejudices of policy makers. At the general level, the complexities presented by cross-cutting linkages, of which foreign policy localization is both cause and manifestation, are familiar. States are not, it is generally recognized, unitary actors: nor are they alone on the world stage. Whether the resultant images of the world that transnationalism and interdependence offer are representative of an impenetrable chaos or subject to their own discernible patterns of operation are, however, issues of debate.[46] This is not, of course, simply a matter of description but also of prescription. What might be for some an undesirable, even dangerous, chaos in international relations created in part by the diversification of actors that foreign policy localization represents can, for others, assume the form of a desirable 'opening-up' of areas for too long the preserve of a policy élite relying on assertions of the specialness of international affairs as a basis for limiting access to them.[47]

This, of course, connects directly to the character of the foreign policy processes themselves. As Karvonen and Sundelius – amongst others – have noted, more attention has been paid to the systemic dimensions of interdependence than to the latter's impact on the foreign policy processes.[48] In part, this reflects disputes concerning the concept and referents of interdependence and more specifically the implications that it carries for the very nature of foreign policy itself given the latter's association with the role of state actors. Not surprisingly, therefore, conclusions as to the consequences of localization for the conduct of foreign policy vary in accord with the perspectives outlined earlier.

At one level, localization may be taken to imply the *rejection* of foreign policy defined as international relations conducted by national governments. On the one hand, it is argued that foreign policy no longer exists as the key focus of international relations because the actor with which it is associated, the nation-state, is itself of greatly diminished significance. Here, to focus on foreign policy is equated with an acceptance of the key assumptions of state-centrism: an emphasis on (a) the discreteness of domestic and foreign policy issue areas, (b) the distinctiveness of the foreign policy processes in terms of those involved in them and (c) the dominance of military security on the international agenda.[49] A preoccupation with foreign policy, in other words, reaffirms the state ideology which some strands of localization arguments would seek to deny or, at least, strongly qualify. Furthermore, the social activist strand of localization will often tend to see official foreign policy as the target which 'local' foreign policies needs to challenge.[50]

Looked at from another perspective, however, localization represents the *expansion* rather than the rejection of foreign policy. With the growth of a wide variety of subnational actors each seeking to pursue objectives that can only be satisfied by involvement of varying kinds at the international level, it seems not inappropriate to extend the term 'foreign policy' beyond the international interests and actions of states alone. Thus the term 'private foreign policy' has entered the vocabulary of international relations. In other words, contemporary international relations is witnessing the emergence of a range of actors each involved in activities to which the term 'foreign policy' can be applied. A key question here, of course, is whether there are special qualities attaching to foreign policy as an activity in which national governments engage, and, if so, whether to so dilute its meaning by applying it to the international activities of the general run of non-state actors is ultimately misleading and unhelpful to an understanding of the nature of world politics.

Rather, it seems more appropriate and helpful to consider foreign policy localization as part of a broader transformation whereby subnational actors in pursuing their international interests are challenging and changing both the content of national foreign policies and the processes through which these emerge and are implemented. The relationship between local interests and patterns of national external relations is complex: in part reflecting tension between levels of political authority, in other contexts involving a complementarity, perhaps mutuality, of interest. What is certain, however, is that the conduct of foreign policy and the diplomacy that gives expression to it is growing ever more intricate.

Taking the case of federal states, the problem is no longer one of simply containing what some have regarded as deviant behaviour on the part of subational authorities but of devising strategies for policy management in a milieu of growing complexity. Each level of government has legitimate interests in maintaining and developing relations with the international system, but at the same time each has its own distinctive problems determined by the nature and scope of its interests and objectives. From the perspective of national foreign policy managers, the involvement of non-central governments represents one manifestation of the familiar problems that flow from fragmentation in the domestic foreign policy environment. Fragmentation, as Hagan has noted, is significant not only because it may reduce the coherence of the decision-making process but because it can prevent the commitment of resources needed for policy action.[51] This, in turn, may lead to an inability to make substantive commitments and to ambiguous behaviour which other actors on the international stage find hard to interpret. Such a challenge is all the more significant where it derives from established 'polities' within the state which may possess well-developed and well-articulated international interests and the capacity to project them outside the confines of national borders.

Two points seem worth making here. Firstly, the argument that growing interdependence, of which foreign policy localization is a key element, implies the redundancy of foreign policy appears to be valid only if one accepts an unnecessarily restrictive definition based on traditional perceptions of the role of the state and its interests in the international system. It is quite possible to reconcile the continuing significance of foreign policy as an activity with conditions of growing interdependence just as the acceptance of the latter need not imply the consignment of the nation-state to the scrap-heap of international relations.

The second point flows from the first: foreign policy is not what it was – or, at least, no longer accords with an ideal type which, when subjected to the scrutiny of historical investigation, possesses less substance than it is often accorded. But the changes that have occurred are not reflective of the clash of two separate worlds: of 'private' and 'public' foreign policies. What is being suggested here is that subnational interests are becoming increasingly involved in the conduct of national public policy which is marked by a heightened international dimension. Neither the local nor the national levels can ignore one another for they have mutual interests which demand a degree of cooperation. Thus whilst subnational interests do indeed have policies that transcend state boundaries, national foreign policy still exists and is characterized by the qualities indicated above. At the same time, national foreign policy has been forced to adapt to a range of forces, both external and internal, of which localization is one. Consequently, whilst foreign policy seems a useful term to retain as indicative of the broad set of orientations and policies that a national government adopts towards its international environment, one of the key changes that has occurred is that those policies have been increasingly modified, in terms of substantive content and process, by local factors: in this sense, foreign policy has become 'localized'.

CONCLUSION

It has been argued in this chapter that foreign policy localization impinges on both the foreign and domestic policy environments. A reflection of international interdependence, it is helping to promote and reinforce the factors that have produced that interdependence. More particularly, it can be seen as a manifestation of a world politics in which accepted hierarchies of political activity which have been regarded as separating the international level from the national and subnational, have been replaced by an intermeshing of all levels in an increasingly unpredictable fashion.

That this should be particularly notable in federal political systems is not surprising given the tensions characteristic of contemporary federalism and the reassertion of the claims of units within many federations to be political entities in their own right rather than mere administrative devices presided over by central governments. Within these political systems, to the growing interdependence between central and non-central government has been added an external interdependence ensnaring both jurisdictional levels. Whilst this has created obvious conflicts as its implications are grappled with, it has also emphasized mutual needs which require the establishment of structures and practices able to deal with the new realities far removed from the assumptions regarding the conduct of foreign policy contained in federal constitutions. Nor is this limited simply to the conduct of foreign relations for it impacts on the fabric of the whole federal structure as its constituent parts respond to external pressures and their relationships are redefined in consequence. The negotiation of the Canada–US Free Trade Agreement, for example, underscored the need to tackle internal barriers to trade within the Canadian federation, just as the image of the single European market drew attention to practices in Australia and the US which deprived these countries of the claim to a 'single market'.

What is being created are scenarios for a much more complex kind of diplomatic activity conducted at a multitude of levels, often simultaneously. It is interesting that Simeon should have utilized a concept familiar to international relations – that of diplomacy – in his seminal study of Canadian federalism.[52] Increasingly, this internal diplomacy is being joined to the more traditional patterns of external diplomacy. Two processes are occurring here. Successful external policy demands internal diplomacy whilst successful domestic diplomacy is evermore dependent on diplomatic interactions within the international arena. It is in this context that multilayered diplomacy is developing; the following chapter examines the place of NCGs within those processes.

2 Non-central Governments and Multilayered Diplomacy

It has been suggested in the previous chapter that related changes in the international and domestic environments within which public policy develops have produced, alongside the internationalization of the policy processes, a congruent 'localization'. This development presents policy makers both with challenges, as local interests and politics intermingle to an increasing extent with those in the international environment, and also with resources which can be mobilized in varying ways to manage the resultant complexity and to achieve policy objectives. In the context of federal political systems, these developments have built on the characteristic internal diplomacy between levels of government and added to them an international dimension in the continuing process of determining the appropriate role and responsibilities of governments in a political environment marked by boundary fluidity and issue complexity.

Consequently, a need for policy makers, both governmental and non-governmental, to engage in forms of diplomacy which span the national and international arenas – a multilayered diplomacy – has developed. The purpose of this chapter is to examine the position and role of non-central governments in these processes, and it begins with an examination of the ways in which NCG international activities have been interpreted in what has become a considerable literature.

PERSPECTIVES ON NCGs AND INTERNATIONAL RELATIONS

Discussions of the place of NCGs in the foreign relations of federal states reflect the more general problems concerning relationships between domestic structures and institutions on the one hand and foreign policy on the other that characterize the study of the foreign policy processes. In this case, the first point to be noted is that the existing literature tends to be fragmented and has failed to build a cumulative body of knowledge and theory. As David Latouche has suggested, there is a limit to the usefulness of observing that things are changing in the international arena: the meaning and significance of change needs to be analyzed.[1] Much of the literature has, however, been descriptive depicting, for example, the presence of regional governments in the international arena and, particularly, noting their trade promotion and investment-attraction activities.[2] This is not to suggest that these are unimportant. However, they have not contributed to our ability to make some sense of the general phenomenon in terms of the shifting movements between various levels of decision-making from the supranational to the subnational.

This can be seen in the apparent confusion which characterizes a good deal of the discussion and is reflected in the concept of 'perforated sovereignties', a term used in one collection of essays devoted to the subject.[3] Despite the editor's attempts to refine the meaning of the term, its precise significance remains hazy. Does it simply refer to the processes associated with transnationalism and transgovernmentalism; is it indicative of a devolution of the foreign policy processes from the centre to a regional level; or is it one aspect of the 'dissolving state' syndrome? In other words, are the transborder political linkages denoted by this term reflective of a conscious and controlled administrative strategy by the central authorities or indicative of the creation of new political entities which are detaching themselves from national jurisdictions – a proposition which forms the basis of Garreau's *Nine Nations of North America*, wherein he identifies north–south regional forces creating nine distinct regions cutting across the national boundaries of Canada, the US and Mexico.[4] Analysts of this mode of NCG international activity are, moreover, by no means agreed on its significance. One study of the linkages between British Columbia and Washington State concludes that the picture they present is 'not exciting nor even terribly interesting'.[5] Similarly, an examination of Quebec–New York and Quebec–New England relations suggests that neither has entailed even the hint of the development of supranational loyalties to the transborder region stronger than to their own countries.[6]

One key to this confusion resides in our frequently conflicting images of the contemporary international system and the roles of the actors within it. Somewhat paradoxically, both sceptics and advocates of the significance of NCGs as international actors have served to discourage us to appreciate the place of the latter in the interactions between domestic and international politics: the sceptics, in emphasizing the primacy of the state as actor, question the significance of subnational authorities within the international arena; the advocates often stress their uniqueness as diplomatic actors and, thereby, place them in a category of their own. One consequence of this has been to stress the conflictual dimension of NCG international activity: the result, on one side, of assumptions that subnational actors are trespassers on an undisputed (and constitutionally underwritten) preserve of central authorities – the conduct of foreign policy; on the other, that state and subnational actors, being quite distinct in their qualities and interests, are locked in a zero-sum struggle whilst NCGs try to expand their autonomy as international actors and central governments seek to limit it.

DEVELOPING AN ALTERNATIVE PERSPECTIVE

The position adopted here is that these approaches are unhelpful to an understanding of the significance of subnational authorities' international involvement. The problem is that the images of the latters' role which they create is limited both in terms of areas of activity in which NCGs are involved and also the ways in which their actions and interests can impinge on the patterns of international politics. Several modifications in approach seem to be necessary if an alternative image which, it will be argued, accords more to the realities of contemporary policy processes is to be developed.

A first step in this process is to abandon the assumption that national governments and NCGs inhabit different regions of Rosenau's 'two worlds of world politics' – the former located in the 'state-centric world', operating according to its rules, and the latter amidst the diversity of the 'multicentric world' of non-state actors. In part it is necessary to do this to accommodate the ambivalent position occupied by NCGs which does not fit comfortably into the accepted categories of transnational and transgovernmental actor and often manage to combine the benefits of residual sovereignty deriving from the evolutionary processes of the federal systems in which they reside, whilst at the same time enjoying the advantages which Rosenau assigns to what he terms 'sovereignty-free' actors.[7]

However, a more all-encompassing reason for developing an integrated image of the respective international interests of national governments and subnational actors, including NCGs, is the linking of the boundaries between the traditional subdivisions of political activity. Whether this phenomenon is denoted as the 'domestication of international politics'[8] or 'internationalising politics'[9] it derives from the fact that actors find it increasingly necessary to operate at all levels of political activity to achieve their objectives, and this includes the international level. In Czempiel's words:

> Because interdependence has intensified the international interaction of governmental and societal actors, politics as value distribution has trespassed more and more upon the territorial boundaries of society. The authoritative value allocation by governments at all levels of their societies has become intertwined with the generation of values in the international environment.[10]

In this context, Manning's oft-quoted observation that to the traditional policy categories 'domestic' and 'international' has been added a third, 'intermestic', tends to obscure the fact that we are not necessarily presented with new categories of policy but with a continuum of policy types which blend together differing elements of the domestic and international located in various political arenas, whether subnational, national or international.[11]

Following the acceptance of a multilevel political arena which transcends traditional boundaries, a second step involves the recognition that the foreign policy processes involve a greater degree of complexity than is acknowledged in much of the literature of foreign–domestic interactions.

The point has been well-made by Ingram and Fiederlein when arguing for the need to adopt a public policy approach to foreign policy.[12] More specifically they suggest that two insights from public policy studies have either been overlooked or inadequately developed in foreign policy analysis. First, that the character of the policy processes varies depending on the issues involved; second, that the role and influence of actors can vary between stages in the policy-making process, from agenda setting to implementation. In other words, when considering the involvement of any domestic political actor in issues with a high level of international input, it is necessary to bear in mind that this will vary both in terms of the type of policy issue and from one stage of the policy cycle to another.

A third step towards revising the place and role of NCGs in international politics is to recognize that the intermeshing of different levels of political activity opens up a much broader spectrum of potential interactions between actors which, in turn, create the possibility of a wide range of strategies based on this expanded web of relationships. Here, Putnam's concept of diplomacy involving 'two-level games' is helpful – an image derived from the observation that negotiators are constrained to operate at two levels simultaneously: with the representatives of their negotiating partners and also with interested domestic constituencies. This, he argues, provides the basis for 'processes of entanglement' between the two levels which turn on the need to ensure ratification of international agreements at the domestic level.[13]

Ratification, however, is not merely restricted to formal processes (such as legislative approval) at the termination of negotiations. Rather, it is a continuous process of building and managing domestic support with relevant affected groups throughout the length of a diplomatic interchange.[14] Such a situation carries implications for interaction patterns, bargaining strategies and power. The interactions between national negotiators and their domestic constituents are the most obvious ones. Negotiating partners have a mutual interest in the attitudes of each other's domestic groupings since these will help to determine the outcome of the negotiations. Hence, for example, the growth of foreign interest lobbying on Capitol Hill. Furthermore, transnational interactions between domestic groupings in the two countries concerned with the outcome of a set of negotiations may well develop and be a crucial influence on the final result.

In terms of bargaining strength and behaviour, the pattern of relations between the two levels has several implications:

- In determining the strength of the negotiator in the sense that building and maintaining a supportive domestic coalition is necessary for acceptance of an agreement.
- In offering bargaining strategies: uncertainty about gaining or maintaining domestic support can be used as a bargaining tactic intended to induce the other side to make concessions.
- Ultimately, in deciding the outcome of a set of negotiations in terms of the ability of both sides to an agreement to gain the support of their domestic constituencies to the terms of an agreement.

NCGs AND MULTILAYERED DIPLOMACY

Adopting these perspectives enables us to move beyond the often unprofitable discussions concerning subnational involvement in international politics generally – and the international activities and interest of NCGs more specifically. They lead us away from the assumption that NCG international involvement is illegitimate, irrelevant, dangerous or portends dramatic change in the international system, and suggest that it is, in fact, one manifestation of developments which, in many contexts, have transcended the distinctions between levels of political activity and question the belief that there exists a hierarchy of political arenas from the subnational to the international each with their designated actors.

Instead, NCGs are located in a complex diplomatic milieu which does not recognize the exclusive territories of the domestic and international but blends both together in various ways at the behest of a range of forces located at differing political levels. Here, international diplomacy is regarded not as a segmented process presided over by undisputed gatekeepers but as a web of interactions with a changing cast of players which will interact in different ways depending on the issue, their interests and capacity to operate in a multilevel political environment. The idea, then, of NCGs as engaged in 'new forms' of diplomacy – whether these be termed 'microdiplomacy', 'protodiplomacy' or whatever – is replaced by an attempt to fit them into the changing patterns of world politics.

As Putnam himself points out, his 'two-level' image of diplomacy is a simplification of a complex reality.[15] Focusing on the place of NCGs in the diplomatic environment is potentially helpful in countering this by moving towards the image of a multilayered diplomacy in which the patterns are more complex. Subnational governments may themselves operate within the international environment so that the permutation of interactions and strategies in any given diplomatic exchange will be more intricate than in the 'two-level' image where national negotiators act as the point of interface with the international system and as mediators between it and the domestic setting.

Some insights into the nature of these developments have been provided by several studies including Mumme's discussions of environmental diplomacy on the US–Mexico border.[16] Another example comes from Greene and Keating who, in writing about Canada–US fisheries relations, focus on the effects of the domestic input.[17] Usually, however, the scope of this domestic input has been drawn in somewhat limited terms. Taking the latter study as an example, Greene and Keating explore the problems confronting Ottawa in dealing with affected domestic constituencies but do not consider the possibilities that (a) domestic interests could have been used as part of a negotiating strategy or (b) that the negotiating partners might have had an interest in managing the other side's domestic interests. In other words, both the patterns of interaction and the strategies which they permit are potentially more extensive than many analyses suggest.

Stages of Involvement and Roles

Table 2.1 sets out in a simplified form some of the occasions when, and ways in which, NCGs can become involved in the three stages of the diplomatic cycle: the pre-negotiation, negotiation and post-negotiation phases. These stages, of course, may not be clear-cut. As Winham, amongst others, has suggested, the character of much modern diplomacy is akin to a management process in which each side is locked together in exploring a problem and devising solutions to it.[18] Here, traditional distinctions between phases of the diplomatic process may be less relevant and, depending on the nature of the issue, the impact of domestic interests will not be limited to the implementation stage alone. Traditionally, discussions of foreign policy making in federal political systems have focused on the problems of implementation at the post-negotiation phase and, specifically, the need to ensure NCG cooperation in passing legislation necessary to the implementation of an international agreement.

It can be seen from Table 2.1 that the possible involvement of NCGs in international interactions extends through the entire policy cycle as illustrated in the case of what has come to be regarded as a crucial stage of the negotiation process, namely the pre-negotiation phase. This is evident from the range of possible roles performed by NCGs amongst which is the creation and maintenance of domestic support for national policy makers' diplomatic goals, particularly important in areas such as foreign economic policy where regional economic interests are vitally affected. As the discussion of multilayered diplomacy earlier in this chapter suggests, this is by no means limited to the closing stages of negotiations but is a continuous process upon which success or failure depends.

Table 2.1 NCGs and trade policy negotiations

Stage in policy cycle	*NCG roles*	*Patterns of interaction*	*CG tasks and strategies towards NCGs*
Pre-negotiation	Agenda setting Aggregating and articulating regional interests	Private sector ⟷ NCG interests NCG ⟷ CG NCG ⟷ NCG	Establish own NCG support Create structures for managing NCG interests Evaluate CG^2's subnational support
Negotiation	Sustaining support for CG goals Focus of opposition as terms of negotiations emerge Surrogate negotiators	NCG ⟷ NCG NCGs ⟷ CG NCG ⟷ NCG^2 NCG ⟷ CG^2	Maximize NCG support internally Externally: stress problems of maintaining domestic support for tactical reasons Maximize CG^2's subnational support to ensure ratification
Post-negotiation	Legitimizing outcome of negotiations (formal and informal processes) Interpreting outcomes to regional interests	NCG ⟷ regional interests	Convince NCGs of acceptability of outcome to ensure ratification and implementation
	Implementing decisions	NCG ⟷ CG	Convince CG and its domestic constituencies that agreement will be ratified

CG = Central government
NCG = Non-central government
CG^2 = Central government of negotiating partner
NCG^2 = Non-central government of negotiating partner

Thus amongst the seven functions that Zartman has attributed to this stage of the diplomatic cycle is the calculation and enhancement of domestic political support:

> Pre-negotiation allows each party to estimate and consolidate its own internal support for an accommodative policy, to prepare the home front for a shift from a winning to a conciliatory mentality. This involves not only changing the public image of the adversary but also putting together a domestic coalition of interests to support termination rather than conduct of conflict.[19]

Domestic support-building, rather than being limited to the final stages of the diplomatic processes, assumes significance from the very beginning. Indeed, support at the final, implementing stage is likely to depend on the effectiveness of coalition-building at earlier phases. Again the significance and nature of these processes will relate to the character of the issue on which a set of negotiations turns but is well-demonstrated in the case of trade negotiations. As Chapter 4 shows, the Canada–US Free Trade Negotiations involved coalition building at the level of provincial and state governments throughout the negotiations. On the Canadian side, one of the key issues in the early phases of the negotiations was the form which any provincial input would take. Provincial officials, whilst not part of the Canadian negotiating team, were certainly informed and consulted as the FTN progressed. Domestic coalition-building was, indeed, a multilayered process as provincial governments sought to establish support amongst their domestic constituencies for their policies on this vital issue. Of course, it follows from this that NCGs can also act as centres of opposition to national goals just as they do in domestic politics. As some of the instances cited in this study indicate, it is most likely that this will occur where subnational interests believe that their concerns have not been taken into account by national negotiators. This phenomenon will be even more marked where such a perception is generated by stuctural asymmetries between the constituent units of a federal state.

Another diplomatic role for NCG arises where the national government perceives an advantage in actually devolving responsibility for the conduct of its relations with other international actors on one or more NCG. This is most likely to occur where transboundary relationships are involved (as with Mexico–US and Canada–US relations) and where an issue touches directly on the interests and responsibilities of subnational authorities. An example of such a situation (discussed below) is provided by Canada–US negotiations on acid rain. Here, to a degree, Ottawa devolved the management of its diplomatic effort directed towards the introduction of enhanced emission controls in the US to provincial governments, particularly Ontario and Quebec. Not only did this offer an additional channel for diplomatic activity, it also provided to a degree a less politicized means of pursuing a policy goal.

A major problem for national policy makers is that NCGs often represent very different types of regional interest; areas representing free trade interests versus areas favouring protectionist policies, for example. This can make the task of managing the domestic coalition an extremely taxing one in which the processes of buying support through payments in the form of concessions to regionally-based groups may be hard to achieve. It is a problem enhanced not only by the sheer physical size of countries such as the US or Canada but also by the nature of the relationship between them. Because there exists an intervening level of legitimate authority between central government and geographically diffuse regional interests, capable of focusing and mediating those interests, more permutations of subnational, national and international interaction become possible as can be seen on the third column of Table 2.1. Here, the potential complexities generated by multilayered diplomacy are very apparent as NCGs become involved in interactions at subnational, national and international levels. The most obvious pattern of relationship will be that between NCGs and central governments, partly because of the desire of national policy makers to maintain domestic support in international diplomacy but also because subnational governments, recognizing the limits of their authority and capabilities, will seek to influence national policy and to exert pressure on the central government to reflect local interests during international negotiations.

Patterns of Interaction

NCG international involvement implies, of course, interactions with international actors. Indeed, it is the growing presence of NCGs on the world stage – as indicated by the growth of their overseas offices – that has generated most attention. As suggested above, this phenomenon can be seen as part of the overall multilayered diplomatic environment rather than as something which is set apart from it. Thus it is quite possible that NCGs will find themselves involved with agencies of foreign national governments (CG^2) and (particularly in transboundary relations) with foreign NCGs (NCG^2). Alongside this, a range of non-state international actors have an interest in NCG policies. Multinational corporations will be concerned with local policies that touch on foreign investment and the general climate in which international business is constrained to operate. Organizations focusing on human rights issues, such as Amnesty International or the World Council of Churches (WCC), may well find themselves involved with NCGs by virtue of the latters' responsibilities. Thus in Australia, the policies of the Queensland government towards its Aboriginal communities became an issue of concern to a number of international organizations, including the WCC.

In short, given the expanding range of issues on the international agenda, including many touching on the powers and responsibilities of NCGs, it is more and more likely that other international actors will find themselves focusing on the subnational level of political activity within the federal state. There are powerful norms of behaviour and practical reasons why such a strategy should be pursued with care: nevertheless, it is by no means unknown. As the study of the unitary taxation issue in Chapter 5 indicates, it was a recognition of the limitations of pursuing a strategy directed at the federal level that led foreign governments and business enterprises to pursue a local strategy focusing on those US state governments employing the unitary method of apportionment.

An obvious conclusion to be drawn from these potential patterns of interaction is that the complex politics of federalism and of international diplomacy have become interlinked. Forces external to the federal system now play a major part in determining the character of central–local relations, thereby producing a situation which is a logical extension of growing interdependence between levels of government. Now, the impact of international events on the character of federalism goes far beyond the frequently noted effect of perceived external threat on the creation of federal compacts. External forces can cohere, fragment and alter the balance between the centres of power in the federal state.

Tasks and Strategies

The final column of Table 2.1 underscores the complexities that multilayered diplomacy presents to both national foreign policy managers and to NCGs in pursuit of their international interests. From a central governmental perspective, these can be viewed in terms of tasks to be performed and strategies which may be adopted in the management of the domestic environment of international diplomacy. High on the list of tasks is the creation of structures and processes through which affected domestic interests can voice their concerns. A failure to do this may cause an international agreement to unravel at the domestic level as opposition to it is voiced and gains political momentum. The logic of multilayered diplomacy requires, additionally, that policy makers are sensitized to the subnational political influences affecting a negotiating partner's position. A deficiency in this respect is as likely to result in failure to achieve a satisfactory outcome as is inattention to one's own domestic constituencies.

Possible tactics flow from these basic factors. First, stressing domestic uncertainty created by NCG interests and involvement may be one way of encouraging a negotiating partner to modify its demands. The fact that federal systems require a more extensive coalition-building and ratification process, it can be argued, potentially enhances the effectiveness of such a strategy for the federal authorities. Obviously, several problems arise here. First of all, it implies an ability to manage uncertainty and to use it at effective points in diplomatic intercourse. In reality, as the case studies included in this volume indicate, NCGs are likely to emerge in unpredictable ways on the diplomatic stage, confounding the intentions of central authorities.

Furthermore, such a strategy has to be regarded as legitimate if it is to be widely employed and, certainly in the case of multilateral diplomacy, it is questionable whether this is so. Such bodies as the ILO, for example, appear increasingly reluctant to allow 'federal reservations' on the grounds that implementing power lies with subnational governments. In the case of the European Community, EC law recognizes only unitary states, a situation which has caused tensions to develop between the German *Länder*, Bonn and Brussels.[20] Additionally, uncertainty regarding the ability to implement an agreement might well constitute a liability rather than an asset. During the various congressional hearings on the proposed Canada–US Free Trade Agreement, the issue of the powers of the Canadian provinces arose repeatedly and was clearly a factor that created doubts on Capitol Hill as to Ottawa's ability to deliver an agreement.

A second possible strategy involves enhancing the chances of reaching an international agreement by attempting to promote support amongst the other side's domestic constituencies. In one sense, of course, this is nothing new. Public diplomacy, understood as the desire to create pressures on national governments by appealing directly to the communities over which they preside, has a long – if not always distinguished – history.[21] What is more recent is the growing trend on the part of a variety of actors, not only governments, to operate much more directly within national policy processes. This at once reflects a perceived need for such activity as the significance of subnational interests in the formulation of policy grows, but also the opportunity to do so afforded by enhanced linkages and communications between national communities.

This focus on the official governmental processes is reflected in the growing debate on foreign interest lobbying, particularly intense in the US where the term is used interchangeably to denote a general pattern of political activity and the techniques used to pursue it (particularly the employment of professional political consultants). As the literature on the phenomenon has developed, we are beginning to learn more about the character of lobbying, its objectives, the means used to pursue it and its consequences both in terms of the international system (regarding the distribution of power, for example) as well as at the level of individual actors.

From this it is clear that lobbying activities have, of necessity, become increasingly diffuse in terms of their targets. Depending on the issue and the precise goals to be accomplished, policy aims will often require action at several levels: the national and subnational and the governmental and non-governmental. These arenas of activity, it should be stressed, are not ordered in any hierarchy of importance and are interlinked: the 'emitters' of influence may well be required to operate in all of them simultaneously or individually as a particular strategy unfolds in response to the uncertainties generated by this many-faceted environment. This characteristic impinges on the key tasks to be accomplished. These involve gaining access to the operational arenas, coordinating the different elements within them and achieving a degree of control in the attempt to direct influence towards the target or targets.

The dangers of direct interactions between a foreign government and the subnational authorities in another state are obvious. It is one thing for a negotiator in one country to act in an interpretative role, explaining the domestic interests of one side to those of the other, as the US Trade Representative, Clayton Yeutter did when explaining during Congressional hearings the role of the Canadian provinces in the Free Trade Negotiations; it is quite another to become involved directly in dealings with subnational authorities, especially where, as is the case with federal systems, the relationships between central and non-central governments are highly politicized and therefore very sensitive. The consequences of overt diplomacy directed towards a subnational government may be to arouse the hostility of the central government (as in the case of Ottawa's reactions to French policy towards Quebec in the past), the resentment of the NCG which may value the insulation from external pressure that constitutional niceties concerning the appropriate channels of international communication provide, or, indeed, both. Nevertheless, as the studies in this book indicate, such communication (within reasonably well-articulated and understood norms and rules of behaviour) occurs and has become an inseparable dimension of contemporary diplomacy.

In short, Table 2.1 emphasizes the variety of ways in which NCGs can become involved in international negotiations at different phases of the policy cycle and suggests that in the multilayered diplomatic environment:

- The role and degree of involvement of NCGs in international negotiations may vary as they evolve through their various stages.
- Patterns of interaction between central and non-central governments are complex and may cut across national boundaries.
- Negotiating strength will, in part, be determined by an ability to sustain and control domestic support as expressed by NCGs.
- NCG international concerns permit and require the development of negotiating strategies which will help to determine the outcome of negotiations.

NON-CENTRAL GOVERNMENTS AS 'HYBRID' INTERNATIONAL ACTORS

The preceding discussion has treated NCGs in an undifferentiated fashion whereas, in reality, their character – and hence their involvement in diplomatic processes – varies considerably. This is true not only in the case of different federal systems, but also between the constituent elements of the same system. A tendency to undervalue the nature of such variations is one factor contributing to the conflicting images of NCG international activity noted earlier in this chapter. Just as nation states are no longer regarded by most observers of world politics as unitary actors on the international stage, so it has to be recognized that the constituent governments in federal political systems are, similarly, complex actors. For this reason, they are not easily accommodated within the accepted taxonomy of contemporary international relations literature.

Largely as a consequence of their status as 'polities' in their own right, a point discussed in Chapter 1, their significance as elements of the domestic political fabric places them in quite a different category from that usually conveyed by the term 'transnational' actor. Rather, they are political settings within which regional interests develop and pursue their goals at various levels of political activity, often in cooperation with agencies at both national and subnational tiers of government. For example the European campaign launched by Canada's forest industries against international criticisms of their tree-cutting practices and of the toxic effluent produced by pulp mills was aided by provincial as well as federal governments. Thus publicity and lobbying strategies adopted by British Columbia's Council of Forest Industries were actively supported by both the provincial government and Ottawa.[22] At the same time, both NCGs, and national governments, are confronted by a wide range of frequently competing interests seeking their support in gaining access to various sectors of the international system.

Nor does the term 'transgovernmentalism' – where this is taken to denote international linkages between agencies of central government – serve to describe accurately NCG international activities. Quite clearly, NCG government departments do interact with other bureaucratic agencies at international, national and subnational levels; but they can do so as representatives of interests quite distinct from, and in opposition to those of central government.

This underscores the fact that non-central governments have at their disposal a range of strategies through which they can pursue their own concerns, and those of their domestic constituencies, within the international system. Adapting Keating's typology of channels of influence available to European regional interests and governments in their dealings with the European Community, we can see that NCGs can further their international interests in two basic ways:[23]

- By exerting influence on national governments to project their interests at the international level.
- By using their own resources, to act directly on the international stage.

Similarly, regionally based domestic interests have at their disposal several routes for influencing external policy, some of which may involve NCGs:

- Through national governments via NCG agencies.
- Directly through national governments.
- Directly through NCG agencies.
- Directly to the international system without any intermediaries.

From this it can be seen that NCGs can be both 'primary' international actors, pursuing their own and their clients' interests by direct international action and 'mediating' actors, using national routes to achieve their aims. The availability of these routes to international activity, the patterns of relationships between non-central and national political arenas and domestic interests in their various forms, means that non-central governments are 'hybrid' actors, possessing some of the qualities associated with nation-states as well as non-state actors. Table 2.2 indicates in general terms the characteristics of NCGs as international actors and participants in the processes of multilayered diplomacy, summarizing points made in this and the previous chapter.[24] But, as noted above, the precise patterns of NCG engagement in multilayered diplomacy will depend on a combination of factors which determine the position of a given NCG within its domestic and international settings. Before considering these, it should be remembered that the central assumption of the discussion so far has been that the significance of NCG international involvement lies not so much in the extent to which they operate as discrete actors in the international arena, but rather relates to their participation in the complex diplomatic processes which span the domestic and international environments and through which public policy evolves.

This impinges on the present discussion since it conditions the criteria of international involvement which are likely to be applied to NCG international involvement. The emphasis on Duchacek's various categories of NCG international activity, such as 'paradiplomacy' and 'protodiplomacy', whilst helpful in distinguishing between different types of relationship, tend to emphasize separateness from national policies and to reinforce the image of conflict between centre and region projected into the international environment.

The factors determining the involvement of NCGs in the forms of multilayered diplomacy described above are more likely to stress patterns of linkage between levels of political authority and activity.

Table 2.2 Characteristics of non-central governments as actors in multilayered diplomatic environments

Aims	Promoting regional interests; interests related to powers and responsibilities, particularly in economic area
Involvement	Continuous but likely to fluctuate in intensity; concentrated on economic agenda
Structure and resources	Non-central government; bureaucratic and political resources; legitimacy among local population; links with national governmental structures
Levels of participation	Governmental and intergovernmental; closely linked to regionally based transnational actors

Equally, whilst conflict between the central and subnational levels is by no means excluded, it is qualified by the imperatives of cooperation if the interests of both levels of government are to be achieved.

MULTILAYERED DIPLOMACY: PATTERNS OF NCG INVOLVEMENT

Bearing this in mind, what factors, then, appear to be significant in determining the pattern of involvement of non-central governments in the processes of multilayered diplomacy?

The Character of the Federal System

Quite clearly, the general character of the federal system will be a major determinant of the extent to which NCGs become involved in the diplomatic process. The degree to which the society on which it is based exhibits what is often referred to as a 'federal culture' is as important as the political arrangements which give expression to them, a point echoed by Duchacek in the following terms:

> As carriers of the territorial diffusion of roles and power, federal and subnational institutions behave, as it were, 'federally', and this appears to be due not only to a federal constitution and pluralistic democracy, but also to that elusive variable, federal culture, mirror-

ing tradition, constant practice, and the belief in the possibility, desirability, and practical value of a cooperative interaction between integrative themes and segmented differentiations.[25]

The extent to which the federal system is decentralized in general terms will, given the closer relationship between domestic politics and external relations, reflect on the management of the latter and the diplomatic processes in which the federal state engages. Taking an overview of federal systems, it is apparent that Canada has, over the last two decades, exhibited the most pronounced tendency for its subnational governments to stake a claim to involvement in external policy issues. By comparison, other federal systems – such as Austria, Switzerland and even Germany – demonstrate the phenomenon to a lesser degree. At the other end of the spectrum we find the example of the USSR under the 1936 and 1977 constitutions which assigned to the Union republics the power to conduct foreign policy, dismissed by Duchacek as a 'confederal facade superimposed on a tightly controlled monolithic centralism'.[26]

It is interesting to note, however, that federal systems are as subject to evolutionary change in this respect as in others. When Harold Stoke published his study of the conduct of foreign relations in federal states in the early 1930s, he predicted that, of all the federations which he examined, Australia seemed destined, by virtue of the constitutional allocation of powers, to suffer from a high level of conflict between national and subnational governments in the conduct of external relations.[27] Sixty years later, a combination of constitutional evolution, differences in the socio-economic profile of regions, domestic politics and a dramatically changed international environment, have produced a situation where, if Stoke were writing in the 1990s, the accolade would pass from Australia to Canada.

Focusing on constitutional evolution, federal constitutions, as the previous chapter indicates, are marked by their characteristic assignation to the central government of the responsibilities attaching to the conduct of foreign relations and also by the limited scope afforded to non-central governments in developing a role on the international stage. Even where a constitution specifies a role for NCGs, as in the case of Article 9 of the Swiss constitution, the word 'exceptionally' is attached to the designated functions.[28] However, as the pressures of foreign policy localization have increased, the apparent constitutional certainties regarding the management of external relations have appeared increasingly vulnerable and subject to contention. But the patterns of adaptation to internal and external pressures have depended on the interaction between the constitutional rules, their judicial interpretation and the demands of politics.

Returning to the examples of Canada and Australia, we can see that the growth of the provincial role in international affairs reflects, in part, very different patterns of constitutional development. In the case of Canada, a decisive event in the emergence of a provincial role for the provinces was the Labour Conventions case of 1937. In this decision, the Privy Council determined that whereas the power to conclude treaties lay with the federal government, the implementing power reflected the general division of powers in the constitution. In other words, Ottawa could not abrogate powers lying in the provincial sphere by claiming that it was necessary to the implementation of an international agreement.[29] Whilst this decision has by no means rendered the federal government incapable of conducting a foreign policy as some predicted, it has ensured the need to involve the provinces in the conduct of external relations which, as can be seen in later chapters, has carried clear implications for the diplomatic processes.

Precisely the opposite trend has been detectable in Australia where the role of the federal government (Commonwealth) in the conduct of foreign relations is underscored by the external affairs power enshrined in Article 51 (29) of the constitution. This has enabled Canberra to expand its powers into areas of state government responsibility, supported by rulings of the High Court, to a degree which has caused concern for the future of the federal system's survival. This trend was greatly reinforced by the High Court judgement in the Koowarta case, discussed later in this chapter, and the events surrounding the proposal by the Tasmanian government to construct hydroelectric power facilities in southwest Tasmania, thereby flooding a unique wilderness area.

The project was ultimately quashed by Canberra's resort to its obligations under UNESCO's Convention for the Protection of the World Cultural and Natural Heritage which had been ratified by Australia in 1974. Arguing that this was a legitimate use of the external affairs power to give effect to an international agreement, the Hawke government passed legislation to prevent the construction of a dam on the Gordon-below-Franklin River, an action challenged by the Tasmanian government in the High Court on the grounds that the Commonwealth had no powers in this area under the provisions of the constitution. The majority view of the Court, however, was that the external affairs power should be interpreted in a very broad sense, thus enabling the federal authorities to legislate in any subject area in giving effect to an international agreement.

It should, of course, be stressed that the issue here has not been the right of the federal government in either country to conduct foreign policy but, rather, the power to implement domestic legislation necessary to give effect to it. However, the contrasting experience of Canada and Australia in this area indicates the significance of constitutional rules in determining the scope for NCG involvement in the interrelationships between domestic and international politics on which the patterns of multilayered diplomacy rest. Put another way, constitutional rules regarding rights of access of NCGs to the international system are one means by which that access is regulated and, consequently, a determinant of the ways in which – and the extent to which – subnational governments are engaged in patterns of communication that span several levels of political activity.

Of course, the rules have had to be adapted to accommodate the realities presented by the growing internationalization of the issue-areas under non-central control. Thus, even in Australia where, as we have seen, the use of the external affairs power has expanded the scope of central initiative, a process of treaty consultation, first introduced by the Fraser government in 1978, has developed. In the case of Germany, as Michelman points out, the Lindau Convention has provided a modus vivendi between the federal government and the *Länder* whereby the predominant role of the former in concluding an international agreement is acknowledged, whilst the *Länder* are consulted on treaties where they have an interest and responsibility. Alongside developments such as these, informal norms of behaviour have developed, most clearly seen, perhaps, in the sometimes sensitive area of direct NCG representation overseas. As Chapter 7 demonstrates, for the greater part, the two levels of government operate in a non-conflictual fashion in terms of their overseas activities, with NCG usually recognizing the limits beyond which such activities will draw opposition from the federal authorities. Thus, although Ottawa has accepted the growth of provincial overseas representation, it has drawn the line at allowing the provinces to open offices in Washington DC, so sensitive is the US–Canada relationship.

As noted earlier, the pattern of formal rules and less formal practices in this, as in other areas of political activity in federal states, is an amalgam of constitutional norms, judicial interpretation and pragmatic political considerations. Taken together, this can produce an uncertain context within which the whole issue of foreign policy localization is debated.

Nowhere is this more obvious than in the US where, despite the apparent constitutional certainties, noted in the previous chapter, regarding the responsibility for the conduct of external relations, the issue appears to have become one of contradictory judicial rulings and conflicting opinion at both policy maker and academic levels. Thus the decision of the Supreme Court in the case of *Zschernig* v. *Miller* (1968) effectively endowed the court with the power to invalidate any action by the states which might impinge on the conduct of foreign relations by the federal government.[30]

This reversed an earlier decision (*Clark* v. *Allen*, 1947) which had taken a far more sceptical view of the claim that state actions with some foreign relations dimension were necessarily incursions on the federal foreign policy power. Since the Zschernig case, various courts have delivered quite different rulings in this area, on such issues as state 'buy-American' legislation, various South African divestment measures, and local nuclear-free zone ordinances. Differing views on the intentions of the Founding Fathers regarding the conduct of foreign relations and the merits of subsequent judicial decisions are well-reflected in the following observations:

> State–federal relations in international affairs have thus become a crapshoot turning not on any defensible principles of democratic decisionmaking but on the whims of judges. In this sense, Zschernig unleashed judicial activism at its worst. It substantially expanded the power of courts in an area that the Framers intended to leave to the political branches of government.[31]

> The US Supreme Court has stayed true to the Founders' essential intentions on foreign policymaking, and has consistently rebuffed state governments where they have acted against the national purpose on foreign policy matters . . . Zschernig remains good law.[32]

Centre–Region Linkages

Alongside the pattern of formal and informal rules impinging on subnational interest and activity in external policy issues, the nature of the means by which local and regional interests are transmitted to the centre and gain expression there will be crucial determinants of the patterns of multilayered diplomacy characteristic of a particular federal system. It may well be the case, for example, that the constituent governments of one federal system are less significant as modes of interest representation and transmission to the centre. In the trade policy area, for example, it appears to be the case that, historically, the Australian states have been less significant than the Canadian provinces as articulators of the interests of domestic economic constituencies, with Australian business seeking direct representation at the centre.

Second, it is relevant to note the differing modes of expression of subnational interests which pertain to federal systems. Quite obviously, in the case of the US, the development of an active congressional role in foreign policy during the last two decades, particularly in foreign economic policy, has offered regional interests a powerful voice at the centre which has acted as a foundation for the supplementary activities of the National Governors' Association. In Germany, the Basic Law provides the *Länder* with a voice (albeit a far less influential one) in the national legislature through the latters' representation in the Bundesrat.[33]

In the Australian case, the extent to which the Senate has acted as a 'states' house' has, traditionally, been questioned. Besides, it has none of the powers in areas touching on the conduct of foreign relations assigned to the US Senate. However, the party system, as Holmes and Sharman demonstrate, acts as a crucial linkage in the pattern of Australian federalism: 'the party system can be seen as congruent with a regional dispersal of power and at most as the major force underpining the continued existence of federalism in Australia'.[34]

Canadian federalism, by contrast, is relatively weak in terms of its representation of interests at the centre. Unlike Germany, where the *Bundesrat*, combined with an elaborate pattern of intergovernmental consultation, has ensured the *Länder* a direct voice in policy decisions, Canada has suffered from the lack of such 'intrastate' mechanisms (that is, representation within central policy-making institutions) for the expression of regional interests. According to Chandler, a resultant insensitivity to regional concerns on the part of Ottawa has spilled over into mechanisms for developing relationships between levels of government with the consequence that these 'have never been integrated into the constitutional order, a situation that has limited the legitimacy and effectiveness of intergovernmental relations as an alternative to intrastate representation'.[35] It would, of course be possible to analyze each aspect of a federal system in terms of its impact on the extent to which regional interests can be represented at the centre, but enough has been said to make the point that the opportunity for NCGs to gain a voice in the shaping of international, as with domestic, policy will vary from one country to another.

Location within the Federal State

Apart from the mechanics of the federal system, NCGs will vary both in terms of their physical location within a federal state and the consequences that this may have for the relationships between subnational and central governments on matters with an international dimension. This is frequently expressed in terms of the existence of 'core' and 'periphery' regions within federal states. Centres of economic and political power, such as Ontario in the case of Canada and New South Wales in Australia, will, it is argued, be identified with a 'national' interest as expressed by the central government, whilst peripheral regions, such as British Columbia and Western Australia, may find their concerns at once different from, and under-represented in, the central power structures.[36]

Taking Australia as an example, the tensions between core and periphery became very apparent in the resources boom of the 1970s. The development of Australia's mineral wealth during the period, Stevenson has argued, resulted in a simultaneous reorientation between the 'outer' states of Queensland and Western Australia and both the core states of the south-east of the country and the international system. As the beneficiaries of changes in patterns of foreign investment and international trade which favoured their resource industries, movements in the international economy 'tended to strengthen the links between the outlying states and the external markets and financial centres of Japan, the US and Europe, rather than tightening the links between these states and the industrialised south-east of Australia'.[37] This served simultaneously to enhance the outer states' interests in international economic policy, particularly in the sphere of foreign investment policy, emphasize differing economic interests within the federal system, and heighten tension between them and Canberra with regard to their international interests.

The extent to which these developments indicated a fundamental shift in the balance of power within the federal system has been questioned by Head amongst others.[38] Nevertheless, for present purposes they offer one perspective on the way in which NCG international attitudes and involvement can differ within a federal state.

International Linkages

From the previous point, it can readily be seen that NCGs are likely to demonstrate differing patterns of interest in, and linkages with, the international system. One of the major variable factors here is that of geography. Where contiguous borders encourage the development of transnational and transgovernmental links between regional authorities in neighbouring states, then the international interests of NCGs are likely to be particularly evident. The classic example is provided by the US and Canada, where the proliferation of cross-border links and transactions largely go uncounted. This is particularly significant for Canada given the pronounced North–South orientation of the provinces with adjacent US states and, of course, the overwhelming importance of the US relationship to Ottawa. As the studies of the free trade negotiations and the acid rain issue indicate, the propinquity of provinces and states presents both a foreign policy challenge to the Canadian government and yet, at the same time, a resource inasmuch as sensitive issues, such as environmental pollution, can be dealt with at a lower level of political authority and possibly, therefore, in a less confrontational manner.

Moving to the other extreme, the extent to which the Australian states have developed international linkages is obviously constrained by lack of opportunity to develop transborder relations. As already indicated, in this case it is economic linkages and the mutual concerns of the states and their domestic constituencies, particularly with Japan, that have proved to be significant to the management of Australia's external relations as noted in the Myer report referred to in the previous chapter.

However, territorial contiguity is not of itself an adequate condition for the development of interaction which might determine the diplomatic environment of a federal state. Despite the transborder concerns of certain Austrian and (West) German *Länder* bordering on states of the former Soviet bloc, such matters as environmental pollution had necessarily to be pursued through traditional diplomatic channels because of the unwillingness of the authorities in these states to allow issues to be managed at a lower level.[39]

Elsewhere in Europe, however, economic linkages between border regions are a major feature of developing patterns of relationships.

Hence the image conjured by the prime minister of Baden-Wurttemberg of a 'Europe of Regions' as represented by the relationships between his own region and those of Rhones-Alpes, Lombardy, and Catalonia, the so-called 'four motors of Europe'.[40] Another example is to be found in the Regio Basiliensis where Basle, isolated from the rest of Switzerland by the Jura mountains, shares boundaries in the Rhine valley with Germany and France.[41] Its location endows Basle with particular concerns on Swiss policy towards European economic integration with the possibility that the opportunity to join the European Economic Area might be rejected as, in the future, might membership of the European Community.

Finally, mention should be made of cultural links in the development of an NCG international presence. The example offered by Quebec is an obvious one as it has sought to establish and develop a role in cultural diplomacy, particularly in the context of *la Francophonie*. In the case of Belgium, the two major linguistic communities have opened cultural offices in other countries, often combining an economic function with their other responsibilities. Amongst the first of these was the creation of a permanent mission in Quebec in 1982 by the French Community and the Walloon region, followed by another in Paris opened in 1985.[42]

Resources

An obvious determinant of the degree to which NCGs are likely to become engaged in multilayered diplomacy lies in the resources which they are able to command. These are very diverse in form and assume both a tangible and intangible form. Under the latter heading comes the political culture and its impact on the foreign policy processes. To the extent they are open and participative, then the greater the likelihood that subnational governments and the interests they represent will gain access to the decision-making processes. Taking the case of Australia, it is clear that foreign relations have been regarded as a relatively closed area of public policy, with limited input from the federal parliament, pressure groups or, indeed, the states. This is reinforced by attitudes to be found in various parts of the bureaucracy with interests in Australia's external environment. Canada, in contrast, although marked by no less a dominant role for the executive in the conduct of foreign relations, has by virtue of its less homogeneous society and more accommodative political culture, offered domestic interests greater scope for influencing the shaping of external policy. This is reflected in bureaucratic attitudes and practices when it comes to consultation with the provinces, as later chapters reveal.

Beyond these general points are to be found the more tangible factors of physical resources. It is an obvious point that NCGs, like nation-states, differ in terms of the resources at their command. California, with one of the world's highest levels of GDP, a network of overseas representation, and a permanent trade policy representative in Washington DC, can hardly be regarded as an actor of the same status as Tasmania, a comparatively poor state in the Australian federation with no permanent overseas offices. But perhaps of greater significance for the ability to influence the shaping of policy at the centre is bureaucratic strength, not simply in size but in terms of expertise. Undoubtedly, one of the key factors in determining the extent to which the central government will feel impelled to grant NCGs a voice in areas touching on external policy is the fact that on many issues they possess bureaucratic expertise which not simply rivals that of central departments, but which the latter may hardly possess. Typical areas reflect, not surprisingly, powers and responsibilities assigned by the constitution to the constituent governments, such as fisheries and the broad range of issues on the environmental agenda.

A further resource that NCGs can turn to their advantage and which therefore becomes significant in determining their capacity to influence the evolution of international policy at the centre is the degree to which they are willing and able to develop cooperative mechanisms. Crucial to the ability of the US states to gain a voice in foreign economic policy, as Chapter 4 indicates, has been the growing role of, on the one hand, the National Governors' Association and, on the other, the development of regional groupings such as the Western Governors' Association, capable of articulating concerns touching on regional interests which span several states.

Taken together, these factors (which do not claim to be exhaustive) help to determine the extent to which non-central governments will find themselves involved in multilayered diplomacy. They underscore the complex qualities that NCGs display as both domestic and international actors, which make generalizations concerning their character and role in political interactions hard to sustain. Rather than constituting a clearly defined category of actor, their activities as they bear on external policy, will vary in response to a mix of domestic and international forces. As Latouche has suggested in the case of Quebec, in evaluating the external interests of NCGs, 'we are operating at the margin of both the domestic and international spheres, a location where what is "inside" and what is "outside" becomes difficult to assess'.[43] Thus an understanding of Quebec's motivations in the international arena:

> must take into account not only the internal articulation of its own state-building process (and the specific configuration of forces which give it life) but also its position within the overall Canadian statist space. We must consider Quebec's federal and regional components, the place of Canada within the international system, and the evolving nature of this system.[44]

SCOPE OF NCG INTERNATIONAL INVOLVEMENT: 'HIGH' POLITICS AND 'LOW' POLITICS

As we have seen, part of the landscape of NCG involvement in multilayered diplomacy is determined by the character of individual issues on the international agenda. It is tempting to simplify this fact by arguing that the impact of non-central governments is confined to the realm of what is often termed 'low' politics. Certainly, it is the case that the dominant interests of the constituent governments in federal states will be related to their responsibilities, particularly in the area of economic development, and that, usually, matters relating to military security will be left to the central government. Thus, whilst it may well be the case that there are distinctive regional defence interests of which NCGs are the major articulators, these are usually expressed through mediation with the centre rather than through any form of primary international action which would be perceived as a challenge to national military security interests.

However, this distinction breaks down where it is taken to imply a low level of importance for NCGs in determining the overall character of a federal state's pattern of foreign relations. On the one hand, as is frequently pointed out, the relative significance of the military security agenda has declined as other issues – in areas where NCGs have clearly developed interests – capture the concern of policy makers. Thus for the Canadian government in the 1980s, the problem of acid rain and negotiation of a free trade agreement with the US were issues at the very top of the foreign policy agenda, and issues in which the provinces were key players. But beyond this the boundaries between issues appear increasingly permeable, with the consequence that even where

NCGs have no clearly developed concerns, they may be drawn into the realm of traditional 'high' politics. This tendency has been reinforced in recent years by the fact that, as the discussion in Chapter 1 suggests, action at the local level on nuclear issues, for example, has been regarded by domestic groups as a route to national and international influence.

In essence there are four factors which influence the overall scope and significance of NCG impact on the conduct of external policy. First, their interests and the generally-held perceptions of what constitutes high politics at both national and international levels have increasingly coincided in recent years. Second, because of the tendency for traditional high politics, that is issues of military security, to become enmeshed with other concerns, particularly in the economic sphere, combined with a growing willingness of domestic groups to involve themselves in defence-related matters, NCGs may be drawn into problems which federal constitutions clearly reserve as the prerogative of the central authorities. Third, as Nossal makes clear in his study of Ontario's policies towards sanctions on South Africa, local political factors, particularly electoral support for the government, combined with party politics at central and non-central levels, will determine the occasions when – and extent to which – NCGs will involve themselves in the realm of high politics.[45]

The fourth factor is to be found in the attitudes of national policy makers, who may have their own motives, related to domestic or foreign policy, for promoting NCG involvement in issues of high policy. Two examples, both taken from the Australian experience, help to illustrate these points.

Human Rights: Aborigines, Queensland and Australian Foreign Relations

Racism, as a central issue on the human rights agenda, has penetrated all levels of political activity, from the local to the international.[46] In the case of federal states, such as Australia, this fact, combined with the responsibilities of non-central governments for native populations, has complicated the conduct of foreign relations in an increasingly sensitive area. This reality was clearly demonstrated during the period of the Fraser governments from 1975 to 1983 as policies pursued by the conservative state governments of Western Australia and Queensland towards their Aboriginal populations came under close international scrutiny.

This issue has to be viewed against both its domestic political and foreign policy backgrounds. In terms of the first set of factors, the realities of federal–state relations combined with the inclination of a conservative government in Canberra to respect states' rights, seeking accommodation rather than confrontation in the management of disputes, provided an important backdrop to the development of Aboriginal politics. With regard to the foreign policy dimension, the problems which the Fraser government was to confront in this area were compounded by the prime minister's attempts to project a foreign policy stance sympathetic to the Third World and one strongly opposed to racial discrimination.

Thus whilst the Labor government of Gough Whitlam, which preceded the Fraser government, had often denounced racism, and South African apartheid in particular, it was Malcolm Fraser who was to voice the strongest condemnation of apartheid in a speech to the Royal Commonwealth Society in London in June 1977. Ironically, it was his criticism of New Zealand's sporting links with South Africa which drew the first open international attack on Australia's own racial policies, made by the New Zealand prime minister.[47]

Central to the problem as it developed in the late 1970s and early 1980s, were two linked issues: firstly, the question of land rights and the terms under which Aboriginal reserves should be held; and, second, the question of mining and oil prospecting on land held by Aborigines, particularly sacred sites. The latter problem had flared up into open conflict during 1980, with the Western Australian government and the mining and oil prospecting companies on one side, and Aborigines occupying land on pastoral lease at Noonkanbah, 1400 miles north of Perth, on the other.

The decision of the state government, led by Sir Charles Court, to assist a US-based multinational corporation, Amax Petroleum, to send in a drilling team to prospect in the area against strong opposition by the Aborigines was met with widespread protest within Australia and warnings of the consequences of such actions on Australia's foreign relations. The *Sydney Morning Herald*, for example, claimed that the Court government's action would 'compromise Australia severely in the eyes of the world, and especially the Third World'.[48]

Additionally, both the Western Australian and Queensland governments were opposed to federal government policy on land rights, the Court government being particularly critical of Aboriginal claims and Canberra's response to them. Whilst the government of Joh Bjelke Petersen in Queensland was somewhat less intransigent than its opposite number in Perth on the question of Aboriginal reserves, it consistently rejected Canberra's policy of granting perpetual leases for reserves and favoured fixed-term leases. No doubt with Fraser's anti-apartheid stance in mind, Bjelke Petersen characterized federal policy as producing within Australia the very same system which the prime minister had so vehemently sought to condemn.[49]

The problem for the Fraser government at the level of foreign relations grew as the international community, both governments and non-governmental organizations, became increasingly aware of this domestic political conflict. Thus, in the US the annual reports on human rights practices presented by the State Department to Congress during the years 1979–81, referred to treatment of Aborigines and, particularly, various policies pursued by the Western Australian and Queensland governments.[50] To a considerable degree, this reflected the success of Aboriginal pressure groups in projecting their concerns onto the international stage both through their own direct actions and by means of gaining the support of transnational groups such as the World Council of Churches (WCC) and the World Council of Indigenous Peoples (WCIP).

In addition, the United Nations and its agencies afforded forums in which Queensland's and Western Australia's policies could be internationalized, to Canberra's discomfiture. Thus in the wake of the incident at Noonkanbah, Australia's ambassador to the UN office in Geneva found himself defending Australia's human rights record before the UN Subcommission on the Prevention of Discrimination and Protection of Minorities to which the case had been referred by the chairman of the National Aboriginal Congress (NAC). This was one move in a campaign to involve the UN in Aborigines' grievances which went back to the latter period of the Whitlam government when the creation of an Aboriginal 'tent embassy' outside the New York headquarters had been proposed.[51]

By the late 1970s, however, lobbying of the UN and its subcommittees had become more systematized, supplemented by a broader campaign facilitated by two events of international significance, both to be held in Australia: the Commonwealth Heads of Government Meeting (CHOGM) scheduled for October 1981 in Melbourne, and the 1982 Commonwealth Games in Brisbane. One of the leading figures in the Aboriginal campaign, Gary Foley, described CHOGM as 'our best-ever opportunity to broaden and strengthen our international links by lobbying as many heads of government as possible'.[52] To this end, Foley was reported as having persuaded Father Walter Lini, the prime minister of Vanuatu, to raise the issue formally during the conference and to lobby other Commonwealth leaders.

In terms of its potential to complicate Australian foreign relations, however, the Commonwealth Games promised to be an occasion of far greater significance. Not only was the Queensland government, as host to the games, directly involved, but sensitive issues touching on sporting links with South Africa, the status of the Gleneagles Agreement and the New Zealand government's stance on both issues, were raised. Moreover, Bjelke Petersen's sympathy towards the New Zealand prime minister's policy (and, specifically, the latter's refusal to stop the 1981 Springbok rugby union tour of New Zealand) on sporting links with South Africa was well-known. He had taken little trouble to conceal his scepticism concerning Malcolm Fraser's condemnation of apartheid, arguing that South Africa's domestic policies were its own affair. The revelation that Bjelke Petersen had received a letter from the South African prime minister thanking him for the support given by Queensland did nothing to lessen the fear that African Commonwealth countries might boycott the games.[53] Their location, together with the broader issues of sporting links with South Africa, ensured that the Commonwealth Games were an excellent opportunity for Aboriginal groups to publicize their cause.

Whilst the NAC called on the black Commonwealth countries to come to Brisbane to see the Aboriginal situation in Queensland at first hand, other leaders were pressing them to boycott the games. A concerted campaign focused on Commonwealth members, particularly the Organisation of African Unity (OAU), was pursued during 1981 and 1982 with a number of Aboriginal delegations travelling to Africa with the purpose of lobbying political leaders, and by February 1982 it was predicted that thirteen or fourteen African countries would participate in a boycott. Claims by Bjelke Petersen that some of these delegations were being trained in terrorist tactics by Libya did little to cool the atmosphere.

The ultimate objective of the tactics employed by the Aboriginal groups was to force the federal government to use its powers to intervene in Queensland and take over control of Aboriginal affairs. As already noted, the Fraser government was disinclined to take such a course of action for domestic political reasons. Opposition to this stance by the Australian Labor Party was to be expected, but some Liberals, such as Senator Alan Missen, chairman of the Senate Committee on Constitutional and Legal Affairs, also expressed reservations as to the likelihood of a change in Queensland's Aboriginal policies being effected by persuasion.[54]

More general pressures for a total boycott were rejected at a special meeting of the Commonwealth Games Foundation in London in 1982. In part this reflected the goodwill which existed in Africa towards the Fraser government arising from the role played by the Australian prime minister at the Lusaka Commonwealth summit in promoting a settlement on the Zimbabwe issue. African leaders appeared to be prepared to distinguish between Canberra's and Queensland's policies regarding Aboriginal issues, reflecting the rather cautiously worded observation of the director of the Nigerian Institute of International Affairs made during a visit to Australia in 1980: 'I get the feeling that the federal government is committed to such programmes [to alleviate the conditions of the Aborigines] but I also get the impression that the state governments do not show the same goodwill on these issues'.[55]

Whilst this interplay of domestic and international politics was being enacted, the High Court, in May 1982, delivered a judgement which not merely affirmed the federal government's power to legislate in the sphere of Aboriginal policy and civil rights generally but (as noted earlier in the chapter) through an expanded interpretation of the external affairs power in the constitution, was of immense potential significance to the future of the federal system. The case turned on the validity of the Racial Discrimination Act passed by the federal parliament in 1975 to give effect to Australia's ratification of the UN convention on all forms of racial discrimination. In response to the case brought by John Koowarta against the Queensland government, accusing it of breaching the act by refusing to approve the acquisition by an Aboriginal Community of various pastoral leases in the Archer River area of Northern Queensland, the Queensland government (supported by Victoria and Western Australia) challenged the validity of the act, arguing that it was not a legitimate exercise of the federal government's powers under the external affairs provision of the constitution. By a narrow majority, the High Court found in favour of Canberra, on the grounds that questions of racial discrimination were now of central concern to members of the international community and that, consequently, Commonwealth legislation in the area was a valid exercise of the external affairs power.

In this instance, the Fraser government was confronted by a problem involving a delicate mix of domestic and international politics which touched on a key theme of its foreign policy. It is worth noting that Queensland's projection into the complexities of international human rights issues came not as a result of its own desire to internationalize the problem, but as a result of the stategy pursued by the Aboriginal organizations and the interests of a number of foreign governments and non-state actors. Here, as Collins has pointed out, a conflict of perceptions exists.[56] For many non-Aboriginal Australians, these problems related to state politics and federal–state relations; to many foreign observers, either unaware of, or unwilling to accept as a legitimate excuse for Canberra's unwillingness to confront the states, the complexities of Australian politics, this was an issue with clear implications for their relationships with Canberra. This demanded a round of active diplomacy on the part of the Fraser government, at both the domestic and international levels. Its success in short-circuiting the threat to the Commonwealth Games by persuading key participants that Australian policy in the area of Aboriginal rights was basically sound and that events in Western Australia and Queensland were not representative of the country as a whole, helped to prevent a boycott of the games by the African states – a particularly embarrassing possibility in the light of Fraser's strong opposition to participation in the 1980 Moscow Olympics following the USSR's intervention in Afghanistan.

Nuclear Ships and the ANZUS Alliance

The 1980s were also to witness another situation where domestic and international politics became intertwined, and on an issue which touched directly on the key element of postwar Australian foreign policy, the ANZUS alliance. The US connection has always been a sensitive and frequently emotive issue in Australian politics, dividing the Australian Labor Party (ALP) from the parties of the right. In particular, the left wing of the ALP has always been concerned with the terms of the alliance, its impact on Australian sovereignty and the presence of US installations on Australian soil, such as those at Pine Gap and North West Cape. In the early 1980s, fuel was added to this debate by the Fraser government's decision to permit Washington to base B52 bombers at Darwin.

The issue of American bases, however, was linked to another area of intense political debate: that of nuclear weapons, nuclear power and the mining and export of uranium. Differences in policy on these issues between the parties of the right, the Liberal and National parties, were underscored when, in 1976, the New South Wales ALP government requested that, on safety grounds, the USS Truxton, a nuclear-powered cruiser, should not be permitted to enter Sydney harbour. Warnings that this action would affect the viability of the ANZUS treaty were speedily voiced by the prime minister, who immediately contacted other state premiers concerning their attitude towards nuclear ships.[57]

Canberra's reaction to what it chose to portray as a major challenge to the conduct of Australian foreign and defence policy was, nevertheless, mild in comparison to its response when, in May 1982, the newly elected ALP government in Victoria under the leadership of John Cain, announced that Melbourne would no longer be available to visiting nuclear ships. The Victorian decision has to be seen in the context of the embarrassment created for the ALP federal leadership by the adoption at the 1982 Victorian state ALP conference of a resolution calling for the termination of the ANZUS treaty and the adoption of a non-aligned foreign policy.[58] Whilst the ALP leadership was certainly critical of aspects of the alliance, the Victorian resolution, which would be carried forward to the ALP federal conference scheduled for July 1982, seemed likely to offer Malcolm Fraser a golden opportunity to portray the ALP as a party wedded to policies whose consequence would be the undermining of Australia's security.

Such fears were amply justified when Fraser, during a visit to the Northern Territory, released the contents of the letter in which Cain had informed him of his government's decision. Although Cain emphasized the domestic context of the decision (Victoria was to be declared a nuclear-free state) Fraser quickly linked it to the future of ANZUS, arguing that port facilities for allied nuclear ships was an integral commitment incurred through membership of the alliance, and announced that legislation would be introduced into the federal parliament to underwrite Canberra's powers in an area so crucial to her defence.

The ALP's traditional sympathy to any diminution of the powers of the states did nothing to lessen its embarrassment at this turn of events. Indeed, within a few days of the controversy emerging, a correspondent writing in *The Age* was able to detect no fewer than four quite distinct positions on the issues of nuclear weapons and nuclear-powered ships circulating within the ALP at state and federal levels.[59] This confusion was compounded by a clear rift in the ALP federal leadership. The leader of the opposition, Bill Hayden, drew a distinction between nuclear-armed and nuclear-powered vessels, suggesting that only the former were unwelcome in Australian ports, whereas his foreign policy spokesman, Lionel Bowen, took a different line, arguing that ALP policy allowed access to both kinds of vessel providing that it was for purposes of refuelling and not conducting exercises. A *Canberra Times* editorial, which observed that 'it is a pity he [Cain] muddied the waters that are murky enough in relation to how foreign governments perceive Australia's would-be autonomous states', must have evinced some sympathy in federal ALP circles.[60]

Of course, the principal foreign government whose perceptions were likely to have been clouded was the US. That the nuclear ships issue arose on the eve of an ANZUS Council meeting helped to ensure that Washington would be drawn into a peculiarly sensitive area of Australian domestic politics. Comments by the State Department critical of ALP policy, alongside observations in Henry Kissinger's recently published memoirs critical of former Labor prime minister Gough Whitlam's views on US bombing in North Vietnam during the Nixon era, did little to calm the atmosphere. Fraser was accused of seeking political capital out of the issue by asking Washington to 'clarify its position' on the question of port access for nuclear ships. That the deputy prime minister, Doug Anthony, happened to be in Washington at the time strengthened the charges of collusion. The US, however, clearly had its own interests in the affair for its nuclear powered ships had recently been denied access to Fiji. The pressures for a nuclear-free South Pacific were growing.

The US representative at the ANZUS Council, Walter Stoessel, lost little time in emphasizing the importance of port access for US nuclear vessels, and he was reported as being 'still concerned' after a brief meeting with Hayden.[61] Not surprisingly, when the Council communique was issued, it was discovered that the third paragraph of the thirty paragraph statement included the observation that the Council members 'recognized the importance of access by United States naval ships to the ports of its treaty partners as a critical factor in its efforts to maintain strategic deterrence and in order to carry out its responsibilities under the terms of the Treaty'.[62] Such an uncompromising position on Stoessel's part left Hayden with little room for manoeuvre, and within five hours of the statement's release he had announced that he now embraced the position already outlined by Lionel Bowen. The July 1982 ALP conference adopted the position that visits by nuclear-powered vessels, but not home porting, would be acceptable, and recognized that the US government could not reveal whether a ship carried nuclear weapons. Meanwhile, the Victorian premier had conceded the federal government's ultimate power in issues of defence and foreign policy.

The nuclear ships issue, however, was by no means dead. Indeed, with the election in 1984 of a Labour government in New Zealand under the leadership of David Lange, the challenge to ANZUS assumed a far more serious dimension. The Labour Party, unlike its Australian counterpart, was committed to banning all nuclear-powered or nuclear-armed ships from New Zealand.[63] As in the earlier case, the US government regarded this a serious problem, and the secretary of state, George Shultz, during a visit to New Zealand shortly after the election, made it clear that Washington saw the Labor government's position as a major challenge to the ANZUS alliance. For a variety of domestic and international political reasons, both governments found themselves locked in an increasingly bitter dispute which escalated with the refusal by New Zealand, in February 1985, to accede to a request by the US to permit the destroyer USS Buchanan to use New Zealand port facilities. In Bercovitch's words:

> like two parties moving along a predetermined course, both countries found themselves moving from a rational to rationalising behaviour with each misperceiving the other's intentions, or feeling betrayed by the other's statements and actions.[64]

In Australia, the Hawke ALP government (which had replaced the Fraser government in 1983) was confronted by the usual political sensitivities aroused by the US alliance, rendered even stronger by disquiet at Reaganite foreign policy and the government's failure – in the eyes of many within the ALP – to take a sufficiently independent stance against Washington. To this was added the tensions that quickly developed between the Australian foreign minister, Bill Hayden, and Washington over arms control issues and US intervention in Central America.[65] In short, this was a taxing domestic and international issue for the Hawke government which, whilst anxious to prevent the growing strains between Wellington and Washington disrupting ANZUS, was well-aware that there was considerable support, both inside and outside the Labor Party, for the stance taken by the Lange government.

It was against this background that state politics emerged as a complicating element in the environment in which Australian foreign policy is conducted. On this occasion it assumed the form of an intervention by the Queensland premier, Joh Bjelke Petersen, whose criticisms of the New Zealand government's position on the nuclear ships issue, and those in Australia who supported it, had been voiced in the clearest of terms. In January 1985, as the New Zealand cabinet was considering its response to Washington's request for port access for the US destroyer later that year, the Queensland premier announced that his state would be adopting its own 'trade sanctions' against New Zealand: 'I don't expect our action will make the New Zealand government change its mind, but at least it will highlight their naive anti-nuclear policies'.[66]

The 'sanctions' assumed the form of a ban on New Zealand chocolates on the grounds that they failed to comply with the labelling regulations of the Queensland Health Department. A few days later, these regulations were also used to impound a consignment of New Zealand beer. These actions were condemned not only by the Australian government, but by the leader of the opposition, Andrew Peacock. Not unexpectedly, the New Zealand government dismissed them as an illegitimate intrusion into the realm of foreign policy:

> The conduct of foreign affairs is in the hands of the Australian government. Under the Australian Constitution Act international affairs are conducted by the government of the Commonwealth of Australia and state governments have no responsibility for it at all.[67]

Apart from this observation by the New Zealand acting prime minister, Wellington, pointing to the balance of trans-Tasman trade in Queensland's favour, hinted at imposing its own trade reprisals, specifically through seeking alternative suppliers for New Zealand's multi-million dollar sugar market.[68] By the end of January, Bjelke Petersen was signalling an end to the bans on New Zealand imports, arguing that they had served their purpose in embarrassing the Lange government and pointing to 'the stupidity of breaking the ANZUS alliance'.[69]

Both problems, Aboriginal land rights and the developments surrounding ANZUS, clearly fell into the category of high politics for Canberra in the sense that they affected key foreign policy interests. Moreover, the ANZUS complications came within the traditional definition of high politics. However, each of these instances demonstrates different circumstances under which NCGs can become involved in patterns of multilayered diplomacy. The Aboriginal land rights and related matters illustrated how what had hitherto been regarded as an essentially domestic political issue, involving state policies, could be elevated to an international issue through the increasingly skilful activities of Aboriginal groups in the international arena. Queensland did not seek to project the issue onto the world stage: quite the opposite. When it was criticized by the WCC for its

Aboriginal policies, the response from Brisbane was, predictably, that this involved a purely domestic issue. For Canberra, however, the problem had to be treated in both political contexts, the domestic and the international. Since it was not prepared to challenge the Queensland government by using its powers to intervene directly, it was forced to engage in active international diplomacy to preserve its position on a key element of its foreign policy, namely support for international human rights.[70]

The ANZUS 'crisis' of 1982 illustrates a different scenario. Here, the Fraser government succeeded in manufacturing a foreign policy crisis for domestic political gain by exploiting US concerns over the port access for nuclear ships issue. Faced with declining popularity, a worsening economic situation and a muddled defence policy, any issue which offered the chance of a federal election on a non-economic theme was welcome. In this context, Cain's actions were a gift to an embattled administration. Once the potentially explosive issue of nuclear ships presented itself, Fraser merely needed to light the touch paper and let ALP factionalism do the rest.

The second ANZUS episode, Bjelke Petersen's so-called 'chocolate war' against New Zealand differed from the first in the sense that this was a direct and conscious intervention in a serious international problem. Again, however, it has to be seen in its domestic context, particularly the tensions between a conservative state government and a Labor administration in Canberra. Its main significance lay not so much in its impact on Australian relations with New Zealand, but in the extent to which it reinforced the domestic controversy surrounding Australia's response to the problem.

CONCLUSION

The chapter began with an of image of NCG international involvement which places a somewhat different emphasis on the phenomenon from that which is implicit in much of the literature. Rather than viewing them as divorced from the main patterns of international diplomacy, this image sees NCGs embedded in them. Indeed, because they stand at a critical juncture between international and domestic forces, their participation in policy issues which span both internal and external policy arenas can become critical to the outcomes of diplomacy. This reflects their hybrid nature as actors which ensures that they no more accord to the picture of a unitary actor than does the nation-state.

Their significant position within socio-political systems, their linkages with the political centre and their status as representatives of regional interests, creates a situation in which both central governments and international actors who perceive access to the political system and society of a federal state as a means of achieving policy goals, will have an interest in coopting subnational governments.

As we have seen, one consequence of this is that NCGs can assume a number of roles in the policy process as it develops. They can be both agent for and opponent to central government in the pursuit of its international goals. At one and the same time, they present national foreign policy managers with a challenge which resides not so much in a threat to the integrity of foreign policy, but in the task of managing the interplay between subnational interests and international actors, and also with a diplomatic resource for dealing with the resultant complex web of public policy. It is this theme that the following chapters explore.

3 The Trade Agenda

One of the first documents bearing on America's foreign relations to land on the desk of newly elected President George Bush came not, as one might have expected, from a federal agency such as the State Department or the Office of the Special Trade Representative, but from the World Trade Commission of the State of California.[1] This memorandum, with its observations and recommendations on state and federal roles in export promotion and the trade policy processes, reflects, as earlier chapters have already suggested, a key factor in growing foreign policy localization; namely, an enhanced interest in foreign trade policy shown by localities and the interests they represent. The impact of this can be seen in a number of forms both at the national and international levels and is underscored by the observation of former US special trade representative, Robert S. Strauss, regarding his role during the Tokyo Round of GATT negotiations:

> The Tokyo Round . . . was, among other things, an exercise in domestic American politics at its best. In fact during my tenure as Special Trade Representative . . . I spent as much time negotiating with domestic constituents (both industry and labour) and members of the US Congress as I did negotiating with our foreign trading partners.[2]

This, of course, should come as no surprise: in Spero's words, 'trade policy is the stuff of domestic politics'.[3] Increasingly, foreign trade and the policies which help to determine it, affect the wellbeing of diverse economic interests and provide a setting within which there is a need for cooperation between national and subnational agencies and interests; yet, at the same time, also create the potential for conflict as regional and national priorities clash.

Given this fact, domestic political and legal structures can assume great significance in determining the position of national communities within the trading system. Such factors as bureaucratic fragmentation in the trade policy area, conflict between executive and legislature, together with the territorial distibution of power, can, moreover, affect the structures of the international economic system itself. As one study of the processes surrounding the implementation of the Tokyo Round has demonstrated, there is a mutual interdependence between the delicate constitutional structures of international economic organizations such as the GATT and the OECD and national political systems.[4] The purpose of this chapter is to consider in general terms that dimension of trade policy localization represented by growing NCG international involvement. The subsequent two chapters pursue the theme in the context of the diplomatic exchanges that developed, firstly during the negotiation of the Canada–US free trade agreement and, second, as British companies attempted to end the practice commonly referred to as 'unitary taxation' employed by some US state governments.

NCGs AND THE TRADING ENVIRONMENT

Potentially, all policies enacted by subnational authorities are capable of affecting the trading environment, particularly in the light of the growing mobility of capital which is a key feature of the contemporary global economy. Policies in such diverse areas as education, employment, taxation and the environment all affect the investment climate and are, therefore, of interest to what Robert Reich has termed the 'global webs' of transnational business enterprises.[5] Indeed, as will be demonstrated later in this chapter, the very character of federal systems, with their regional economic differences and political tensions, condition the environment in which international trade is conducted and investment decisions made. This can be clearly seen where industry and government come into close contact, as in the awarding of major defence contracts such as the replacement of the Oberon submarine fleet in Australia and the proposal (ultimately abandoned) of the Canadian government to purchase up to twelve nuclear powered submarines.[6] In both cases, a complex pattern of interactions between the contenders for the contracts, their 'home' governments, the federal authorities responsible for awarding the contracts and the subnational governments competing for the construction work, developed.

Furthermore, as the focus within the international trading system has moved in recent years away from protectionism created by tariffs towards that sustained by non-tariff barriers, increasing attention has been directed to locally administered policies which might be regarded as distorting the free movement of goods. Consequently, both international business and international organizations, such as the European Community (EC) and the General Agreement on Tariffs and

Trade (GATT), have found themselves concerned with NCG policies, as in the case of Canadian provincial liquor policies discussed later in this chapter.

Looked at in reverse perspective, the interactions between the international economy and local economies is reinforced by the marked growth in NCG activities directed towards export promotion and investment attraction. This creates a scenario in which complex diplomatic relationships embracing international, national and subnational actors are fostered. This is reflected in situations where local issues become internationalized, as in the case of the unitary taxation issue or local government procurement policies. On other occasions, perhaps more rarely, local national conflicts can become projected onto the international stage. This was the case when the Queensland government, during the period when the Australian Labor Party of Gough Whitlam ruled in Canberra, attempted to pursue its own brand of resources diplomacy towards Japan, bringing it into open conflict with the federal authorities.[7] More recently in Canada, a storm of protest erupted around Prime Minister Brian Mulroney when, during a visit to Tokyo in May 1991, he openly criticized policies adopted by the recently elected New Democratic Party government in Ontario as likely to create an environment hostile to foreign investment.[8]

Instances such as these are always likely to hit the headlines and have conditioned perspectives on the role of NCGs in the international system, both in general terms and, more particularly, in the sphere of foreign trade. It is, indeed, the case that federalism, given the division of powers characteristic of federal constitutions and the responsibilities alloted to subnational governments in the area of economic development, will be marked by diverging interests between regions and the centre. One study of Australian resources diplomacy makes the point that differences between state and federal government objectives in this field can result in both foreign investors and Australian citizens being subjected to conflicting demands. Not surprisingly, then, 'foreign businessmen and policy-makers alike have had considerable interest in how the Australian federal system works in relation to resources trade and development'.[9]

As discussion in Chapter 2 has suggested, however, cooperation between centre and regions is at least as likely to characterise NCG–centre relationships, and this is as true of the foreign economic policy arena as it is of others. In fact, as elsewhere, the patterns of relationships which emerge depend upon the precise nature of the area of activity. Bearing this in mind, the ensuing discussion will examine three dimensions of local activity in the trading environment:

- Export promotion and investment attaction.
- Local influence over national trade policy.
- Local trade policies.

EXPORT PROMOTION AND INVESTMENT ATTRACTION

The growing international focus displayed by subnational governments is no more clearly indicated than in their attempts to enhance economic development through promoting exports and attacting foreign investment.[10] The growing international orientation of NCGs is captured in the Governor of Virginia's introduction to the National Governors' Association series of reports entitled *America in Transition: The International Frontier*, published in 1989. Noting the emergence of the global marketplace and the changing position of the US within it, Governor Baliles points to the growing role of state governments:

> Twenty years ago, states were bystanders as international events changed the economic landscape. That, too, has changed. Our boundaries are no longer the borders of our states, but every corner of the globe. As Governors, we are challenged to confront this new reality.[11]

Allowing for necessary differences of circumstance and location, these sentiments could well have been expressed by any state/provincial politician, indeed by city leaders, concerned with the economic future of their citizens. The general trends in the world economy which have produced this situation have been identified in earlier chapters and do not need repeating here. It is, perhaps, sufficient to note, as has one study of foreign investment in the US, that the expansion of state overseas offices follows the major periods of recession and consequent unemployment during the 1970s and 1980s.[12] Official reports from subnational departments of economic development are replete with indices of the growing reliance of local economies on the international economy. Hence, in the case of California, the value of traded goods passing through California's customs districts has increased four-fold; the number of foreign companies located in Georgia has risen from 150 in 1975 to 1257 in 1988.[13] In the Australian state of Victoria, a real growth in non-primary exports of 53 per cent was recorded between

1985 and 1988, whilst in Ontario merchandise exports increased by 13 per cent per annum during the period 1976–87.[14] By far the most detailed information regarding NCG international activities comes from the US in the form of the National Association of State Development Agencies' State Export Program Database. Figures for the fiscal year 1987–8 show an increase of 195 per cent in state expenditure on trade development; the average state budget for international trade in 1988 had grown by 141 per cent since 1984.[15]

In broad terms, NCGs in each of the three countries which are the focus of this study engage in similar activities in pursuit of trade promotion and investment attraction. These include a variety of programmes designed to provide information on export opportunities for local businesses: thus Ontario's Ministry of Industry, Trade and Technology runs a series of international marketing seminars throughout the province intended to provide potential exporters with information on market opportunities. More extensive courses are offered through the provincial universities.[16] NASDA's survey shows that virtually all US state governments operate this form of counselling service.[17] In addition, NCG development departments typically seek to assist firms by developing overseas trade leads, channelling these to appropriate companies, and offering financial assistance to exporters. In California, the California Export Finance Office provides loan guarantees for companies taking up export orders which cover up to 85 per cent of a maximum loan amount of $411 000. In 1988, CEFO provided 79 guarantees covering $60 million in transactions.[18] Similarly, Ontario, through its Development Corporation, operates an Export Support Programme to help exporters by means of bank guarantees, term loans and incentive loans. It also operates an Export Success Fund which matches, dollar-for-dollar, marketing costs up to $35 000 ovcr a twelve month period.[19]

These various strategies are frequently brought together as programmes targeted on specific markets such as Ontario's New Exporters to Border States programme which is aimed at helping potential exporters to get their products marketed in the US.[20] In Australia, Victoria has a similar series of 'export facilitation programmes' such as the North American Market Entry Program established in 1985 and, in the first instance, focused on the Pacific North West area of the US and Canada.[21] The success of this programme (estimated to have produced exports of A$61 million and technology development of A$11 million between 1986 and 1989) encouraged its replication in a European Community Market Entry

Program with a target of establishing 100 Victorian companies in the European market intended to generate additional export sales of A$50 million over a three year period.[22] In the case of Japan, the 1988 report set as its goal the strengthening of existing programmes to focus on the export of value-added products and services. On the investment front, the aim was to secure a shift in Japanese investment away from its traditional areas such as property and financial services towards 'investment opportunities strategic to the development of the Victorian economy'.[23]

Undoubtedly, it is the overseas presence of non-central governments which has alerted observers to their role on the international stage. And, indeed, the general trend over the last fifteen years or so has been for overseas offices to increase in number as the NASDA figures reveal in the case of the US. Between 1986 and 1987, 42 new overseas offices were opened by state governments, increasing the total to 108.[24] In terms of the number of offices, Illinois is revealed as the most 'international' state with six offices, whilst the average figure is slightly over two per state. Of the five largest Australian states, Victoria, South Australia and Queensland maintain four offices, New South Wales three and Western Australia two. In Canada, provincial international offices range from Ontario's sixteen, through Alberta's six to Newfoundland's sole international representation through a 'condominium' arrangement whereby the province is represented in the Canadian High Commission in Hong Kong.[25]

The emergence of a variety of terms to identify the activities of these offices – such as 'microdiplomacy' and 'global paradiplomacy' – has tended to endow them with an aura which distorts the realities of the work in which they are engaged. In some instances, the politics of separatist aspirations, as in the case of Quebec, does provide a political gloss to their activities, but for the most part, the offices are one element in the accomplishment of NCG trade and investment strategies combined with tourist promotion work. A recent survey carried out by the California World Trade Commission, whilst pointing to the similarity in terms of the broad range of functions undertaken by the offices, also notes some differences:

> Many part-time contractors merely answer telephones during given hours. Smaller offices may seek trade leads or distribute tourism material. The larger offices generally devote time to some combination of trade promotion, investment attraction, market research, networking, and, at times, tourism. State representatives attend

> trade shows, trade and investment seminars, promotional events, business association meetings; offices host special gatherings of industry representatives and/or policymakers; staff speak at various functions.[26]

One international office with a long history, British Columbia House in London, describes its activities as:

- Providing detailed information to European businesses on sources and supply of BC products and services.
- Informing BC companies of commercial prospects, market conditions and opportunities in Europe.
- Providing assistance to BC companies seeking to access European markets.
- Providing an operational base for BC companies visiting London.
- Arranging visits to BC for European business people to meet suppliers and explore direct investment opportunities.
- Linking manufactuturers to possible joint venture, technology transfer and licensing opportunities in British Columbia and in Europe.
- Facilitating business immigration programmes.
- Promoting the travel industry and the marketing of tourism to BC.[27]

This range of functions is reflected in the information provided to the author during interviews with staff at overseas offices. One of the words most frequently used by staff when describing their role was that of 'facilitator' in promoting export and investment and opportunities. Most state representatives see this role in 'reactive' terms (that is, responding to enquiries from the home base and target areas) and 'proactive' (for example, identifying markets and home companies that might seek to exploit them).

The precise nature of these activities appears to depend in large measure on resources available to the offices. Not surprisingly, operating internationally in this way is expensive: in 1988, California spent $1.5 million on what was then its three offices.[28] During the fiscal year ending in 1987, Ontario spent in excess of C$16 million.[29] Expenditure on Victoria's four offices was estimated in 1989 to be in the order of A$1 million each.[29] Less wealthy states and provinces find such costs hard to sustain, particularly in times of economic recession. Tasmania closed its London office in the mid 1980s; Saskatchewan followed a similar course in 1991, whilst Nova Scotia downgraded its UK representation from that of full-scale agent-general to trade mission. Typically, NCGs appear to experiment with different forms of overseas representation, using a local consultant here, closing an office there or relocating in a region perceived to be of growing significance. In the case of all three countries' NCGs, Tokyo is the location most frequently targeted; Europe follows with offices usually placed in Brussels, Frankfurt or London.

Partly for this reason, officials tend to find themselves less well-placed to devote time to developing stategies and more likely to be reacting to external requests, a point frequently made by trade officials. Victoria's London office had seen a reduction in its staff from 34 in 1983 to 14 in 1989. The actual number of overseas offices maintained by an NGC can, however, be misleading both in terms of its international interests and its capacity to fund them. California, despite its economic strength, did not open its first offices (London and Tokyo) until 1987. The Californian survey referred to above makes the point that the strategy pursued by what it terms the 'top states' is to establish well-funded offices employing full-time staff. It contrasts this approach with that of Minnesota 'which has the advantage of eight locations overseas, but is represented on only a part-time basis, with no budget for promotions or advertising.[31]

Given the cost of maintaining overseas offices and the fact that all dimensions of economic development are likely to be politicized issues, it is not surprising that international aspects of development are frequently intertwined with local politics. One example can be found in the conflict that arose beween Governor Schaefer of Maryland and the state legislature during the 1988 legislative session over the funding of a state World Trade Institute intended to provide export support services for local business. Although the issue in dispute was the demand by legislators that private industry should eventually assume the cost of the Institute, it was generally seen as one manifestation of the continuing dispute between between the two arms of government as to their respective powers.[32]

Politicization has often been reinforced by the tendency, particularly in the case of the Canadian and Australian offices in London, to appoint former politicians to head their operations, implanting an aura of political patronage in the activities of overseas offices. In the case of Australia, where the Labor Party, traditionally opposed to federalism, has looked with suspicion on the role of such offices, the question of their cost, indeed the need for them, has frequently found itself on the political agenda. Thus it is quite likely that an incoming Australian state government will carry out a review of its overseas operations as did that in Victoria in 1982 and in New South Wales in 1989. One of the most notable developments in Australian state representation, however, is to appoint professionals to preside over offices; it is now far more common to find state representatives with experience in business and commerce and in the diplomatic and commercial services than it is former state politicians. Thus the new agent-general for Queensland in London, appointed in 1991, had previously served in the Australian trade commissioner service, Austrade, before taking up his post.

Alongside the overseas offices, the most obvious manifestation of the NCGs' international presence is the growing number of trade and investment missions led by prominent state political figures, particularly US state governors and Australian and Canadian premiers. A recent National Governors' Association survey revealed that, in 1989, 41 governors had made 82 trips to 35 countries.[33] During a single month in 1987, 15 governors made official visits to Japan.[34] This reflects the central role of chief executives in the formulation, coordination and implementation of economic development policy within their jurisdictions, partly because of its intrinsic significance, partly for obvious political reasons. As one observer of the changing role of the US state governments in economic development has suggested, the governors are 'in a unique position to bring together a variety of actors to structure economic development policy and build coalitions to support economic initiatives'.[35] Similarly, in Australia, the emergence of what has been referred to as the 'strong premier type' has been identified as closely related to the growing significance of state development:

> They sell themselves with skill and fervour. State development has been a primary policy objective for all, and they have competed with one another in seeking to attract investment. They have been supersalesmen for their states, undertaking diplomatic missions and bargaining by offering attractive concessions to prospective investors.[36]

In some instances, as in the case of Queensland and California, the close association between economic development and the premier or governor is reflected in the administrative structures which have been created to pursue international trade and investment objectives. (California's overseas offices are administered by the Governor's Office.)

The involvement of the chief executive in trade and investment missions is also perceived to be a mark of the significance attached by the NCG to its relations with particular markets and potential investors.[37] An account of a mission headed by Governor Baliles of Virginia to Japan, South Korea and Taiwan provides a flavour of the kinds of activity involved: selling the advantages of the state to potential investors; trying to persuade firms to shift their exports from other East coast to Virginia ports.[38] Similarly, Australian state and Canadian provincial premiers are regular figures on the international circuit.

Thus, in 1988, the premier of South Australia, John Bannon, led a mission comprising officials and industrialists on a two-week European tour.[39] In this case, the agenda reflected both concerns common to the trading community as a whole (the impact of the Single European Market and the desirability of opening a trade office in Brussels) as well as the South Australian economy in particular. Special emphasis was given to Sweden in the light of two factors: first, the emergence of Sweden as Australia's largest overseas wine market and the location of major wine exporters in South Australia; second, the awarding to the Swedish shipbuilder, Kockums, of the contract to build – in Adelaide – six diesel-powered submarines. Given the industrial base of the state, Bannon's main emphasis was on attracting high-tech companies, particularly those in the defence-related sector such as Plessey and Ferranti.

Competition and Cooperation

The picture presented by these overseas extensions of NCG state development activities appears to be confused and untidy. At first sight, it offends against both logic, which suggests that centralization in the federal government would provide a more rational approach, and innate assumptions regarding the undesirability of having a multitude of voices speaking for countries overseas. In some senses this is true. Federalism, it is often observed, is inherently untidy; and, it should be added, world politics is becoming increasingly so. As noted in other parts of this study, it is not simply federal systems that are demonstrating a growing internationalization on the part of local jurisdictions. Cities, prefectures, provinces, regions in the most centralized of political systems are demonstrating their wares in the international marketplace and competing to attract foreign investors to their localities.

A not atypical view from the centre is to be found in the 1989 report of the Committee for Review of Export Market Development Assistance in Australia. Having considered the export programmes of the states, it concludes that:

> there was competition rather than complementarity, particularly in overseas representation. Buyers overseas are frequently confused by overlapping State and Commonwelath representation. Total expenditures are small and administrative costs are therefore relatively high. Because of these factors it is doubtful whether State efforts add much to the development of exports overall.[40]

This image is reinforced by the director general of the United States and Foreign Commercial Service, who, whilst arguing for a partnership between federal, state and local export development programs, indicates the problems that can arise:

> More often than not, states and localities show up on our doorstep overseas with little or no advance notice. While state and local trade programs are increasing in sophistication, and some have the the highest level of professional expertise, others are still in the 'adolescent' stage of development. Yet some of these unprepared groups undertake the extremely complex and ambitious task of leading overseas trade missions and heavily tax US & FCS staff and time resources.[41]

NCG trade officials are quick to acknowledge the shortcomings of the system but frequently make two points: first, there is considerable cooperation between the offices in a given location, and, also with the federal trade authorities; second, that a centralized system, not attuned to the needs of the localities, simply could not carry out the task alone. To the European director of New York's London office, there is 'no real alternative to the present situation; the system is efficient and it works'.[42] A commonly heard observation is that federal trade departments cannot provide the intelligence required by local trade officials and business interests; 'too slow and out-of-date' is a typical description, (in this case, of the information provided by the US Department of Commerce). It also has to be remembered that one of the reasons behind the growing role of NCGs in this area has been either the contraction of the federal role or its failure to meet the perceived needs of the regions. Certainly, in the case of the US, Washington has not merely tolerated an enhanced role for the states but has actively encouraged it. It has little choice, as the director general of the US & FCS recognizes in arguing for a partnership beween the centre and the regions in the overall US trade effort:

> No matter how broad our field network of domestic offices is, there will always be more companies we cannot reach that are capable of expanding into foreign markets but don't know about the range of programs and services available to help them to do so.[43]

In fact, in each of the countries examined, there is, despite problems generated by political and bureaucratic conflict, a high degree of cooperation between the levels of government which are reflected, for example, in the frequent attachment of federal trade officers to NCG trade departments. Both tiers of government need services and information that are best provided – or can only be provided – by the other. Beyond this, there are clear signs that NCGs are recognizing the need to cooperate with one another in the international marketplace; that, particularly in the investment-attraction game, competition has reached a point where it has become of questionable value. This is not to say that the activities of subnational governments overseas have entered an era of benign harmony, but there are signs of the elements of cooperation which are as much part of the overall picture as those of conflict, may be developing.

This is most clearly the case in the US. Indeed, one of the themes of the NGA's major policy document on exploiting foreign markets stresses the need for cooperation, arguing that 'even in this competitive arena, there is room for cooperation':

> In Brussels, Tokyo, and other world commercial capitals, directors of state overseas offices should be asked to propose cooperative projects. Joint market research initiatives or reporting are possible initiatives.[44]

Given the much larger number of subnational jurisdictions in the US than in either Canada or Australia, it is not surprising that regional cooperation bringing together groups of states has become a notable feature of their international operations. In 1983, the international development agencies of Alabama, Arkansas, Mississippi, Tennessee and Louisiana together with the World Trade Center in New Orleans, formed the Mid-South Trade Council, stimulated by the belief that 'by combining the products and services of an entire region, more benefits may be gained by all the states involved'.[45] In similar vein, the governors of the western states have been considering the possibilities of regional cooperation in their overseas efforts. A report commissioned by the Western Governors' Association advocates, amongst other things, coordination of governors' overseas missions, joint overseas trade offices, and the creation of a joint export finance service.[46] For some observers, this regionalization of the US trade effort is linked to processes of growing regional cooperation between nation-states, as the following comment made by the executive director of the Council of State Governments suggests:

> I think the regional revolutions going on in the European Community in 1992 and in the nations of Southeast Asia, which are trying to band together, are important models for states that can pool their resources to compete around the globe.[47]

The picture is different when one turns to investment attraction, an area noticeably missing from the WGA's study on state trade cooperation. Here the situation is characterized by conflict between NCGs and, not infrequently, between NCGs and the federal authorities. As one would expect, this derives from competition for the scarce resource, foreign investment, and the differing priorities of the centre and the regions. The point is well-made in a survey of the Australian states' role in industry promotion which, having noted the 'beggar-thy-neighbour' policies accompanying the quest for investment, goes on to indicate the tension which may arise where the goals of national policy are 'to increase overall (national) economic production and efficiency and to facilitate some redistribution of wealth to the poorer regions'.[48] In brief, the arguments revolve around the efficiency (or lack of it) of a situation where NCGs are offering packages of locational incentives to industry; the weakening of a national community's overall position vis-à-vis international business where rival subnational jurisdictions are competing for its favours; and the clash between local and national priorities.

Considerable discussion has taken place on the costs and consequences of NCG incentive policies. Critics argue that they are wasteful in the sense that interregional rivalries to attract industry creates duplication, especially where, as in the case of Canada and Australia, there is a small domestic market. Second, locational incentives can produce a highly expensive auction as firms play off one jurisdiction against another. Robert Reich provides one classic example in the case of the US forklift truck manufacturer, Hyster, which, having announced to the five US states and four countries in which it operated that some plants would be closed, acquired $72.5 million in various forms of aid from the jurisdictions involved.[49]

Glickman and Woodward, in their study of the impact of foreign investment on the US economy, make another point; namely, that the use of direct subsidies to attract firms does not actually influence investment decisions.[50] Their survey of foreign companies reveals that sudsidies were amongst the least important factors influencing investment decisions: amongst the most important being labour costs, good infrastructure and the intangible consideration, 'quality of life'. Not surprisingly, then, the authors question Kentucky's wisdom in paying Toyota an incentive costing in excess of $108 000 per job created to move to the state. Adjusting for the specific economic context, similar points are made in the cases of Canada and Australia.[51]

Turning to the argument that competition amongst NCGs in the international marketplace enables transnational business enterprises to play-off one jurisdiction against another, we confront one aspect of the proposition that centralized control over foreign investment negotiations enhances the bargaining power of host governments and that fragmentation has precisely the opposite effect.[52] In the case of the US, the argument that national sovereignty is being eroded by state activities in the field of foreign investment is a key part of the 'selling of America' fears represented in writings such as those of Martin and Susan Tolchin, which emphasize the costs of a lack of coordination in US foreign investment policy:

> Faced with such disarray among states and between the federal government and the Congress, foreign investors find it easy to drive a wedge into American markets. By the time policymakers discern a pattern of disadvantage and attempt to remedy it, it is often too late; the investor is solidly established, with all the political protection of an American business.[53]

The particular investment needs of the resource-endowed Australian states and Canadian provinces have, over the years, generated similar concerns. Thus, for example, the interstate competition to attract aluminium smelters allowed companies to exploit these rivalries to their own advantage.[54] For some observers, the scramble for foreign investment needed to develop these resources has resulted in the subnational governments becoming agents of international business.[55]

Clearly, these arguments are closely linked to the third issue noted above: the divergence between local and national interests. Local élites in effect become coopted by transnational business interests, thereby becoming key actors in processes which undermine the interests of the national community as a whole. It may not, however, be necessary for transnational firms seeking favourable investment terms to consciously play-off the various levels of government competing for their favours since their very presence may be enough to set in train patterns of intergovernmental conflict.[56]

In other words, one does not need to subscribe to the more extreme forms of these arguments to recognize that tensions exist between the central and subnational authorities regarding foreign investment. As Stevenson has pointed out, the level of economic development of the regions within a federation will be one factor determining a subnational government's attitude towards investment.[57] Thus Western Australia and Queensland in Australia, and Alberta in Canada have found themselves in conflict with Canberra and Ottawa respectively regarding federal policies relating to foreign investment which the former have sometimes regarded as detrimental to the attraction of investment necessary to the development of their mineral resources.

TRADE POLICY: LOCAL AND NATIONAL

From what has been said above, we can see that there is a very thin dividing line between NCG economic development interests directed towards the international arena and subnational interest and involvement in broader issues of national trade policy. Indeed, it would be surprising were this not so since the factors which have stimulated the former lead, inevitably, to the latter. The economic interests of local constituencies have naturally extended to issues of foreign economic policy as the traditional regional differences regarding free trade, protection and tariff policy bear witness. As one observer of the US states' growing role in trade development has noted, the governors' greater prominence in this sphere exposes them to a welter of protectionist pressures. Hence the demands by US pork producers in some states that their governors ban the growing import of Canadian hogs on the ground that feed treated with chemicals banned in the US is permitted under Canadian law.[58]

At the same time, NCG trade interests and activities are of concern to the federal authorities, for at least two reasons. First, local policies can affect the trading environment in which national policy makers are forced to operate, particularly where these affect the interests of other international actors. This as we have already seen is reinforced by the growing significance of non-tariff barriers on the trade agenda which has focused attention on local policies such as government purchasing policies favouring local producers. Central governments will then find themselves squeezed between external demands relating to policies and actions over which they may have little or no control.

Second, national policy-makers need to involve subnational interests, both for constitutional and practical reasons. Both of these factors came together in the case of the Canada–US free trade negotiations. Here, the potential role of the provinces in implementing an agreement combined with the practical necessity of developing channels of communication with local economic interests to ensure the need for the creation of processes for federal–provincial consultation. Moreover, foreign policy managers are often reliant on the cooperation of subnational authorities for the implementation of measures crucial to the success of foreign policy. This is particularly true where economic sanctions are involved, as in the case of sanctions policies towards South Africa and China in the wake of the Tiananmen Square massacre in 1989.

National Trade Policy

For these reasons, processes of intergovernmental consultation have become a growing feature of the trade policy environment in recent years. These are discussed at some length in Chapter 7, but it is relevant to the present discussion to note their general features. The goals of such influence, from the NCG perspective are often clearly stated in NCG trade policy documents, as in the case of the statement of the western Canadian provinces' trade objectives presented to the 1989 Western Premiers' Conference:

> The historical impact of Canada's import tariff structure on Western Canada has been well documented. Federal tariff policies have hindered economic development in British Columbia, Alberta, Saskatchewan, and Manitoba. The current 'Uruguay Round' of Multilateral Trade Negotiations (MTN), therefore, represents an excellent opportunity for the four western provinces to influence national trade policy in such a way as to enhance economic development and diversification in Western Canada.[59]

Consequently, there have been consistent pressures for the creation of adequate consultative structures through which domestic constituencies can express their views in the context of trade negotiations. In the US, the industry consultation processes were established by Congress in 1974 and strengthened in the Omnibus Trade and Competitiveness Act of 1988. As noted elsewhere, the primary expression of state and regional trade interests is Congress itself, but the state governors have become increasingly involved in trade policy issues as a natural extension of their trade promotion activities, as the following extract from a National Governors' Association briefing document for new governors makes clear:

> A governor's role in the making of U.S. trade policy is that of a participant in the national debate on the issues. Governors participate through direct lobbying of Congress and the White House regarding their state's needs, through membership on various intergovernmental trade policy advisory committees, through co-operation with other Governors at the national level (NGA), and through their work with federal agencies.[60]

Clearly, the extent and form of consultative processes will depend on a number of factors reflecting the general patterns of intergovernmental relations within the federal system. Of the three countries which have provided much of the data for this study, it is Australia where the subnational governments seem to be least involved in formal consultative structures. In his analysis of the Australian states' involvement in tariff policy, for example, Warhurst suggests that the growth in state involvement which has been apparent since the 1970s, has not been reflected in the development of adequate consultative arrangements between Canberra and the states.[61]

A similar tendency is observable in the patterns of consultation established in the context of international trade negotiations. Whereas in Canada, the Tokyo Round of GATT negotiations witnessed, partly as a result of provincial pressure, the creation of the Canadian Trade and Tariffs Committee as a channel of communication between industry, the provinces and Ottawa,[62] the processes in Australia have been much less extensive and formalised. When non-tariff issues emerged on the trade agenda, one federal trade official recalled touring the states to discuss standards codes and government purchasing policies, a venture which he found was not always welcomed by state officials.[63] Whereas this can be understood to some extent in terms of the politics of federal–state relations in Australia, it is also the product of the fact that there is a tradition of industry and unions going straight to Canberra, either individually or through the various peak organizations which have emerged in recent years:

> The industry peak groups can influence Australian trade policy in various ways. For example, the National Farmers' Federation suggests to the Bureau of Agricultural Economics that it carries out research on the European Community and the effects of the Common Agricultural Policy on Australia. This work then influences government policy.[64]

Again, studies of the tariff policy processes appear to make a not dissimilar point, suggesting that Australian state governments tend to act as a supplementary, rather than primary, route of influence over trade policy.[65]

These consultative processes are characteristic of the information-gathering and coalition-building which, as we have seen in earlier chapters, are an integral element of multilayered diplomacy. In fact, they are part of a staged process of information gathering and dissemination combined with consensus formation which begins at the local level and can extend to the national and even international levels. The process can be seen in operation in the case of consultations with the private sector conducted by British Columbia's Ministry of International Business and Immigration in the context of the Uruguay Round of multilateral trade negotiations, the aims of which were 'to seek information to supplement the Ministry's internal analysis' and 'to establish a communication link with private sector groups'.[66] One of the main findings of the survey (which attracted a far lower response rate to a similar exercise conducted for the free trade negotiations) was the low level of awareness shown by the private sector of the potential influence of the negotiations on the provincial economy.

In the US, California has produced a series of guides for California business leaders and policy makers on key trade issues such as the Canada–US free trade agreement, the Uruguay Round, the Pacific Rim and the Single European Market.[67] As one would expect from a major actor in the world economy such as California, these documents are impressive, the GATT report being used by the US negotiating team in Geneva as a key study of the potential impact of GATT negotiations on American industry.

The policy and research section of the California World Trade Commission also works with industry to promote changes in trade policy as in the case of the electronics industry's campaign to have US export controls on 'dual-use' products such as personal computers relaxed. In this instance, the CWTC helped to establish, in conjunction with electronics industry leaders, a set of priorities for reforming US export controls, including an enhanced level of involvement of the Commerce Department in the licensing process and the transference of munitions control administration from the Department of State to Commerce.[68] At a more formalized level, the CWTC was instrumental in the creation of the CAL–AG Committee on International Trade (CACIT), a coalition of agricultural interests, whose aim is to provide information to its members on the Uruguay Round and to strengthen their influence over the formulation of trade policy.[69]

Of course, it is easy to construct a picture of a highly rational policy process in which local interests are channelled from the local to regional to national and from there to the international level. As has been suggested repeatedly in this study, however, such an image oversimplifies the intricacy of the relationships and the cross-cutting interactions characteristic of so much of contemporary diplomacy. Nevertheless, it is undoubtedly the case that national policy makers rely on the information provided by processes such as these and that they are essential to the establishment of the domestic consensus which is vital to the effective implementation of trade negotiations.

The costs of inadequate consultative mechanisms can be high as the fisheries section of the Australian Department of Primary Industry (DPI) discovered during the long-line fisheries negotiations with Japan in 1979. In this case, the DPI had engaged in the usual round of consultations with state fisheries departments, but as a federal official involved in the negotiations noted, found it difficult to communicate with the fishing interests themselves to convey the significance of the issues at stake and, thereby, to gain their confidence. This reinforced other problems:

> the DPI team were not sufficiently prepared and not well-enough informed. We were overstretched and preparations for the negotiations had not started early enough. In retrospect the critical error was not to include the states and the fishing industry in the first round of the negotiations.[70]

Because of what one observer has described as 'the relatively closed nature of the debates' pressures from the regional fishing interests, particularly the Queensland game fishermen who wanted a wider exclusion zone imposed on the Japanese fishing industry, built up at the end of the negotiations.[71] This severely embarrassed the DPI negotiators, who were confronted by a unified Japanese team resentful of these last-minute problems. As a result of this experience, the DPI took the decision to include a state observer (usually a state director of fisheries) in the second round of negotiations. Consequently, the Australian negotiators were better prepared than they had been in the first round, domestic issues were confronted at an early stage and tensions between Canberra and the fishing community reduced.

The growing complexity of international business linkages produces ever greater opportunities for localities to project their concerns in national trade policy, often in quite unpredictable ways. The pattern of events which followed attempts by the US Congress to penalise Toshiba for illegal sales of US-designed milling machines (used in the production of submarine propellors) to the USSR is a case in point. The Senate quickly voted to cut off Toshiba's American market estimated to be worth some $2.5 billion per annum, whilst a group of congressmen symbolized much of the frustration felt by many Americans towards the Japanese by publicly smashing a Toshiba cassette recorder in the grounds of Capitol Hill. It soon became apparent to US legislators, however, that they were not dealing simply with a foreign corporation but a global industry with powerful US domestic allies. As a result, Congress was besieged not only by lobbyists acting for Toshiba America, but for firms such as Tektronix, Hewlett-Packard and Compaq which were either dependent on Toshiba products (particularly semiconductors) or sold imported Toshiba goods under their own brand labels. Whilst Toshiba did not seek to coordinate this domestically based lobbying campaign, it did not need to do so, for its impact in political terms could hardly have served Japanese interests better. In the words of one congressman, 'they came in waves, first the Washington lobbyists and then people from companies in my own district'.[72] Given these domestic pressures, it was not surprising that by April 1988, Congressional 'punishment' of Toshiba had been reduced to the imposition of an annual ceiling on its US sales of £200 million. The pattern of events clearly came as a surprise to all those involved, not least Toshiba, who had not appreciated how closely its interests were linked to those of American companies and how action in Washington might stimulate counter-action by the localities within which affected American firms were operating.

Local Trade Policies

Whilst centre–NCG relations are often marked by a high degree of cooperation on trade issues, tensions and conflict can arise, largely as a consequence of the different contexts in which trade policy questions are approached at local and national levels. Problems emerge where local policies, reflecting relatively narrow economic interests, attempt to pursue goals which the centre deems as incompatible with the interests of the national economy as a whole and injurious to the international trading system.[73] Foreign policy managers will be far more inclined to relate specific trade policy issues to their broader diplomatic settings, as the following observation regarding the differing perspectives on Canada–US relations held by Ontario and Ottawa suggests:

> In most cases Ontario can take a narrower, more parochial and focused view on Canada/U.S. issues and respond to them in terms of their implications for the province's economic development objectives. In contrast, the federal government may have to balance economic considerations with diplomatic or strategic ones. This adds another reason why the Ontario perspective may not necessarily be identical with the Canadian one.[74]

At the same time, both levels of government are linked by a common concern for a stable trading relationship so that each has a vested interest in ensuring that such differences of perspective are not allowed to weaken the overall trade effort.

Nevertheless, as noted in earlier chapters, conflicts do occur and are more marked where the external economic interests of the NCG diverge from that of the centre due to factors such as geographical location and economic structure. Where these are reinforced by political differences, then the potential for disruption to external policy can become very marked. An extreme example can be found in Australia where the tensions between Canberra and the Queensland government under its long-serving premier, Joh Bjelke Petersen, helped to complicate foreign relations in several areas. This became most obvious when the Labor government of Gough Whitlam was in power in the early 1970s.

Given the clash between Whitlam's centralist tendencies and Bjelke Petersen's firm advocacy of states' rights – or, more precisely, Queensland's rights, and the latter's belief that Canberra was veering towards 'communism' in both its domestic and external policies – it was not too surprising that these differences should spill over into the sphere of foreign economic policy. Thus in early 1975, following the Japanese government's decision to ban imports of Australian beef, the Queensland government announced that it was contemplating refusing

Japan coal-mining leases in the state unless the decision was reversed. Such a move met strong opposition from most quarters on several grounds, not least that the extension of resources diplomacy to the subfederal level could endanger the complex fabric of Australia's most important trading relationship, opened up the possibility of Japanese retaliation and clouded the environment in which negotiations for an Australia–Japan Treaty were being negotiated. In the event, the Japanese ban was lifted and so a potentially embarrassing intrusion of domestic conflict into foreign economic policy avoided. However, this, together with other incidents in which Queensland ventured into the realm of unilateral economic diplomacy, indicates the problems that can arise for the management of trade when uneasy federal–state relationships extend to the international sphere.[75]

The tendency for incidents such as this to arise is, in part, a reflection of the fact that, as with national governments, NCGs are confronted by various economic interests with conflicting attitudes towards the international trading environment. On the one hand, they are concerned, as we have seen, with expanding trade opportunities: on the other, they may well be presented with demands for the introduction of protectionist measures to secure the interests of industries which find themselves threatened by overseas rivals. As Hills points out in the case of Ontario, one of the major dilemmas confronting provincial policy makers is the trade-off between its import vulnerable and export interests.[76]

Given this division of economic objectives, subnational governments are quite likely to speak with more than one voice when it comes to expressing opinions on national trade policy. West Virginia offers a clear example of such divided interests. Here, the trade issue is central to the state's future but its economy is so structured that conflicting messages on national trade policy emerge from its representatives. Job losses, partly the result of foreign competition, have been heavy in the steel, glass and petrochemicals industries; yet West Virginia depends to a considerable extent on exports, 20 per cent of its output being exported compared to a national average of 12 per cent.[77]

The attitudes of the state's two senators, Senate Majority Leader Robert C. Byrd and John D. Rockefeller, towards US trade policy as Congress considered trade legislation during 1987 reflected the differences of approach resulting from this duality of economic interests. Byrd was a clear advocate of measures designed to protect declining industries such as steel and textiles threatened by centres of production with low labour costs whereas Rockefeller's emphasis lay in enhancing US competitiveness as the solution to growing import penetration and the trade imbalance.

In general terms, it is where local protectionism gains expression in various forms that conflicts between subnational, national and international interests will arise providing scenarios for the kinds of multilayered diplomacy discussed in this study. As Spero has suggested, the opportunities for this to occur have been enhanced by the success of the GATT in liberalizing international trade through the reduction of tariffs and quotas.[78] This, in turn, has led governments to resort increasingly to the use of non-tariff barriers (NTBs) in various forms with the aim of protecting industry and promoting exports. As we have seen, the consequent shift in the trade agenda towards the reduction of NTBs has brought with it formidable negotiating problems. This is due in some measure to the fact that many trade barriers of this kind are inseparable elements of social and regional policies. Additionally, and this is of central importance to the present discussion, it is not only national governments which are involved in this area but a wide range of sub-national actors, including NCGs.

Looming large amongst the galaxy of NTBs operated by subnational governments have been government procurement policies. The stakes are large: it has been estimated that more than 25 per cent of the world's gross national product is accounted for by government procurement.[79] Both US state and Canadian provincial governments operate systems of government preference; Australia, after difficult negotiations between Canberra and the states, finally concluded a National Preference Agreement in 1986.[80]

In the case of the US, where some states have operated 'buy-American' laws for decades, Kline has pointed out that these proliferated during the 1970s, so that by 1981, the State Department estimated that thirty-two states had adopted such legislation.[81]

Given its overall significance on the trading agenda, it is not surprising that increasing attention has been given to government procurement. Whereas early GATT negotiations were largely concerned with tariff reductions, the 1973 Tokyo Round adopted a code on government procurement. However, although the possibility of extending the code to subnational governments in federal states was considered, in the event no such action was taken. According to one study of the negotiations, this was not due to US government opposition since Washington was confident that it had the authority to adopt the provision.[82] Rather, it reflected the concerns of other federal states, such as Canada and West Germany, regarding the problems of implementing an agreement of this kind. According to one trade official, the Australian government, confronted by a mixture of apathy and hostility from the states on this issue, was prepared to resort to the external affairs power vested in it by the constitution should intergovernmental negotiation at the domestic level prove fruitless.[83]

More recently, the issue has reemerged in the context of the Uruguay Round and the Single European Market. The issue of reciprocity has received considerable attention from the European Community (EC) as European companies turn their attention to the regulatory and legislative obstacles to trade with the US, including government preference legislation which effectively limits their ability to bid for government contracts. Increasingly, the problems that state and local policies and practices present are gaining attention at state and local level and the extent of the problem debated by governors and economic development officials. As one author has noted, it is not simply a matter of NCGs enacting preference legislation, for even where no such legislation exists, there is still powerful political and social pressures for governments to buy from firms who are located within a specific jurisdiction and pay taxes to it.[84]

One example of multilayered diplomacy generated by NCG non-tariff barriers can be found in the dispute between Canada and the EC concerning provincial liqour-pricing policies. This was a classic case in which Ottawa found itself pressured between the demands of the international trading community in the form of the EC and the GATT and the domestic political realities of federal–provincial relations.

Although in Canada the federal parliament is granted power over international and interprovincial trade, this power excludes local products within the provinces. Consequently, the provinces are empowered under the Constitution Act to enact legislation controlling the supply and distribution of alcoholic beverages within their borders.[85] Thus, taking Ontario as an example, it has an agency (the Liquor Control Board of Ontario) established under the provincial Liqour Control Act, which enjoys exclusive authority over the import of alcohol from any source. The LCBO operates liqour stores in Ontario which have a monoploy on the sale of imported beer and wine whereas Ontario wine producers are able to sell their wine through their own stores supervised by the LCBO. Amongst the protectionist regulations adopted by the provincial liquor agencies are 'mark-ups' on imported alcoholic beverages (a 66 per cent mark-up was being applied by the LCBO to imported wines in the 1980s), regulations that restrict the number of foreign brands on sale, and a range of discriminatory distribution practices.[86]

Predictably, discrimination against imports of alcohol maintained by the provinces have been strongly opposed by Canada's trading partners, particularly the EC and the US. Following the Tokyo Round, Ottawa negotiated statements with overseas suppliers regarding these practices. In the case of the EC, the 1979 Provincial Statement of Intentions offered by Ottawa on behalf of the provinces made a commitment that, by 1 January 1988, differential mark-ups on imported spirits would reflect only commercial considerations such as handling costs, and those on wine would not be increased above current levels except where similar commercial considerations justified it.[87] However, the status of this undertaking was never clear since the federal government had no authority to make such an undertaking on the part of the provinces, but was relying on the successful outcome of domestic diplomacy to meet an international commitment. Indeed, some of the provinces attempted to eliminate a number of the disputed practices although the major wine producers, Ontario and British Columbia, resisted international and federal pressures to do so.

Negotiations between Canada and the EC during the 1980s failed to resolve the dispute and were complicated by the US–Canada free trade negotiations whose agenda also included the alcoholic beverages issue. Brussels therefore requested the GATT Council to set up a dispute-settlement panel in February 1985 which reported to the Council in March 1988. Its findings, in summary, were that the 1979 Statement did not alter Canada's GATT obligations and that the provincial practices were contrary to certain provisions of the Agreement. Having accepted the ruling, Ottawa negotiated a settlement with the EC in which the former agreed to have discriminatory provincial mark-ups on foreign wine phased out over seven years, as agreed under the Canada–US free trade agreement. Additionally, foreign and Canadian wines were to be subject to the same listing procedures.[88]

Managing the problem presented the Canadian government with a difficult situation embracing international and domestic political considerations. Failure to satisfy trading partners on this issue invited retaliation. Moreover, as noted earlier, the EC case could not be taken in isolation given the problems that alcoholic beverages had presented in the free trade negotiations with the US. Here, the particular case of beer, a secondary consideration to the EC but also on the agenda, was of central concern. Following a strong lobbying campaign by the Canadian brewing industry, beer was exempted from the final agreement. However, under an agreement with the EC, US brewers would be entitled, as GATT signatories, to similar treatment, thus resuscitating the US threat which the Canadian brewers had successfully averted in the free trade negotiations.[89] From Ottawa's viewpoint, there was a very real danger that the EC and the free trade negotiations would become linked by this dispute causing the deal with the US to unravel as the provinces with small regional breweries found their existence threatened by the inevitable rationalization that would follow the dismantling of protection.

This reflected the complex domestic politics of Canada's trade policy which was underscored by internal divisions of interest and attitude on the wine and beer issue as reflected in differing provincial responses.[90] The centre of opposition to compliance with EC demands was Ontario, which insisted on the need for a twelve-year phase-out period for its pricing policies and vehemently opposed the agreement reached with the EC in December 1988.[91] Provinces with smaller wine and beer industries such as Quebec were ready to comply with the GATT ruling as was British Columbia, the other province with a significant interest in the issue. Even within the brewing industry – where some 19 000 jobs were at stake – splits were reported on the desirability of maintaining the interprovincial trade barriers.[92]

Thus the challenge for Ottawa was to pursue a linked diplomatic strategy at the international and domestic levels which could exert pressure on Ontario, partly by means of the other provinces, whilst holding the ring with the EC and demonstrating to Brussels the very real constraints that constitutional and political realities imposed on it. As an official in the Department of External Affairs explained, Canadian negotiators were presented with the dual task of negotiating with the provinces and getting them to understand the significance of the problem in its broader dimensions and educating EC representatives as to the nature of Canadian domestic politics.[93] Moreover, the negotiations with the EC, as we have seen, had to take account of the free trade deal with Washington so that the domestically sensitive beer issue was not put back on the agenda. In the event (and despite the fear in December 1988 that Ottawa would have to take the matter to the courts following the statement by Ontario's Consumer and Commercial Relations minister, William Wrye, that the provincial government would ignore the free trade and EC agreements and adhere to its own twelve-year phase-out pricing plan) an agreement was reached in March 1989. In return for Ontario's acceptance of the seven-year phase-out period contained in the free trade and EC agreements,

Ottawa established a compensation fund to which the federal government would contribute $Can5 million.[94]

Local trade policy and social activism

Local trade policies may be the product of influences other than protectionist interests, however. Earlier chapters have pointed to the impact of social activism on the localization of foreign policy and this is reflected in the trade policy agenda. Two factors come together here to reinforce the involvement of NCGs and local authorities in foreign economic policy. Firstly, the developing role of a variety of activist groups in international issues and their use of the locality as a route to participation in, and influence over, external policy. Second, the opportunity to develop local policies afforded by the economic powers and financial structures of subnational authorities. The conjunction of these two factors can be clearly seen in the attempts by a diverse range of groups to encourage institutions and organizations to adopt economic sanctions in pursuit of human rights objectives, as in the cases of South Africa and Northern Ireland.

In the US, where this phenomenon has been particularly noticeable, it has assumed several forms: pension fund disinvestment, bank deposit denial, procurement denial and (in the specific case of South Africa) regulation of the Krugerrand.[95] Amongst these, pension fund divestiture appears to be the most potent. In the wake of the 1976 Soweto riots, a number of communities in the US enacted measures to remove investments in companies operating in South Africa and which did not adhere to a code of practice known as the Sullivan principles from the portfolios of pension funds.[96] Michigan was the first state to adopt sanctions legislation but with the 1984 disturbances in South Africa, it was joined by a growing number of state and local governments. In 1989, one author noted that 'some 23 states, 14 counties, 80 cities and the Virgin Islands have enacted various kinds of divestment or procurement legislation or ordinances directed at South Africa's apartheid policies'.[97]

As such sanctions policies became more popular, their scope extended to other countries, including the USSR and Iran, whose actions attracted the disapproval of various interests. In later years, the list has included Northern Ireland. Unemployment amongst the Catholic population of the province has become an issue on state and local political agendas, particularly in communities containing significant Irish–American populations. Again, pension funds have been used as weapons, in this case to persuade US companies to implement the MacBride principles drafted by the New York City Comptroller's office in 1984. These principles are intended to protect the interests of religious minorities in the Northern Ireland workforce and to relieve the high levels of Catholic unemployment through such measures as increased representation of religious minorities and bans on religious and political emblems in factories. During 1989, the MacBride campaign gathered momentum with 10 states and 12 cities having passed legislation in support of it by February of that year.[98]

The precise impact of the divestment policies is the subject of debate with arguments depending on assumptions regarding the efficiency of the financial markets.[99] It is, of course, hard to attribute the causes of company investment policies, and to determine the extent to which divestment has affected the behaviour of US firms or whether, if it has, this is due to the desire to avoid unfavourable publicity rather than fear of any economic consequences that might result from it. Nevertheless the chairman of the American Chamber of Commerce in Johannesburg has been reported as stating that divestment activity at the state and local level 'poses the most serious threat to a continued U.S. corporate presence inside South Africa'.[100] For the South African government, whatever the economic costs, the divestment campaign has demanded that an active diplomacy directed towards the state, as opposed to federal level, be pursued. In an attempt to counter the spread of divestment legislation, its regional consulates throughout the US were strenghtened to oversee state lobbying campaigns. During 1985 alone, more than $1 million dollars was spent on employing lobbyists to coordinate the anti-divestment campaign.[101]

Similarly, the MacBride campaign presented the British government with a diplomatic challenge. MacBride-inspired legislation was of concern to London on two counts: first, because it furthered the Irish Republican cause in the US and, second, because of its impact on foreign investment in Northern Ireland. As in the case of South African divestment, the highly diversified character of the campaign presented great problems to diplomatic efforts to counter its spread. A British diplomat explained to the author that it was of little use dealing with Washington on this issue.[102] For both political and ideological reasons, the Reagan administration was reluctant to intervene in state politics, especially on such a sensitive issue. Moreover, Washington does not have the resources or the time to deal with a problem at the bottom of its agenda. Given the nature of the problem, the goal of the British diplomatic effort was not to 'solve' it but to contain it by staging a series of 'fire-brigade' campaigns, using local lobbying firms, as legislative proposals emerged. Whereas the British Embassy regarded this strategy as reasonably successful, the interaction of international and local politics presented some obvious challenges. In Boston, for example, Mayor Flynn was using the MacBride issue as one element in his campaign for the governorship and any intervention by the British or their agents would have been counterproductive.

CONCLUSION

The pressures towards the localization of the trading environment go hand-in-hand with those which have accompanied its globalization. On one side, these originate in the activities and interests of the actors operating in the trading system. As we have seen, both business enterprises and international institutions, such as the GATT and the EC, have found themselves ever more closely enmeshed in the domestic political structures and processes of national communities. At the same time, sub-national political authorities, such as NCGs, partly in response to these external interests but, more generally, in recognition of the implications of economic interdependence for their local economies, find themselves constrained to operate on at least two levels in pursuit of their objectives. First, they seek to establish a more vocal presence in national trade policy; second, they attempt to project their interests directly onto the international stage. In doing so, they are revealed as pursuing a mix of trade-expanding and protectionist goals: attempting at one and the same time to act as agents of trade promotion and investment attraction whilst insulating their domestic economies from perceived external threats.

As the following comment suggests, the consequences of enhanced local involvement can be confusion:

> If foreign businesses in America sometimes feel confused about the American reaction to them, no wonder . . . On one hand, the overseas offices of state governments in London, Brussels, Tokyo and elswewhere offer every inducement to foreign business to invest in their states. On the other, politicians in Congress are pondering no fewer than 24 bills to shut them out in one way or another.[103]

The challenges that such confusion presents is operative at several levels: that of the institutions which seek to regulate trading relations; international business and commerce, which are constrained to operate in an increasingly complex political environment; and, not least, that of national policy makers. At this level, the task of managing simultaneously domestic pressures and conducting international negotiations is a testing one and produces patterns of complex multilayered diplomacy which are the central focus of this study. In the next two chapters, we shall look in greater depth at these complexities, firstly in the context of the domestic and international negotiations attending the conclusion of the Canada–US Free Trade Agreement and, secondly, by examining the interactions which developed as British industry sought to end the use by certain US state governments of worldwide unitary taxation.

4 Multilayered Diplomacy and the Canada–US Free Trade Negotiations

From the discussion in the previous chapter, we can see that in the complex world of contemporary trade diplomacy, subnational actors, such as NCGs, will fulfill a variety of roles, become enmeshed in a web of interactions and involved in diplomatic strategies of both their own and others' making. In the process, they may be seen to be agents of national foreign policy implementation, a part of central strategy. On the other hand, in pursuit of local interests, they may be hostile to national goals and cause international negotiations to unravel at crucial stages. However relationships between the representatives of national and subnational interests develop, whether these are conflictual, cooperative or, as is more likely, a mixture of the two, what is certain is that the task of reconciling domestic and international demands in the context of trade negotiations, of conducting a multilayered diplomacy, is a taxing one. This fact is amply demonstrated in the context of the Canada–US free trade negotiations (FTN) which are the subject of this chapter. What roles did the Canadian provinces and the US states assume as the negotiations proceeded and what patterns of interactions between the respective central and non-central actors developed?

The Emergence of the Free Trade Proposal

The proposal for the FTN came from the Canadian government following the announcement by the prime minister, Brian Mulroney, in September 1985 that Ottawa would seek to negotiate a new trade agreement with Washington. In terms of the evolution of Canada–US relations the issue, of course, was a phase in a well-established and continuing debate that goes to the roots of Canadian identity.[1] In the more immediate context, it followed a period of introspection on the general direction of trade policy stimulated by the uncertainties of the 1970s, the recession of the early 1980s, the depressed state of demand for Canada's natural resource exports and the impact of these developments on Canadian prosperity.[2] Furthermore, attempts to achieve trade diversification in the 1970s through the 'Third Option' had clearly been unsuccessful; Canada was now more, rather than less, linked to the US in trading terms. More immediately, there was the growing protectionist mood on Capitol Hill generated by the publication of monthly trade figures recording an ever-larger US trade deficit.

Even in the specific area of trade relations, FTN did not occupy the highest place on the White House agenda, however, coming a long way below US–Japan trade relations. Yet, apart from whatever predisposition that might have encouraged President Reagan to accommodate the objectives of a Canadian prime minister far more congenial to Washington than his predecessor, Pierre Trudeau, a bilateral trade agreement held certain attractions. First, it might be valuable as a means of diminishing protectionist pressures in Congress, demonstrating tangible results from the Administration's trade liberalisation stance. Second, it could serve as an element in a 'plurilateral' strategy whereby the US's trading partners were nudged towards the goal of multilateral trade talks by means of a series of bilateral trade negotiations.[3] In this sense, the Reagan Administration's multilateral trade objectives were consistent with, and worked in favour of, Canada's bilateral trade objectives.

Nevertheless, despite a degree of mutual interest in engaging in free trade talks, it was clear that there was an asymmetry of interest between the two national governments both in terms of the importance they attached to the substantive issue and their precise motivations for addressing it. To use Winham's words, 'there was an imbalance in the negotiation at its more profound levels that made the endeavour all the more difficult'.[4] At root, this lay in quite different perceptions of the trade policy agenda in the two countries. In the US, the focus of attention was on a range of practices seen as constituting legitimate regional policies by Canadians but regarded as trade-distorting subsidies on Capitol Hill. For Canada, on the other hand, the key objective was to limit the effects of US trade remedy measures such as countervailing duties by the creation of some form of binding dispute settlement mechanism.

Canadian and US Subnational Interests

Given a mutual interest in pursuing bilateral trade talks – even though the incentives to do so might be very different – both national governments had to be concerned with subnational interests and the means by which they would be expressed. As with most trade agreements, the results of FTN were likely to threaten the well-being of economic constituencies with a regional base. In the case of Canada economic policy and regionalism are intertwined reflecting, on the one hand, a complex emotional mix of resentments, jealousies and local 'patriotisms' and, on the other, differences in resource endowment and patterns of economic activity.[5] Although regions – whether viewed as political or economic phenomena – cut across provincial boundaries, the provinces have a key role as channels for the articulation of economic interests. To this political factor was added the constitutional dimension and the fact that whereas the federal government might enjoy exclusive jurisdiction over international trade, the provinces through control of their natural resources are empowered to implement legislation giving expression to taxation, royalty, subsidy and regulatory policies which can affect international trade.[6]

Since the focus of both the new GATT round and any Canada–US bilateral negotiations would be concerned with non-tariff barriers produced by such policies (and supplemented by other practices such as government procurement policies) the involvement of the provinces was inevitable. Moreover, the precedent for consultation was well-established through the federal–provincial consultative mechanisms constructed for the Tokyo Round. Finally, the significance of the provinces was assured by the importance attached to provincial practices viewed by Washington as constituting disruptions to its 'level-playing field' conception of international trade.

On the US side, the basis for state participation in the formulation of international trade policy appeared rather different. At one level, the constitutional allocation of powers places Washington in a far stronger position vis-à-vis the states than is Ottawa when confronting the provinces. Article 1 of the constitution gives to Congress power 'to regulate commerce with foreign nationals', providing it with the basis for a preeminent role in trade policy, a role which it resumed in the 1980s.[7] Furthermore, although state policies in certain ways could well be affected by any free trade agreement (for example in the services area where state governments regulate, amongst others, banking, insurance and legal services), state interests in the outcome of the FTN seemed very much understated when contrasted with the situation of the provinces.

A second factor determining the role of the states in the trade policy sphere is organizational capacity. It is only during the last decade or so that the US state governments have become conscious of their international interests, as reflected in growing trade promotion and investment attraction activities.[8] With this has come an expansion in bureaucratic infrastructure but this is uneven and not necessarily directed towards making an input into the trade policy processes. Few states emulate the contribution made by California whose California World Trade Commission has produced impressive documentation on trade policy issues and which is the only state to maintain a full-time trade official in Washington.[9] According to one official in the office of the US Trade Representative (USTR), 'a key problem for US trade negotiators wanting to consult or inform the states is that the necessary staff work is not done; they do not have the capacity to do it'.[10]

In part, this has to be seen as a function of the sheer number of subnational governments in the US. As a British Columbia trade official explained to the author, it is far harder to operate a system encompassing fifty states as opposed to ten provinces.[11] This factor may help to explain the growing importance of organizations such as the National Governors' Association, able to act collectively on behalf of the states in – amongst others – the trade policy area.

Attitudes are also crucial. The same provincial trade official noted a greater acceptance of the preeminence of the federal government in the trade policy sphere by US state representatives together with a more obvious readiness on the part of business interests to accept a national as opposed to a regional viewpoint. The difference in the relative positions of the US states and Canadian provinces in the trade sector is summed up in the words of a trade adviser to the Governor of Colorado: 'The Canadian provinces are sophisticated and constitutionally secure relative to states. State activities and institutional competence are just beginning to mature in the international arena'.[12]

In short, the direction and character of the domestic level negotiations which would make up the multilayered character of the FTN were different for the US and Canada. The situation is, of course well-understood and underpins many interactions across the 49th parallel. Its essence lies in a recognition that the crucial power cleavage in Canada runs along federal–provincial lines whereas in the US it is expressed in executive–congressional relationships. Doran, amongst others notes the consequences of this fact for Canadian–US diplomacy and the problems in the form of misunderstandings and unexpected consequences to which it gives rise:

> The United States is often hindered in the formulation of bargaining initiatives by the awareness of the critical split between the authority of Ottawa and of the provinces. Canada is frequently disappointed in bargaining outcomes because of the split in authority between the President and the Congress.[13]

Doran goes on to argue that both sides are linked in a misplaced belief that these fissures are aberrations which will disappear under normal circumstances rather than fundamental characteristics of the two political systems. Whether or not this is correct, it is certainly the case that, in the context of FTN, both sides were aware of the other's domestic interests and, as the pre-negotiation phase developed, were keenly concerned as to how these would impinge on negotiations.

The Prenegotiation Phase

Amongst the seven functions that Zartman has attributed to this stage of the diplomatic cycle is the calculation and enhancement of domestic political support.[14] In his analysis of the events leading up to the decision to negotiate a free trade agreement, Tomlin notes the fluctuations between domestic and external preoccupations in the phases of prenegotiation and the concern of both sides for the other's bases of domestic support as well as their own.[15] For both the US and Canada, time was of the essence here.

For somewhat different but related reasons, Ottawa and Washington were both concerned to act before the protectionist thrust in Congress developed and was strengthened by the 1986 mid-term elections. In January 1985, Trade Minister Kelleher, while assuring parliament, the provinces, the business community and the general public that adequate consultations would precede any talks, emphasized that Canada's 'window of opportunity' to engage the US in trade talks was limited to early 1986.[16] By that stage, he argued, the president would be a lame duck and the political agenda dominated by the Congressional elections. As already indicated, the White House also perceived a strong element of urgency as it watched protectionism grow in Congress with the publication of each month's trade figures.

Both Washington and Ottawa shared an interest in isolating trade talks from the domestic political minefield of international trade relations. It appeared increasingly likely that there would be moves within Congress to create links between Canada–US trade talks and specific issues such as alleged subsidies to the Canadian lumber industry. These two factors – concern with time constraints and the fear that Congressional interests might engage in 'linkage' diplomacy whereby the politics of trade would become even more complex – encouraged both sides to support the utilization of the so-called 'fast-track' negotiating procedures, established in 1984 through an amendment to the 1974 Trade Act, providing a form of delegated Congressional authority for negotiating trade agreements. Not only does the procedure enable expeditious action on the results of the negotiations, Congress can only accept or reject a treaty negotiated under it, thus avoiding the unravelling of a negotiated package at the implementation stage. In other words, the framework for negotiation provided by the fast-track system was regarded as a major element in the management of domestic forces impinging on trade relations. Both Ottawa and Washington were confronted by the problem of divided jurisdictions. In the case of the latter, Congress constituted the challenge; it was, moreover, a challenge demanding the active attention of the Canadian government as well as the White House.

Congress

Ottawa was clearly presented with several dilemmas when dealing with Congress. In the broad strategic sense, it needed to gain Congressional attention at a time when the major issues occupying Capitol Hill were those of the budget deficit and tax reform. Certainly, trade-related issues hovered in the background, but there was always the danger – a very real one as events were to prove – of providing a focus, in the form of an FTN proposal, for potent interests concerned with imbalances in US–Canada trade. On the tactical front, the climate for political lobbying on Capitol Hill was becoming more difficult as the concern grew at the use of lobbyists (especially former White House staffers) by foreign governments. While lobbying of Congress was clearly essential and a major role for the Canadian embassy in Washington, presided over by Allan Gotlieb, potential costs as well as benefits clearly had to be taken into account.

What appeared obvious to observers of the Congressional scene was the general climate of 'friendly indifference' on the Hill to the prospect of FTN. Whereas the White House had completed a favourable internal assessment of the proposal by the time that Ottawa made its formal request to Washington to begin talks, no such conclusions had, it seems, been reached by the members of the two key committees who would review any request by the Administration for fast-track approval. These were, in the House, the trade subcommittee of the Ways and Means Committee and, in the Senate, the Finance Committee. Predictions of their reactions suggested that the House Committee would offer little problem, but that because of the presence of several representatives of lumber states, some seeking reelection in 1986, the Senate Finance Committee might present more difficulties.

Generally, however, the feeling in late 1985 and early 1986 was that the White House would secure fast-track approval. As noted earlier, one of the key variables would be the direction and speed of protectionism in Congress. Few of the three or four hundred protectionist measures circulating on Capitol Hill were of any consequence. Some, indeed merely took the form of press releases. Others, such as those in textiles, clothing and footwear, could have had a great impact on the international trading system.

Engaging the White House and Finding (or Manufacturing) a Consensus

The essence of the Mulroney strategy in promoting FTN and dealing with other bilateral issues such as acid rain was to reactivate the concept of a 'special relationship' between Canada and the US. A central component of this strategy was to be the establishment of annual summit meetings between prime minister and president by means of which Canada could force Washington to focus, if only briefly, on the key issues affecting the relationship. In the context of FTN, there was an associated desire to engage White House support in dealing with growing Congressional protectionism – a strategy also advocated by Premier Lougheed of Alberta at the first ministers' conference in February 1985. Obvious dangers attached to such a strategy. Given the sheer diversity of issues on the White House agenda, Ottawa could hardly be sure of sustaining Washington's interest. Second, relations between Executive and Congress were becoming increasingly tense and it was by no means certain that the Reagan Administration could build and sustain the necessary coalitions to ensure the utilization of the 'fast-track' process. Nevertheless, as suggested above, observers at the time seemed to believe that Congress would accede to a request from the president for approval to begin negotiations.

While the White House, on the official level, awaited a formal initiative from Ottawa, it was, in fact, conducting soundings amongst

US business interests through the International Trade Commission and the Office of the Special Trade Representative.[17] These revealed considerable support both from individual groups, such as the brewers, and organizations, particularly the US Chamber of Commerce. A key stage in the prenegotiation phase was the Quebec City summit meeting between Mulroney and Reagan on 17–18 March 1985, which appeared to many (if not in the eyes of the opposition parties) a vindication of the prime minister's success in encouraging Washington to look towards its northern neighbour. (Before the summit, the White House had ordered a full National Security Council review of its relationship with Canada.) The two-page statement emanating from the summit served a symbolic as well as a practical purpose. It demonstrated to the Canadian public and to economic interests that bilateral trade talks were on the agendas of both governments. One cloud did, however, loom over the horizon – the resignation, in March 1985, of William Brock from the position of US Trade Representative. Brock's experience in the trade policy arena together with his background as a senator would be hard to match, and fears were expressed that his transfer to the Department of Labor would weaken the White House's capacity to influence trade policy and hence any Canadian trade initiative.[18]

Following the summit, Ottawa's attention turned towards the domestic front. Already, in January 1985, Canadian business had established a task force on Canada–US trade relations to 'advise' the government on trade relations with the US. This body favoured a comprehensive rather than a sectoral agreement. But, as discussed above, it was clear that there existed a range of views on the desirability and/or the precise form of any agreement. If any free trade initiative was to survive the stresses and strains of the domestic political processes, then they would have to be based on, at least, the appearance of consensus. And so, two days after the Reagan–Mulroney meeting, Trade Minister Kelleher began a six week tour during which he visited 15 cities. The objective, as stated by Kelleher, was to alert the public to the importance of an FTN initiative.[19] The process of establishing the image of a consensus was aided by the publication of the Macdonald Report in June 1985 which added to the general impression of widespread support for what was, after all, a very vague proposition. Thus when Mulroney issued his request to the White House to start the negotiation processes, he could claim that it had been legitimized by consultation and by the authority of a $20 million royal commission. It was rather unfortunate that a document produced by a task force in the prime minister's office should have been leaked at that moment, appearing to suggest that the government was less interested in informing and consulting the public than in engaging in a propaganda exercise.[20] Whereas the claims from the Liberal opposition that Mulroney's five-page statement said very little about the agenda for discussion ignored the essential nature of such negotiations, there did appear to be some substance to the accusation that the government had deliberately avoided a parliamentary debate. In terms of the practical politics of FTN, however, the main domestic preoccupation of the Mulroney government in the ensuing months was the provinces.

The Provincial Dimension

As indicated earlier, Ottawa and the provinces have mutual objectives in the trade policy sphere, better access to overseas markets being an obvious one. At the same time, constitutional and political factors combine with differing economic interests and a natural wariness of the impact of national policies on regional economies to produce tensions between federal and provincial power centres. The uneasy balance between the two sets of impulses – the recognition of the need for cooperation and deep-seated rivalries – was well-expressed in a 1986 C.D. Howe Institute paper:

> For its part, the federal government desires the provinces' participation in an eventual agreement while seeking to affirm its primacy in international relations. For their part, the provinces wish to exercise and protect their own areas of jurisdiction while ensuring that benefits of more secure access to export markets are not jeopardized.[21]

With this in mind, the attitudes of the various provinces towards the prospective FTN were crucial. As time elapsed during 1985, it became increasingly clear that whereas the majority of the provinces supported some form of negotiation and agreement, this was heavily qualified in important respects. Ontario, not unexpectedly given its economic profile, was the province most cautious regarding a free trade deal. In October 1985, the Ontario assistant deputy minister for trade indicated that his government entertained grave doubts concerning the impact of free trade on the provincial economy, referring to studies which suggested that industries which could be seriously affected by any free trade agreement employed 280 000 Ontario residents.[22] Quebec, less dependent on the US in trade terms, and faced with the effect of NTBs in key areas such as mass transit and electrical equipment, appeared much more supportive of the notion of a comprehensive free trade agreement. The Atlantic provinces, such as Nova Scotia, seemed disposed to favour FTN in which all issues, including regional development subsidies, were subject to discussion but emphasized that provinces outside the industrial core would need federal assistance if they were to compete in a continental market. In the West, traditionally a bastion of free trade, it was to become increasingly clear that there was no clear consensus on the issue, either amongst the provinces or the various economic interests within them.[23] During its travels in the West, a parliamentary committee seeking opinions on FTN found a variety of views. British Columbia, Alberta and Saskatchewan seemed more supportive of a possible agreement than did Manitoba. But in each case, it was evident that the provinces had lists of items that they did not want to have placed on the negotiating table. Generally, labour and agribusiness seemed to be opposed to FTN, business divided, and oil, gas and chemicals favourably disposed. Such a situation gave Trade Minister James Kelleher's claim that there was a consensus to begin comprehensive trade talks something of a hollow ring. Whatever the final outcome of trade talks, it became manifestly evident during 1985 that the interests focusing on them and the interactions generated by them would present policy managers with taxing problems.

The Provinces and the Negotiating Machinery

The key issue confronting the Mulroney government, apart from the diversity of interests which it represented, was that of the provinces' role in the actual negotiations. Apart from the Tokyo Round experience already referred to, in which the provinces had been consulted but had not actually participated, there were other models – such as the Atlantic fisheries negotiations of the mid 1970s where the provinces were present, as necessary, during the actual negotiations.[24] This issue was addressed in a preliminary fashion at the February 1985 first minister's conference, but was to become a crucial issue at the November meeting held in Halifax. The agreement hammered out these referred to 'full provincial participation' without spelling out what that ambiguous phrase meant. The parties to the Halifax agreement were given 90 days to establish a meaning and to outline their objectives within the context of FTN. During the ensuing weeks it became quite clear that there were marked differences not only between the federal government and the provinces, but amongst the provinces themselves as to their role in the trade negotiations. Ontario and British Columbia took a 'maximalist' position, arguing that the federal and provincial governments were equal partners in policy formulation. Such a position appeared unacceptable to Ottawa, but was also questioned by the smaller and bureaucratically weaker provinces who feared that they would be overwhelmed by the interests of the larger provinces in the negotiating room.

The battle over provincial representation was carried on in late 1985 and the early months of 1986, both through political channels but also in the bureaucratic machinery created for the conduct of the negotiations presided over by a former deputy finance minister, Simon Reisman. Appointed in November 1985, Reisman was given carte blanche to establish his own staff. That such a large office (nearly 100 members) was established by April 1986 indicated the significance attached by Ottawa to the negotiations, but was also, perhaps, a reflection of some disquiet concerning the trade policy machinery in the wake of the transfer of trade to the Department of External Affairs in 1982.[25] The Trade Negotiations Office was given the dual task of conducting the negotiations and consulting domestic interests through an International Trade Advisory Committee (ITAC) and Sectoral Advisory Groups on International Trade (SAGITS), panels of representatives from specific industries.

Added to his brief, Reisman found himself responsible for the task of reaching an agreement with the provinces over the sensitive issue of their role in the negotiations. Closer discussions between Reisman, provincial trade ministers and officials during January and February did not appear to be productive. The provinces reacted to what was reported as Reisman's 'firm line' on the primacy of the federal government's role and began to press for a meeting with Mulroney. Led by Alberta, they developed an eight-point plan based on the equal partnership notion which Ottawa had already rejected. Of equal concern, and more difficult to resolve, was the thorny issue of interprovincial trade barriers, an issue inseparable from that of any Canada–US free trade deal, as Washington had repeatedly pointed out. The prospect of removing these barriers to internal and external trade, while keenly supported by Ontario was not embraced with equal enthusiasm by other provinces. In answer to a question on the subject, the Alberta minister for intergovernmental affairs suggested that the provinces would convince Washington and Ottawa of their willingness to remove trade barriers 'at the appropriate time'.[26] Both issues, provincial participation and interprovincial trade barriers, were high on the political agenda as the prenegotiation phase entered its final stage in Congress.

The Congressional Arena

The key factors conditioning Congressional attitudes towards the Reagan request for authority to start trade talks with Canada – general indifference, preoccupation with taxation and the budget deficit, and growing tension between the White House and Congress on trade issues – have already been outlined above. As Brock's replacement, Clayton Yeutter, began consultations with Congress, the general feeling appeared to be that both the key committees would allow the talks to proceed. There was, however, the lumber issue on which great sensitivities had been aroused and which had encouraged the formation of one of the most powerful lobbies on Capitol Hill, that representing the US lumber industry. By 1985, Canada had captured 31 per cent of the US lumber market, with exports to the US worth over $3 billion. US producers accused the Canadian provinces of levying low stumpage fees (the levy charged on felled timber), thereby creating a subsidy to the Canadian industry and undermining the US industry.[27] This was a sensitive issue in the House, where Sam Gibbons (Democrat, Florida), chairman of the trade subcommittee of the Ways and Means Committee, had urged the White House to levy tariffs or quotas on Canadian lumber. But, more significantly the Senate Finance Committee contained a number of 'lumber state' senators – including a prime mover on the issue, Max Baucus (Democrat, Montana) and the chairman, Robert Packwood (Republican, Oregon). Moreover, Packwood, together with three other Republicans, was up for reelection in 1986. In the early months of 1986, both committees were heavily involved in the taxation and budget deficit issues. The Senate Committee could have chosen simply to let the deadline for consideration of the request pass. But only a few days before the 21 April deadline, Packwood announced that the Committee would refuse the White House request. Quite clearly the decision took Yeutter and US trade officials by surprise and seemed to demolish at one blow the whole Mulroney strategy. It was to take 12 days of intense lobbying by both the White House and Ottawa before the request was passed in a 10-10 tied vote on 24 April 1986. The closeness of the vote reflected the passions that trade policy had aroused in Washington, a fact also reflected in the high level lobbying which had involved the president, vice president, treasury secretary, commerce secretary and the secretary of state.

From the Canadian perspective, the key problem appeared to be that as events developed, Ottawa was placed in a position where it needed to manage not only its own domestic environment but that of the US as well, while clearly constrained in its capacity to do so. For political and constitutional reasons, the main actor in dealing with Congress had to be the White House, but there were limitations and dangers for the Mulroney government in relying on the Reagan Administration, given the turmoil surrounding executive–congressional relations in the trade policy sphere. Even so, frequent suggestions were heard in early 1986 that Ottawa had relied too much on the assurances from the Administration that fast-track approval would be forthcoming and had failed to anticipate the degree to which the lumber issue would complicate the processes involved.[28]

Whether or not Ottawa had any greater degree of scope for initiative in smoothing the path of FTN during this crucial phase, it was obvious that the White House itself was faced with a growing dilemma in building the necessary Congressional coalition to allow the negotiations to begin. In promoting FTN as part of a broader trade strategy, it succeeded in raising the political temperature on sensitive issues in US–Canada trade relations. Throughout 1985 and early 1986, Yeutter found himself impelled to talk the language of protectionism while arguing the case for bilateral trade talks with Canada. It was, moreover, Ottawa's misfortune that FTN was, inevitably, caught up in the general debate concerning the relative powers of Congress and president in the trade policy area.

These difficulties impinged on the management of domestic political forces within Canada, for the Mulroney government found it increasingly hard to keep the free trade issue couched in the very general terms that it clearly preferred. As specific issues arose, some generated internally, some inspired by US actions or statements, so the ambiguous and low-key language used by Ottawa came under increasingly critical examination. The danger was that establishing and maintaining a domestic consensus would be much more difficult as domestic interests and the general public became alerted to well-defined problems. And yet, at the same time, the provinces had to be involved and encouraged to confront the extremely thorny issue of interprovincial trade barriers. Simply establishing consultative mechanism with the provinces and key interests was to prove difficult enough and aroused regional and industrial divisions of interest.

NEGOTIATIONS

Structures for Federal–Provincial Consultation

The question of provincial involvement was unresolved as the negotiations began on 21 May 1986 and required intensive efforts by Reisman and Mulroney before a formula was accepted at the June 1986 first minister's conference. This added quarterly meetings of first ministers to a multi-tiered structure which comprised a Continuing Committee on Trade Negotiations (CCTN) made up of federal officials, trade representatives from the provinces, the Yukon and the Northwest Territories and chaired by Reisman (this had been created in January 1986), irregular meetings of trade ministers and continuing bilateral exchanges at the official level. The system of private-sector consultation interacted with and supplemented the federal–provincial consultative structures. Although the 250 representatives serving on the ITAC and SAGITS were federally appointed, a British Columbia trade official explained that they were to become part of the federal–provincial linkages during the FTN as, in this case, BC sought to pass on information to the relevant groups and when, on occasions, a chairman might contact provincial officials on a specific issue.[29] Despite earlier pressures to do so, by this stage the provinces had accepted that they would not be represented in the actual negotiating teams.

Predictably, opinions on the value of this consultative structure varied. During the twenty months or so of the negotiations, Reisman himself was to make comments which suggested a mixture of resignation at the inevitability of the process tinged with exasperation and some doubts as to whether the information he was able to impart at CCTN meetings found its way from the official to the political level. Looking back on the process, Reisman's deputy, Gordon Ritchie, described it in the following terms:

> the provincial governments became deeply involved in the process, short of actually sitting at the negotiating table. Every month Reisman chaired day long sessions with the designated senior trade representatives from the ten provinces and two territories to review the negotiating positions. The premiers themselves, while keeping

> their freedom to manoeuvre, were extensively briefed in three regular First Ministers' Conferences and eight special meetings on the trade negotiations, meetings that often ran for eight hours or more.[30]

Interviews with provincial officials, on the other hand, tended to reveal reservations. Having made the point that opinions were likely to vary depending on attitudes towards the outcome of the negotiations, a consistent theme was that, despite the good rapport that developed, the process involved information dissemination rather than consultation. According to one Ontario public servant, little sense of the interplay of the negotiations, trade-offs and developing priorities was conveyed through the CCTN process. To a senior TNO official, however, this reflected the style of provincial operations. Claiming that there was 95 per cent divulgence of information during meetings, he had found that, on the whole, the provinces were 'passive rather than active participants' with Ontario the least, and BC and Quebec the most, active. Some provinces, such as Alberta, had chosen to operate at the political rather than the bureaucratic level.[31] In part, roles depended on personalities. Quebec employed as its trade advisor and representative on the CCTN Jake Warren, a former ambassador to Washington and coordinator of Canadian negotiations within GATT. His highly active and interventionist role in promoting Quebec's position was contrasted by an observer to the clearly different role perceptions held by Ontario's adviser, former senior federal official Bob Latimer, who was described as seeing his role much more in terms of providing advice.[32]

These processes were part of a highly complex pattern of multilayered interactions bringing together domestic and international diplomacy. Not only were provincial trade ministries engaged in federal–provincial consultative processes, they were also important channels of information and advice between regional interests and the centre. In this sense, they acted as both transmission channels to the centre as well as 'educators' of local interests regarding the broader implications of free trade. Moreover, there were the challenges of provincial bureaucratic consultation and coordination paralleling those at the centre presided over by the TNO.[33]

FEDERAL–PROVINCIAL INTERACTIONS

The attitudes and position of the provinces ran as a continuing theme through the negotiations. They could never be far from Reisman's and

Mulroney's minds because of the domestic political realities that underpinned them but also because the US – more specifically Congress – ensured that they remained on the front burner. Throughout congressional committee hearings in 1986, 1987 and 1988, the issue of provincial NTBs were at the forefront of discussion and at various stages Yeutter and Reisman's opposite number, Peter Murphy, found themselves acting as interpreters of Canada's federal–provincial trade politics.[34] Witnesses appearing before, and written statements considered by, the committees underscored the concern felt on Capitol Hill at a range of provincial policies that could be subsumed under the broad term 'subsidy'.

This was symbolized and underscored by several cases brought against Canada under the contingency protection provisions of US trade laws, particularly those concerning imports of cedar shakes and shingles and softwood lumber which were to be major irritants in US–Canadian relations during 1986.[35] The latter (concerned with the charges on timber – 'stumpage fees' – levelled by provincial governments and regarded by the US lumber industry as too low and, consequently, a subsidy) proved to be by far the most serious, creating tensions not only between Ottawa and Washington but between Ottawa and British Columbia as the province with the most obvious interest in the outcome of the case.[36] The relationship between this case and progress in the free trade negotiations was clearly expressed by Trade Minister Carney when she warned an audience of Boston businesspersons that such protectionist actions as the imposition of a 15 per cent countervailing duty on Canadian lumber threatened the outcome of the negotiations.[37]

For Canadian federal negotiators, this two-dimensional aspect of provincial involvement – domestic and international – meant that in one sense the two levels of diplomacy would always interact with one another. The provinces would be demanding to know what kind of a deal was being constructed, whilst the Americans would need to be assured that the provinces would support – and implement – the measures contained in an agreement.

During the early months of 1987, there seemed to be two key issues relating to the role of the provinces in the negotiations: the implementation of the measures contained in any agreement and the related question of what would constitute provincial approval of an agreement. On the first of these, a good deal of discussion reflecting differing opinions had already emerged, ranging from the view that the federal government possessed the necessary powers to implement an agreement to the argument that provincial involvement was essential and that the provincial governments therefore possessed an effective veto.[38] Mulroney's strategy appears to have been to avoid turning the issue into a constitutional confrontation, one to which the premiers, despite murmurings to the contrary, seem to have been willing to subscribe.

Presumably the hope was that indirect involvement in the negotiation process would, for the moment defuse the issue and that, in any case, areas touching on provincial jurisdiction would, in the final event, be minimal. According to a comment reported in an issue of Maclean's which appeared during the March 1987 first ministers' conference, this seemed to be reasonably successful:

> Their [the provinces'] guys are totally up to date. In fact, they have been playing a role in designing what is going on in the negotiations. A lot of the provinces got into the meeting and said, 'What are we talking about ratification for? We're part of the process.'[39]

By the time of this meeting, however, the premiers were demanding 'hard facts' on the progress of the negotiations, fearing that they would be presented with a fait accompli which they would have little option but to approve. At the same time, it was reported that Reisman was under pressure from Washington to complete the negotiations and that he needed a firm mandate to do this.[40] The premiers, having been assured that the areas under their own jurisdiction involved in the negotiations were limited, appeared to be willing to set aside the implementation issue until later first ministers' meetings. Mulroney's position was clearly articulated: acceptance of a free trade deal required a consensus amongst the premiers and that no single province could exercise a veto. In the light of this, Quebec's Premier Bourassa appeared to soften his stance on the need for provincial ratification during the meeting whilst Newfoundland's Premier Peckford was supportive of the consensus proposition. Manitoba and Ontario, however, contrived to assert a right of veto if an agreement went against the interests of their province. Although it is hard to determine the pattern of provincial tactics – if one can speak of a unified approach – it seems not unreasonable to suggest that the premiers were willing to leave the negotiations to the federal government so that if they collapsed – or their outcome was in some sense unacceptable – they could disclaim any responsibility.

This left the provinces as fluctuating centres of support for and opposition to specific dimensions of a possible free trade agreement as the negotiations developed. The focus of support came, notably, from the three far western provinces and particularly British Columbia, together with Quebec. Ontario was the focus of opposition. The stance adopted by the premier of Ontario, David Peterson, hardened as the negotiations proceeded and was clearly affected by the provincial elections to be held in September in which free trade was the key issue. In this context, Peterson set out six conditions which would need to be met before he would subscribe to an agreement. Amongst these were the creation of a dispute settlement mechanism and an assurance that the twenty-five year old auto pact between the US and Canada would not be affected.[41]

It became obvious, however, that neither of these stipulations would be met. The chairman of the powerful Senate Finance Committee, Lloyd Bentsen, reflected strong congressional sentiment when, during a visit to Ottawa, he unequivocally opposed exempting Canada from US trade laws on the grounds that this would set a precedent for other countries.[42]

When it became clear that the White House regarded the establishment of a dispute settlement mechanism as politically impossible to achieve given the growing protectionist sentiments on Capitol Hill, Peterson advocated leaving the talks. Reports of the July first ministers' meeting suggested that, on the other hand, Bourassa and a majority of the remaining premiers were in favour of continuing the dialogue. Peterson's overwhelming victory in the September election (from being a minority government, the Liberals won 95 out of 130 seats in the Ontario legislature) strengthened his position in the free trade debate at a crucial time. By October 5, under the fast-track procedures, President Reagan was required to send the final draft of a treaty to Congress for ninety days of deliberation, and Senator Bentsen, amongst other prominent figures in Congress, was emphasizing the importance he attached to unanimous provincial approval. Nevertheless, observers were careful to note Peterson's caution. His six 'principles' were drawn in broad terms and were very similar to those that Mulroney himself had set out earlier in the year.[43]

Peterson's concerns were, however, underscored when, during the September first minsters' conference, it was revealed that Washington was insisting that the auto pact be placed on the negotiating table. This combined, with a lack of progress on the dispute settlement issue created a pall of gloom over the meeting, with the premiers agreeing that any deal was likely to be much more restricted in scope than expected. These problems, together with a political impulse to distance themselves from Mulroney in the event of total collapse of the negotiations, were reflected in the observation of Premier Bourassa to the effect that all the provinces could do now was to leave it to the prime minister and 'hope for the best'.[44]

This provincial detachment from the flow of events was reinforced when, following Reisman's withdrawal from the negotiations on 23 September, Newfoundland's premier Peckford's musings as to the motivations underlying the decision were recorded.[45]

The most obvious explanation was that Ottawa was seeking to resolve some of the key points of disagreement by engaging the Reagan administration's attention and moving the discussions from the official to the political plane. Indeed, Reisman had stated in August that Mulroney and Reagan might need to meet to iron out these problems. An intense round of shuttle and telephone diplomacy between Washington and Ottawa in which Treasury Secretary Baker became involved resulted in a tentative deal being struck at ten minutes before midnight on 3 October. An emergency first ministers' meeting had been convened in Ottawa on the previous day, and was variously seen as an attempt to spread the blame with the provinces in the case of failure, a simple briefing exercise and/or an attempt to pressure the premiers into agreeing to any compromises necessary to reach an agreement with the US.[46]

PROVINCIAL REACTIONS TO THE AGREEMENT

When the premiers reassembled in Ottawa on 6 October to hear the outcome of the final, frenzied diplomatic round, it was clear that whilst both Mulroney and the Americans were concerned to obtain provincial agreement, in fact there were relatively few issues that would require formal implementing action by the provinces. One of these (which Ottawa had tried to keep off the table but had been forced to address at US insistence) was that of provincial liquor policies discriminating against the sale of US wines. Opinions differed on the degree to which the provinces would need to be involved, some observers arguing that provisions in such areas as energy, services and investment would also require action at the provincial level.[47]

The real issue, however, lay in the political realm. Whatever the constitutional position regarding implementation of specific items within the agreement, the task facing Mulroney was one of establishing and sustaining the provincial consensus which, as noted above, he had substituted for the notion of a provincial veto. The response of the premiers during October and at the November first ministers' conference was not unexpected and reflected regional interests that had been articulated with increasing clarity during 1987. Amongst the keenest supporters were Quebec's Bourassa, Saskatchewan's Devine and British Columbia's Vander Zalm. Both Bourassa and Devine announced during October that they would be prepared to engage in a national campaign to 'sell the deal'.[48] New Brunswick and Newfoundland were regarded as wavering in their support. Opposing the deal were Prince Edward Island, Manitoba and, of course, Ontario.

The latter represented the most serious political challenge to Ottawa as the debate moved into the realm of federal politics during 1988. However, the situation was as taxing for Peterson as it was for Mulroney. It seemed that Peterson had little option but to sustain the position that he had held to over a period of two years: namely, that whilst he did not support the agreement, he would not actively oppose the federal government in its implementation. In fact, it was suggested, Peterson never believed that Ottawa would negotiate a deal and that if a compromise were achieved, it would be unacceptable to Congress.[49] Now he was confronted with a dilemma created by his opposition to free trade, expectations amongst anti-free-trade groups that this had produced, conflicting attitudes amongst economic interests within the province and an inability, in practical terms, to do much about the agreement. Even in the area of provincial wine and liquor pricing, it was suggested that a refusal by Ontario to remove markups on imports might well bring US retaliation against Canadian whisky distillers and their $400 million market in the US. The agony was prolonged, however, by the Ontario government's decision to hold province-wide hearings on the free trade agreement whose outcome, given the fact that Peterson described its function as 'educating the public to its flaws' seemed predetermined.[50] Predictably, these hearings became the focus for opposition groups, some of which were urging action by the provincial government that was politically unrealistic. The National Action Committee on the status of women, for example, suggested that Peterson should 'ignite a constitutional crisis', something that he had clearly no intention of doing.

Confronted with differing provincial reactions and the difficulties in Ontario, Mulroney's strategy appears to have been two-fold. First, to emphasize the political costs that would accrue to any premier whose actions endangered the agreement. Hence Trade Minister Carney's warnings during November 1987 that any provincial government that failed to support the free trade deal would face the charge of contributing to national disunity. Second, to employ the well-tried techniques of horse-trading. For example, Newfoundland Premier Peckford's support might be bought, it was suggested through federal help in resolving the dispute between his province and Quebec over the transmission and pricing of electricity. Similarly, a link was suggested between Saskatchewan's support and a $1 billion federal grant to grain farmers. An announcement that federal funds would be made available to build a bridge between Prince Edward Island and the mainland had, according to Premier Ghiz, no connection with the domestic politics of free trade.[51]

CONGRESS AND THE STATES

Several factors limiting state involvement in trade have been noted above. An observer of the negotiations has suggested one lesson to be drawn from the experience: namely that 'Congressional concern was episodic and that the states could not use the federal formula for leverage in the same way that the Canadian provinces fell back on their constitutional prerogatives'.[52] That this was so reflected the fact that firstly, the channels between the states and the negotiators were undeveloped and contacts highly episodic. A report from the 49th Parallel Institute for Canadian–American Relations claimed that one USTR official had revealed during a conference on US–Canada trade issues that the administration had no strategy for accommodating state interests or for gaining the governors' support in the event of an agreement.[53] This could be explained on one side by an assumption (a Canadian trade official suggested that it was a 'gamble that paid off') that issues directly affecting views of state jurisdiction would be kept off the table. In the event this proved to be the case. Had an agreement required a general elimination of NTBs as was at one time assumed, then changes to state laws would have been inevitable and 'the ensuing complications would have been challenging to state and federal authorities alike'.[54]

A second factor which limited both congressional and other subnational inputs into the negotiations was the adoption of the fast-track procedure. Once the Senate finance committee had accepted this, the role of congress and the interests using it as a channel of expression, whilst by no means insignificant, were constrained. Thus during June and July, fears were being expressed that Congress would have little opportunity to amend the provisions contained in any legislation. Certainly, the most intensive round of committee activity was to come during the early months of 1988 as committees considered the various aspects of the agreement and heard evidence from a variety of regional economic and business interests. By this stage, however, it was suggested that only cosmetic changes could be made. Certainly, to the TNO in Ottawa, state interests seemed to surface late in the negotiations and then assumed the character of an 'ad hoc rifle-shot approach'.[55] As in earlier phases of the negotiations, a major concern expressed by Congress was whether the provinces would comply with the agreement. In mid May 1988, the Senate finance committee approved a provision that would require President Reagan to certify that Ottawa could ensure provincial cooperation.[56]

A further constraint on the states' involvement was created by the lack of any unified position amongst them, a reflection of differing regional concerns. The impression gained during interviews with state officials was that individual states were pursuing their own interests, California focusing on the wine industry, for example. Regional coalitions of states found their voice weakened by differences of approach on key aspects of the free trade agenda. The Western Governors' Association, for instance, whilst registering a growing awareness of the significance of international trade, did not operate as a coherent pressure group on this occasion since the interests of Dakota, Idaho and Montana were too distinct.[57] To the extent that the states had a coherent voice, this assumed the form of a task force created by the National Governors' Association.

One of the most notable examples of regional coalition building came in the form of the powerful congressional bloc of 38 senators and 200 members of House of Representatives known as the Northeast–Midwest Coalition which appeared to be the central factor in forcing the sensitive issue of the auto pact on to the negotiating agenda. Mulroney had assured the House of Commons in March 1987 that he could prevent this happening, clearly aware that this was one of the crucial aspects of the free trade debate in Ontario.[58] To leading congressional voices, including John Dingell, the Michigan chairman of the House Committee on Energy and Commerce, was added that of John Blanchard, governor of Michigan and an outspoken opponent of the auto pact. Blanchard was reported as having presented US trade representative Clayton Yeutter and the leader of the US negotiating team, Peter Murphy, with a position paper which, in essence, said that Michigan would oppose any agreement that failed to revised the auto pact, a condition subscribed to by the Council of Great Lakes governors as representatives of auto parts manufacturers in their states. Behind-the-scenes trade-offs in the final hours of the negotiations helped to lessen this opposition but did not remove it. When Congress finally approved the agreement in August 1988, Dingell – along with other Michigan legislators – described himself as a 'reluctant supporter' and expressed disappointment that US interests had not been more vigorously presented.[59]

STATE–PROVINCIAL INTERACTIONS

Given the highly developed patterns of transboundary relations between the states and the provinces, it might have been assumed that these would have assumed a significant role in the course of the negotiations. The available evidence, however, suggests that this was not so. Exchanges between state and provincial capitals were generally at the bureaucratic level and did not appear to represent subnational strategies which materially affected the course of the negotiations. In the case of British Columbia, a trade official recalled that 'there was some dialogue between the premier and the governor or Washington but nothing of great substance; it probably took up a few minutes of a meeting'.[60] The reasons for this are not hard to find. Within the office of the USTR it was seen as a reflection of the states' awareness of constitutional niceties: 'the states are sophisticated; they know the federal government is the way to solve problems of this kind. Generally, they don't go it alone – unlike business and the banks . . .'[61] This was supported by the experiences of a staff member in the California World Trade Commission who pointed out that whilst the state would engage in lobbying actively in Ottawa, it was sufficiently aware of federal–provincial tensions not to engage in a dialogue with the provinces. Furthermore, the same official could recall no occasion on which the provincial offices in California had contacted the CWTC.[62] At the federal level, a similar view prevailed: 'the federal position is quite clear; we are dealing with Ottawa. That is not to say that we won't speak to the provinces, we will. Carla Hills [the current USTR] recently had a fifteen minute meeting with Peterson at his request. But we won't negotiate'.[63]

An interesting sidelight on this arose in the context of the softwood lumber dispute referred to earlier. Given BC's high stake in the issue, Premier Vander Zalm's anxiety to reach a settlement with US

Commerce Department on the stumpage fee issue was clear and, it was suggested, effectively undermined Ottawa's strategy of resisting US demands. According to one press report, Canada's ambassador in Washington, Alan Gotlieb, was alerted to discussions occurring between members of the department and BC officials and sought to neutralize any provincial intervention by pressing the Americans to give a undertaking not to talk to BC. Despite the fact that both Federal Trade Minister Pat Carney and the BC premier's office denied that any negotiations (as opposed to exchanges of information) had taken place, the belief that Ottawa's response to the lumber issue had been greatly complicated by BC's actions persisted.[64]

A more central factor determining state–provincial interactions lay in the nature of the issues on which the free trade talks turned. If it was the case, as suggested above, that subnational coalition building was limited by regional diversities, then this was even more so in the case of provincial–state relations where many of the key issues (such as lumber and the auto pact) emphasized differences of interest. Such a situation limited the opportunity and the perceived value of transboundary diplomacy and distinguishes the free trade experience from other episodes in Canada–US relations (such as the acid rain dispute) where state–province relationships appear to have been central to the overall pattern of diplomacy. Given the sensitivities encompassed in the FTN, the natural 'allies' of subnational economic interests were the federal authorities and however unhappy with the nature of the negotiations these appeared to be, on the whole they seemed not unwilling to allow Ottawa and Washington to take the responsibility for shaping an agreement.

The main formal link between the states and provinces during the negotiations assumed the form of the Governors and Premiers Task Force on Trade created at the 1985 annual meeting of the NGA held at Boise, Idaho. Originally this comprised six governors and four premiers; by 1988 the group had expanded to include all ten premiers and twenty governors. Assessing the role of this body is difficult given a lack of information and the semi-secrecy which has surrounded some of its meetings. The guidelines adopted in 1985 are bland and unrevealing: (a) defining areas of cooperation in trade, (b) recommending action to the respective federal authorities on the resolution of trade differences, (c) searching for ways of increasing trade opportunities.[65]

At the 1988 meeting held in Traverse City, Michigan, David Peterson clearly sought to use the occasion to press his views on the auto pact issue and reached an agreement with Michigan's Governor Blanchard to set up a joint task force to determine the effects of the pact on Ontario and Michigan. A further meeting between the two was scheduled for the autumn of 1988. Generally, however, it seems that these meetings have not represented serious attempts at 'regional diplomacy' intended to exert pressures on federal negotiators or to solve regional economic differences at the subnational level.[66] More realistically, the task force has probably assumed the role – by no means insignificant – of a forum for mutual education which:

> will engender greater understanding of two distinctly different governing systems intertwined though extensive and increasing economic interdependence. State and provincial officials, after all, probably know less about one another's political structures and economic policies than do their federal counterparts.[67]

Elsewhere, provincial-state interactions were highly episodic. An attempt to develop a cooperative approach amongst the states and provinces to promote lumber exports in the Pacific Basin lost its impetus and a 1987 meeting of the Conference of New England governors and Eastern premiers expressed general support for the FTN but decided to avoid discussion of specific issues.[68]

CONCLUSIONS

What lessons does the experience of the Canada–US free trade negotiations offer which might facilitate an understanding of multi-layered diplomacy and the place of NCGs within it?

Firstly, the most obvious point: both Ottawa and Washington confronted the problem of managing very significant subnational interests in the context of the FTN. These represented regional economic interests which gained their primary expression in the Canadian instance through the provinces, and in the case of the US through Congress with associated pressures from representatives of state interests such as the National Governors' Association. Furthermore, to achieve their goals in the negotiations, both sides had to maintain an interest not only in their own subnational interests but in those of the other negotiating partner. In this sense, success or failure would be determined as much by events within the two countries as between them. For both Washington and Ottawa, the problem lay in the realm of ratification and implementation of the agreement, not simply in a constitutional but in a broader political sense. Bearing this in mind, it is possible to identify patterns of interactions, strategies and roles embracing these subnational interests as the negotiations progressed through the prenegotiation and negotiation phases.

In terms of the patterns of interactions, one notable feature of the FTN process is that the two national negotiating teams were the dominant foci for interactions between the US and Canada. Given the extensive transboundary relations between at least some of the states and provinces, it might have been assumed that the various forms of 'micro' or 'para' diplomacy identified in the literature of NCG international activity would have come into operation. That this was not so is largely a reflection of issues on which the negotiations turned. Certainly, some states and provinces were linked by virtue of regional economic interests but these were conflictual rather than cooperative in nature as symbolized by the softwood lumber dispute. This fact limited diplomacy at the subnational level and inclined both sets of interests to view their own federal governments as the appropriate negotiators, even though doubts might have existed in some quarters as to whether these would act as adequate articulators of regional interests. Such contacts as there were, in the form of the Governors–Premiers Task Force, appear to have been information-exchanging exercises rather than any serious attempt to influence directly the negotiations from the subnational level.

Far less were there interactions between one set of subnational actors and national policy makers on the other side. Again, this is not to say that communications did not exist; statements by several premiers during the negotiations were clearly based on information gained through the web of communications crossing the border. The point is, however, that there is little evidence of attempts to influence the negotiating teams. The exception referred to in this paper is the claim that British Columbia sought to intervene directly with the US Department of Commerce during the softwood lumber dispute. The denials that this amounted to anything approaching 'negotiations' made not only by Premier Vander Zalm but also by the US Commerce Department and Canadian Trade Minister Pat Carney, would, to say the least, seem to weaken the significance of this episode as an example of NCG diplomacy.

However, the fact that the states (together with their main channel of influence, Congress) and provinces did not assume the role of primary actors in the negotiations does not lessen their importance to an understanding of the flow of negotiations and the constraints and opportunities that each presented to their national negotiators. The logic of multilayered diplomacy requires each side in a set of negotiations to take an active interest in the other's domestic constituencies where these affect the likelihood of reaching an agreement. In the case of the FTN, the problems confronting Washington and Ottawa were compounded by the fact that the norms governing Canada–US relations, combined with political prudence, strictly limited the extent to which either negotiating team could involve itself in the other's domestic political processes. The picture is complicated by the fact that domestic interests in Canada–US trade could, in the context of the negotiations, be at once a negative and positive factor in fashioning a negotiating strategy. This can be seen if we examine the relationships between the negotiators, their own subnational interests and those of their opposite numbers.

Taking Canada first, in terms of international management, the major issue confronting Ottawa was the need to develop a framework within which provincial interests and aspirations could be accommodated whilst limiting any weakening effect that this might have on its position in the negotiations. The first step here was determining the form and level of provincial involvement, denying the provinces a place at the negotiating table whilst creating a consultative structure at both political and bureaucratic levels. Associated with this was the attempt to defer the thorny issue of the provincial role in the implementation of the agreement. Here, of course, Mulroney confronted conflicting impulses: a desire to leave this in abeyance until the shape of an agreement became clear set against the need to assure regional interests represented in Congress that the provinces would support the final result. The position finally adopted – one that did not appear to convince Congress – was that Canadian compliance need not rest on unanimous approval but on a provincial consensus. When the terms of the agreement reached between Ottawa and Washington were finally revealed, it became clear that both sides had sought to avoid as far as possible issues impinging on the powers of subnational jurisdictions and that this comprised a major element in their strategy for dealing with domestic demands. In this sense, subnational interests constituted a set of constraints on what was regarded as politically possible within the trade negotiations arena.

The Ottawa government was helped in managing these internal problems by the varying interests and attitudes of the provinces themselves. Not all the provinces – especially the smallest – were ardent advocates of a major role in the negotiations, fearing that their voice would be drowned by the most powerful. Similarly, reactions to the federal government's position on agreement by consensus rather than unaniminity, whilst opposed by Ontario, was subscribed to by Quebec and British Columbia.

At the external level, Ottawa did not confront complications created by essays in provincial diplomacy. Even Ontario, the main focus of opposition to the FTN, was extremely cautious in the way in which this was presented. Peterson's stance at one and the same time emphasized his hostility to the talks and yet made it clear that his government's power to act was limited and that, in any case, he would do nothing to undermine the prime minister's position. Quite obviously, the provincial factor created problems for both sets of negotiators in dealing with Congress since interests represented on Capitol Hill continually emphasized the importance of the implementation issue. Nevertheless, in one sense, the demands placed on Ottawa in constructing a firm domestic negotiating base constituted one of its few strengths given the asymmetries of power and interest on which the talks rested. The point is emphasized by Deputy Chief Trade Negotiator Gordon Ritchie who, in his survey of the negotiating process, argues that the elaborate consultative structures presided over by the TNO with its pattern of private sector and provincial consultations, constituted the sole resource that Canada could mobilize against the 'sheer economic clout' of the US.[69]

Ottawa's real problems on the external front lay in Washington's incapacity to control its own major subnational interest in the form of Congress and the regional interests represented therein. As already noted, Canada's negotiators were, ultimately, forced to rely on the Reagan administration's ability to deal with Capitol Hill. However, as Aho points out, the White House failed to mobilize its allies within Congress and its overall consultations with relevant domestic interests was, to use his term, 'spotty'.[70] How serious a problem this was for Canada can be seen in the near-failure of the Senate to approve the fast-track procedure in May 1986 and the need clearly felt by Reisman to force a crisis in the negotiations on 23 September 1987 in order to engage the attention of the administration to the impasse that had been reached.

Turning to the US, the fast-track procedure offered the framework within which the main expression of subnational interests could be contained. As noted earlier, however, the problem for the White House was that the Canada–US trade talks were overshadowed by the broader trade issue and the executive–legislative tensions generated by it. When combined with the low level of resources devoted to the negotiations and the weakness in domestic consultations just noted, the problems confronting the US negotiating team were severe. In no sense did the congressional factor appear to be used as a negotiating tactic to pressure Ottawa during the talks. On the contrary, the evidence such as it is would suggest that Murphy was forced to respond in an ad hoc way to congressional pressures. It is tempting to speculate that there was a greater identity of interest between the US team and their Canadian counterparts than with the forces ranged on Capitol Hill. In this context, Clayton Yeutter might have been forgiven a wry smile when, in appearing before the Senate finance committee shortly before its crucial vote on the fast-track procedure, he was told by its chairman, Senate Baucus, that a motion of disapproval would enable him 'to sit down at the bargaining table with more authority, more leverage, more bargaining power'.[71]

As has been demonstrated throughout this discussion, at the external level, Murphy and Yeutter were repeatedly forced to consider the role of the provinces and to act as interpreters of the situation in Canada to congressional committees, acting as interpreter of one set of subnational interests to the other. Ultimately, however, each national government had to rely on the other to manage its own domestic political and economic interests as best it could. Apart from the occasional speech delivered in Canada during which Yeutter could gently remind his audience of the importance attached by Congress to the provincial dimension of the trade talks, there was little that the US team could – or would want to – do to strengthen the hand of its Canadian counterparts in the negotiations. In this respect, given the elaborate consultative procedures established by Ottawa combined with a certain amount of luck in the latter's dealings with the provinces, the US team were more fortunate in the Canadian subnational component of the FTN multilayered negotiating environment than was Ottawa with that of the US.

Overall, it is clear that provincial and state interests were pivotal to the development of the multilayered diplomacy which made up the free trade negotiations. Far from displaying patterns of behaviour contrary to accepted constitutional norms, their involvement reflects the character of much contemporary trade diplomacy wherein domestic and international interests are closely interwoven. It needs to be stressed, however, that the free trade negotiations do not represent in some sense a model of NCG involvement in multilayered diplomacy;

rather the opposite. Indeed, each situation is likely to be unique, involving NCGs and other subnational actors in a variety of ways and endowing them with roles which reflect the character of a specific issue, the interests of the actors, and the diplomatic tasks confronting national negotiators.

5 British Industry versus US State Governments: The Politics of Unitary Taxation

The focus of the previous chapter was on the pattern of negotiations at two levels – the domestic and international – in the context of traditional intergovernmental trade negotiations. It demonstrates the point made in earlier chapters, namely that non-central governments can become enmeshed in complex diplomatic processes and, in so doing, discharge a number of roles. But, clearly, there are a wide range of circumstances outside those imposed by formal negotiations in which NCGs are likely to find themselves involved in interactions with a variety of international actors. The point was made in Chapter 3 that, as authorities possessing the capacity to make rules capable of affecting the operations of the 'global web' of international business, NCGs are likely to find themselves the focus of the latter's interest. Consequently, international business enterprises are increasingly constrained to operate in a variety of political jurisdictions at both national and subnational levels.

This chapter develops the theme by focusing on attempts by British interests to end the 'unitary taxation' policies operated by certain US state governments. In so doing, it is intended to cast further light on the growing international involvement of NCGs by examining a situation where the two worlds of governmental and non-governmental actors intersect as UK companies and financial interests sought to mobilize their power to influence the policies of certain US state governments and, in so doing, found themselves caught up in a complex web of political interactions.

UNITARY TAX: THE ISSUE

The term 'unitary tax' is misleading in the sense that it refers not to a tax but to a system for calculating the profits which are to be taxed.

(Since, however, it is a convenient shorthand term for a complex subject, it will be used throughout this discussion.) The essence of the issue lies in the emergence of business enterprises operating in a number of taxing jurisdictions. This poses one of the most controversial issues in company taxation: how should a taxing authority, be it national or subnational, determine its share of such an enterprise's taxable income? In the case of the US, where companies are taxed both by the federal authorities and each of the states in which it operates, the state taxing authorities employ formulas which apportion a corporation's income amongst these states. In doing so, it is necessary to consider the business enterprise as a 'unitary' entity in the sense that it is a single enterprise no matter how complex its structure might be. The unitary principle developed in the nineteenth century as the US railroad, canal, telegraph and express systems expanded and the states sought to determine their share of company profits.[1] Operating the opposite principle, known as 'separate' or 'arm's length' accounting, whereby corporations are taxed on their operations within each state, resulted in a situation where railroad and other multistate enterprises could reduce their tax liabilities by basing their income calculations on operations in low-tax jurisdictions. In the case of the railroads, companies reduced their tax liabilities in high-tax California by calculating their income on the basis of track length in each state. Conveniently, this meant that their tax liabilities were highest in low-tax states such as Utah and Nevada where the companies had constructed long stretches of track but carried relatively few customers. The use of the unitary principle, however, meant that the railroad companies' operations could be considered as a single business enterprise, and states could calculate company tax liabilities on their overall value, apportioning tax due to them on the basis of track length within the state taken as a proportion of the total length of the system.

By the 1930s, the unitary method had become common practice within the US. It was its gradual extension during the 1960s and 1970s to foreign business enterprises that placed the issue firmly on the international agenda. More specifically, it was one method of calculating the nature of the unitary business, referred to as the 'worldwide combination' system that has been at the heart of the controversy. State authorities, such as those in California, employing this form of the unitary principle took the total world income of corporations with overseas operations in calculating tax liabilities. Put at its simplest, this meant if 10 per cent of the total or worldwide business activities of the unitary business occurred in a particular state, then 10 per cent of the group's worldwide combined income would be taxable by that state. This practice was first applied to multinational corporations (MNCs) operating out of the US; by the 1970s, however, some states such as California had extended it to cover foreign-owned MNCs with US subsidiaries. This stood in contrast to the 'water's edge' approach in which only the income of related business enterprises located in the US is used as the basis for computing tax liability.

Objections to this system were to gather momentum during the 1970s and 1980s and rested on a series of arguments about its nature, consequences and constitutionality. Amongst these were the contentions that it was at variance with the international practice of separate accounting for avoiding double taxation; that it created an uncertain climate for investment by MNCs, thereby threatening investment and trade; that some tax authorities, such as the California Franchise Tax Board, applied the system in an arbitrary fashion, and that it burdened companies with considerable – and costly – administrative burdens. As will be shown below, it engaged the attention of numerous governments and business interests around the world, but became a prominent issue in UK politics in the context of the renewal of the UK/US Double Taxation Treaty.[2] Article 9(4) of the treaty, supported by both the UK and US governments, would have eliminated the application of the worldwide unitary system by the states to British-owned businesses. In the event, the Senate, as a result of intensive state lobbying, effectively removed the clause and the treaty eventually passed by the Senate in June 1978 did not contain Article 9(4). The British parliament had already ratified the treaty, and approved a revised version in February 1980 on the understanding that the unitary issue would be dealt with in Congress. In the words of one senior British executive closely involved in the unitary issue, 'lulled by sweet sounds Parliament ratified prematurely and threw away Britain's bargaining power. The active lobbying and the sympathetic noises faded: it was presidential election year.'[3]

Indeed, during the next two years, in which a number of bills were introduced into Congress concerning the unitary issue, the Reagan administration, seeking legislative support for other tax measures, displayed no sense of urgency. Clearly, this was a highly sensitive political issue, touching the raw nerves of states' rights on the one hand and taxation on the other. Increasingly, the White House found itself squeezed between powerful domestic pressures represented by US corporations with their own set of concerns relating to worldwide unitary tax, and the states operating such methods. In addition, the Administration was confronted by mounting international concerns. Hopes that the problem might be resolved through the courts suffered a setback when the Supreme Court in the Container Case, upheld the right of the states to use the unitary formula in the case of US MNCs but reserved its judgement on foreign MNCs.

Following this, the international and domestic politics generated by the unitary problem moved into higher gear both at governmental and non-governmental levels. This was stimulated by fears that the use of the worldwide combination system might spread not only within the US (Florida decided to adopt it in 1983 in the wake of the Container decision) but in other countries, particularly in the Third World. Given the fact that only three states were using the method in 1978, compared with fourteen in 1983, there appeared to be some substance in such fears. In the case of the UK, the focus of British MNC efforts was the Unitary Tax Campaign, created very much on the initiative of one person, Peter Welch, finance director of Foseco Minsep.

Pressures were also directed by the British parliament towards the British and US governments. These resulted in the adoption of a 'retaliatory clause' in the 1985 Finance Act which would have removed certain taxation advantages enjoyed by US companies operating in the UK.

The groundswell of international opinion was largely responsible for the creation in 1983 of a working group on the unitary tax issue, chaired by Treasury Secretary Donald Regan, which brought together federal, state and business interests. This was generally regarded as a means whereby the nettle of legislative action could be brushed aside rather than firmly grasped as many international interests believed was necessary if the problem was to be resolved. The working group, after numerous meetings of its technical task force, failed to reach agreement on a recommendation to the president. Rather, it delivered six options, all assuming that the problem should be resolved by voluntary action on the part of the states. In August 1984, Regan announced that he would deliver his own report to the president and in it, to the annoyance of the states, recommended federal action if they had not made progress on unitary reform within one year. Against this background, activity at the state level increased. In some cases, such as Florida, Indiana and Oregon during 1984, worldwide unitary legislation was either not enacted or repealed. In the Californian case, regarded as the the most crucial by the international business community, Governor Deukmejian supported a bill which, after one major interruption, finally passed into law in September 1986. However the compromises on which this was based produced features in the legislation which did not satisfy foreign multinationals and the battle continued through the courts in the form of a series of cases such as that brought by Barclays in California.

ISSUE CHARACTERISTICS

This brief survey of the origins and development of the unitary issue suggests certain characteristics which were to prove significant in the development of the multitiered lobbying processes and the strategies accompanying them: it is helpful to note these before turning to the patterns of interactions which developed as events unfolded.

First of all, the most obvious point: the unitary tax problem developed, in a clear-cut form, all the facets of a classic multilevel political issue. This is true not simply in the sense that the relationships which developed around it spanned a variety of arenas and bridged the domestic and international divides, but also in that they brought together the worlds of business and government in a shifting set of relationships as the former sought to achieve their objectives. Secondly, differences and similarities of interests between the major protagonists spanned the various arenas of activity, creating complex adversary–partner relationships. US-based MNCs, for example, whilst concerned with the unitary issue, had their own specific objectives which distinguished them from foreign MNCs with US operations. Third, unitary tax is a complex and technical issue which the simplistic treatment rendered in this discussion belies. However much it might excite coteries of accountants poring over its finer points with quasi-theological fervour, it was never an issue likely to interest a mass public, far less stir the populace into action. As we shall see, this was a significant factor in the development of lobbying strategies.

Yet, at the same time, it became an issue of high politics for the governmental actors and showed a remarkable capacity for survival over, in political terms, a quite considerable time period. It was dealt with not solely at the bureaucratic level but involved the most prominent political figures in the UK and US. Furthermore, partly because it was a technical issue, it appeared to offer an opportunity to groups with other interests to attach their causes to it.

THE BRITISH CAMPAIGN: TASKS

As noted earlier, the British were by no means alone in their concerns with the unitary tax issue. Indeed, the sheer variety of interests spanning various political arenas was one of its key features. Nevertheless, the UK was to become a leading actor for several reasons. One of these, of course, was the high level of British investment in the US which not only underpinned the attitudes of British companies as the unitary issue unfolded but ensured that British policies, both official and unofficial, would gain a hearing in the US at both federal and state level. It was always clear, however, that changing the worldwide unitary system presented a daunting task; or more accurately, a set of tasks embracing several tiers of political activity.

Within the home arena, there were two main tasks confronting the opponents of unitary tax. One of these involved building and sustaining a coalition of governmental and non-governmental interests over a period of time where those interests were not entirely identical and opinions might differ on questions of strategy. A second major task lay in gaining the support and active involvement of the British government. The ensuing discussion will make clear why this was important in the context of the parliamentary campaign which was to be central to British efforts, but it was also crucial in pressuring the US federal authorities and using the international governmental networks provided by, for example, the IMF and World Bank meetings and Group of Seven (G7) summit meetings.

At the US level, there were tasks to be accomplished at the corporate, federal and state levels. Identifying allies and opponents amongst US business interests would be essential in applying internal pressure at the national and state levels. With regard to the federal government, one of the most difficult tasks lay in establishing the issue on the crowded White House agenda. Here, as mentioned earlier, the support of the UK government would be vital. When it came to the states, several points had to be borne in mind. Not least amongst these was gaining access to the political processes in these diverse theatres. This was partly a constitutional issue where governmental operations were concerned since the conventions of international diplomacy dictated that the UK government dealt only with the federal authorities. Moreover, great dangers existed in becoming embroiled in the sensitive politics of federal–state relations. Beyond these factors, however, lay the obvious problems of operating in a variety of subnational political settings, each marked by their own characteristics and requiring local knowledge if activities at this level were to succeed.

At the broader international level, it was obvious that the larger the range of international voices which could be mustered on the unitary issue, the greater the chance of success. Thus one set of tasks lay in identifying sympathetic international interests and, where possible aligning them with those in the UK. The most that could be hoped for here, given the diversity of interests involved, was that they could be coordinated where a lack of coordination could weaken the overall campaign. It was also necessary to bear in mind the potentially negative effects of, firstly, exerting too much pressure on the US which could easily generate strong resentments, and, second, the need to distance British interests from those of other foreign actors whose involvement might not always be regarded as a positive factor. Taken overall, then, the tasks confronting British companies were those noted earlier: access to a variety of actors and arenas, coordination of activities, and – to the extent that this was possible – controlling the exercise of influence on the target arenas.

ACCOMPLISHING THE TASKS

Bearing in mind the scope of these tasks, a fluid and adaptable strategy was clearly of the essence. Amongst other things, this would need to take account of the issue-characteristics noted earlier. As Moon has suggested in his typology of transnational lobbying, a variety of approaches are available to actors wishing to operate in foreign political theatres, some requiring direct involvement in the political processes, others relying on indirect techniques.[4] In each case, familiar lobbying tactics are employed. Moon distinguishes between what he terms the 'access to power' approach (the attempt to gain direct influence through the use of power-brokers) and the 'technocratic' approach which relies on the use of experts where highly technical issues are involved. On the indirect front, the two main tactics are the familiar ones of seeking out allies in the target arena and mobilizing public interest groups of various kinds. Given the nature of the unitary tax issue, its technicality, low appeal to a mass public audience and the involvement of several political power centres within the US, one could expect that the first three techniques would be significant and the fourth less so. How, then, did the British campaign develop and how were these several modes of access to and influence within the relevant US and other theatres achieved?

DEVELOPING THE CAMPAIGN: THE HOME FRONT

In the wake of the failure to eliminate the unitary tax problem through the renewal of the UK/US Double Taxation Agreement, it was clear that some form of 'control centre' was necessary if British industrial and financial interests were to succeed in projecting their interests in the various arenas involved in the issue. This was achieved through the creation of the Unitary Tax Campaign (UTC) which, as noted earlier, had been established on the initiative of Peter Welch, the finance director of a British company, Foseco Minsep. In part, his motives for doing so were the slowness of the Confederation of British Industry (CBI) to act and the hesitancy displayed by the British government. Welch recalled the founding of the UTC in the following terms:

> In the late 1970s my company was proposing to invest in California and I became very aware of the unitary tax issue. I decided that action of some kind was necessary but had absolutely no idea how to tackle the problem and no experience at all of action at the political level. So, I rang around the directors of companies who had an interest – there were five initially – each subscribed money and we set up the UTC. The problem at this stage was we didn't know what to do![5]

In seeking political advice, Welch and his compatriots sought out one of the most influential and highly regarded firms of political consultants, Ian Greer Associates. IGA, in effect, became the operational headquarters of the UTC which was established as a limited company with a board of directors largely comprising the finance directors from leading UK business and financial institutions. At the height of the campaign, the original membership increased to over sixty companies, each subscribing sums of between five and ten thousand pounds to a campaign fund. A technical committee and campaign strategy committee were set up, the latter meeting regularly and including figures crucial to the development of the campaign, such as the Conservative member of parliament and chairman of the Conservative backbench finance committee, Michael Grylls. The advantages of this arrangement are not hard to find. It provided coherence and continuity in the development and application of a strategy, and, through the expertise and contacts provided by IGA, offered access to several levels of political activity in the UK and overseas. Indeed, for one participant in events, serving as economic counsellor at the British Embassy in Washington, one of their most notable features was the apparent access and influence that IGA enjoyed in London.[6]

One of the key tasks of the UTC was to engage the interest of the government for the reasons noted earlier. Although the Labour government of James Callaghan – replaced in 1979 by the Conservatives under Margaret Thatcher – was opposed to unitary tax, it was not high on its agenda. Nor was the Thatcher government, which it might have been assumed would have been more attuned to industry's concerns, particularly active in its early years. This situation began to change in 1982, very much as a result of the personalities involved. John Moore, financial secretary of the treasury, was deputed by the chancellor of the exchequer to take responsibility for the issue and was a key figure in the interactions between the UTC and the government over the next few years. Furthermore, there were sympathetic faces at the bureaucratic level, particularly within the Inland Revenue. But one of the key elements in gaining the government's attention was the ability of the UTC in cooperation with prominent backbenchers, such as Michael Grylls and Sir Graham Page, to develop a parliamentary campaign.

Parliament, as we have seen, had been involved through its role in the ratification of the US/UK tax treaty and members such as Grylls and Page had managed to keep the issue simmering, if not on the boil, since that period. Given that this was hardly a vote winner, securing a reasonable degree of parliamentary interest was no mean task, yet one that seems to have been accomplished with a considerable degree of success. The pressure on government was kept up by the usual means of contributions to debate parliamentary questions and the tabling of Early Day Motions (EDMs) asking the government to take action on the unitary tax issue and a series of meetings between UTC members and the financial secretary, John Moore.

The key feature in the official arena, and the event that linked together government, parliament and industry, was the passing by the House of Commons of the so-called 'retaliatory clause' in the 1985 Finance Act. Pressure had steadily grown at Westminster for positive action by the government but had received a cautious response. A central factor here was that any attempt to include such a measure in the Finance Act could only come from the government through a

'Ways and Means' motion. The government continued to resist pressure to take such a course of action during 1983 and 1984, its preferred strategy being to encourage Washington to sponsor, or at least support, legislative action. The tabling of two EDMs in 1984 and 1985, each bearing over two hundred and fifty signatures together with a delegation of Conservative backbenchers, led by Michael Grylls, to the financial secretary, appear to have played a part in changing the government's attitude. Given the sensitivities involved in London–Washington relations, the parliamentary anti-unitary forces had to tread carefully: in late 1983, the Treasury, in pointing out the action that the government had taken, warned Grylls that he should not press it too strongly on the question of the retaliatory clause as this might give the appearance of disunity in the British camp.[7]

Government policy on the clause changed between the meeting held between John Moore and the UTC in February 1985 and that which followed in June when Moore informed Welch and Grylls that it had decided to table the necessary Ways and Means resolution. Consequently, parliamentary, combined with UTC/CBI, pressure and the lack of real movement in the US, prompted the UK government to endorse the passing, in July 1985, of a provision (Section 54, Finance Act 1985) under which the UK could withdraw from US parent companies situated in unitary states the entitlement to tax credits relating to dividends paid by UK subsidiaries. This would come into force through a statutory instrument to be passed at some future date by the House of Commons. In other words, this was a threat hanging over US companies with UK interests, and the clear hope was that they would exert pressure on Washington to take action. In succumbing to pressures to adopt the retaliatory clause, the Treasury was emphatic in its insistence that it be seen as a cross-party parliamentary action, thereby limiting the tensions that such a move might generate at the governmental level.

The UTC played a key role in the drafting of the clause but needed to be aware that adopting such a strategy might well reveal the fact that its membership was by no means totally united when it came to matters of strategy. Here, it has to be remembered that not all the UTC subscribers held identical interests in the Unitary tax issue. For some, their support derived as much from a belief in the rightness of the cause as from the impact of the worldwide unitary system on their operations. Were the use of retaliatory measures to lead, in turn, to retaliation by Washington, then consensus might quickly vanish. Differences of opinion were reflected in the advice that individual members of UTC were providing to the strategy committee and also in the CBI's attitude which, whilst not opposing the adoption of retaliatory powers in the Finance Act, did not favour their use. Taking a more definite stance, the British Insurance Association did oppose the adoption of the clause, arguing that the correct approach was through negotiation and persuasion at a broader international (particularly European Community) level.

The fact that the BIA's representative in the House of Commons, Sir William Clark, refused to endorse the Association's position and voted in favour of the clause is, perhaps, one measure of the strength of support that this strategy of potential retaliation enjoyed. Certainly, by the March 1985 meeting of the UTC strategy committee which considered the report of a UK business mission to California arguing the case for the assumption of retaliatory powers, the UTC had decided that it was essential to press the government to take this course of action.

It was the adoption of this strategy which helped to turn the UK into a target arena for US interests. Whilst the retaliatory clause was being drafted, UTC advisers had sounded out the reactions of two US corporate giants, Mobil and Exxon. They appeared to have no objection to the adoption of the clause as a means of exerting pressure on Washington and those state governments using the worldwide unitary system, but, obviously, their attitude would be different were its provisions to be implemented. The reaction of the American Chamber of Commerce in London, however, was strong in its condemnation. In a letter to John Moore at the Treasury, sent shortly after the adoption of the clause, the Chamber argued that this was a 'slap in the face' to those US companies which had supported the repeal of unitary tax, and would have a severe impact on US/UK relations.[8] Along with some UK interests, the Chamber argued that the proper course of action was the pursuit of negotiations in Washington for the restoration of Article 9(4) of the Double Taxation Agreement.

Alongside the parliamentary campaign, the UTC sought to capitalize on the close relationship between Margaret Thatcher and Ronald Reagan. From 1983 onwards, a regular exchange of letters between the prime minister and Michael Grylls on the unitary tax issue developed, and this helped to ensure that the matter would not be forgotten in Washington. Of course, this could not overcome the pressures directed at the White House from the US domestic arena: in October 1983, the prime minister pressured Reagan to file a supporting brief in the Container case, which it did not do. In June 1984, following the publication of the Regan Working Group report, Thatcher raised the question of the Administation's intentions during a meeting with Reagan. She did so again during her 1985 visit to Washington and this was regarded by the UTC as a major factor in the publication in December 1985 of draft legislation to limit the states' use of the unitary method to the water's edge principle.[9]

THE INTERNATIONAL FRONT

Quite clearly, the broader the international pressure that could be brought to bear within the US, the greater the chances of a successful outcome in the struggle over unitary tax. For British interests as represented in the UTC, this meant attempting to develop and maintain contacts with the various official and non-official bodies involved and to establish, where possible, common positions. Caution needed to be exercised here, of course. Foreign trade and investment are highly sensitive issues, not least on Capitol Hill, and it would be only too easy to generate a domestic backlash against what was frequently portrayed as special pleading by foreign MNCs looking for a tax-break. In particular, caution needed to be exercised in relations with one other major player, Japan. Both at state and federal levels, resentment at the Japanese trade imbalance and growing investment was, and remains, a key feature of US politics. Distancing themselves from any negative consequences of the intensive Japanese lobbying effort would be as much a consideration in the minds of British interests as establishing a common front with Japan.

As far as the original founders of the UTC were concerned, there had been no intention of operating directly at an international level.[10] The assumption had been that the aim of the campaign was to encourage government to government negotiations to resolve the impasse that had developed in the wake of the elimination of Article 9(4) of the Double Taxation Agreement. As it became clear that this was unlikely to occur, the need for direct action, both in the US and on the broader international front, became apparent. In the case of the latter, international coalition-building occurred at several levels. One was that of individual companies sharing a concern with the issue. In early 1984, for example, the UTC decided to invite Hoechst and Wormalds (an Australian company) to join its ranks. Regular meetings occurred between UTC representatives and Japanese industry. Thus, in 1984,

Peter Welch met Akia Morita of Sony to discuss the campaign in California and Florida and the possibilities of greater cooperation through the Committee on Unitary Taxation (CUT), one of the California-based international coalition groups. In March 1985, he held a further meeting with representatives of the Keidanren at which strategy in California was discussed and the possibility of cooperation through CUT and other coalitions was again canvassed.[11] The reactions of foreign business interests to UTC overtures varied depending on a variety of factors, not least the personalities involved. The Swiss were not anxious to be involved in these international efforts; the Dutch preferred to act separately.

A second level of international coalition building was provided by international industry groupings such as UNICE (Union des Industries de la Communauté Européenne). Here the UK assumed a major role within the Steering Group on Unitary Tax, the UTC being represented at its meetings.[12] Representatives of another US-based coalition of foreign interests, the Organization for Fair Taxation of International Investments (OFTII), also attended these meetings and the minutes of OFTII meetings were regularly considered at them. In turn, UNICE-related developments were reviewed at UTC strategy meetings. One can begin to see here the intricate networks of relationships that the unitary tax issue fostered.

International governmental actors were also to prove important. Amongst these was the OECD. UTC interests were served here by virtue of the fact that one of its major allies within the Inland Revenue was also chairman of the Fiscal Affairs Committee within whose remit the unitary tax question fell. This was to prove valuable in keeping the issue on the international agenda and also in mobilizing OECD pressure in Washington. (This will be dealt with in the subsequent discussion of operations within the US.) The European Community was also to play a role, but one that was reactive rather than active.[13] In 1985, the UTC sent a delegation to see Christopher Tugendhat, vice-president of the EC Commission, who whilst sympathetic to their cause, made it clear that there was relatively little that the EC as an independent actor could do. In the event, its major role was to be in Washington as an added voice in the diplomatic pressures being applied to the administration. Mention should also be made here of other forums through which influence could be exerted. The British chancellor of the exchequer, Nigel Lawson, raised the unitary issue with Treasury Secretary Baker at IMF and World Bank meetings and it was also discussed at G7 meetings.

THE US ARENA

The key feature of the target arena was its diversity and complexity. Any succesful strategy needed to take account of three levels of activity: the US domestic corporations with an interest in the unitary issue, the federal arena, and the states operating the worldwide unitary method. Each of these contained a variety of actors and interests, both private sector, governmental, legislative and bureaucratic. It was against this background that British companies developed the US arm of their multitiered lobbying strategy. This presented the UTC with a major task, particularly in the period from 1983 to 1986 during which it was seeking to achieve legislative action at the federal level and in several states, whilst managing the home and international arenas.

Relations with the US Domestics

Nothing could be achieved on the unitary front without the cooperation of those US corporations (the 'domestics') who had a direct or indirect concern with the outcome of the dispute. Both British industry and the domestics, together with the broader international business community, shared an interest in the unitary issue. Yet, at the same time, those interests did not entirely coincide; on the matter of the taxation of the dividends received by US companies from their overseas operations ('foreign source dividends'), for example. As will emerge in the analysis of state-level activities, this was to prove a crucial issue since, whilst not of central concern to the British, it affected the attitudes of state politicians to the whole unitary question. Maximizing the points of linkage whilst insulating against any negative effects that might flow from such linkages was one task that coloured the coalition-building processes on the industrial front. Another lay in assuaging the fears that the adoption of the retaliatory clause might have aroused in the minds of the US corporate community.

Part of the processes through which the clause emerged had involved, as we have seen, some discussion with the domestics. Nevertheless, the prospect of its implementation appears to have remained in their consciousness, particularly as the failure to make progress at the federal level during 1986 made this a real possibility. So, for example, executives from Esso/Exxon, representing one of the domestics' major groupings, the California Business Council (CBC), visited officials of the Inland Revenue during 1985. They offered the following proposition: in return for the abandonment of the clause, they would join with UK interests in pressing the Reagan administration to pursue a legislative solution which would restore Article 9(4) which Senate opposition had removed from the US/UK tax treaty.[14] The clause remained but a considerable degree of contact and cooperation, in the event, developed over the next two years. This embraced both federal and state theatres. In September 1985, for example, Exxon made an approach to Treasury Secretary Baker regarding the need for federal legislative action and proposed to the UTC that representatives of both organizations meet with the American Chamber of Commerce in the UK to develop a united front in their representations to the US Treasury.[15] With regard to strategy at the states level, regular meetings were held between UTC and CBC representatives in London and Sacramento concerning developments in California. One proposal made by the CBC was that all the industry groupings operating in California send Governor Deukmejian a 'demarche' on the unitary tax issue, a course of action rejected by the UTC's Sacramento lobbyist on the grounds that it would align UK interests too closely with divisive domestic issues, such as foreign source dividends.

One very real problem lay in the relationships between the multiplicity of actors spawned by the unitary issue, particularly the groupings representing foreign and domestic corporate concerns. A bewildering array of names and acronyms confronts the observer. On the US domestics side, the main organizations were the California Manufacturers Association (CMA), the Committee on State Taxation (COST) of the State Chambers of Commerce, and the California Taxpayers' Association (CALTAX). Alongside these were sectoral organizations such as the American Electronics Association. These were joined by coalitions created to fight the unitary battle, such as the California Business Council mentioned above, founded in 1984. The CBC, representing over 90 major US MNCs, each paying into a campaign fund, had as its aim (in the words of one of its lobbyists, Revell Communications): 'to serve as a broad-based, consensus organization to garner strong business, community, legislative, media and general constituency support for an equitable approach to the unitary tax problem through effective, timely, political advocacy and an active public relations/media campaign'.[16]

Representing foreign concerns were several coalition groups. The Committee on Unitary Taxation (CUT), overseen by the UTC's

Sacramento lobbyist, A–K Associates, comprised mainly foreign MNCs. The California Unitary Coalition (CUC) was supported mainly by international giants such as Sony, Barclays and Royal Dutch Shell. The California Investment Environment Committee was dominated by Japanese interests. OFTII (Organization for Fair Taxation of International Investments) was set up in 1984 partly to balance the active Japanese lobbying campaign and was dominated by UK MNCs. In addition, many of the large US and foreign MNCs such as Sony, IBM, Shell and Kyocera International, retained their own lobbyists in pursuit of their goals.[17]

Not surprisingly, simple communication, far less coordination of activities, was a major problem with such a large and disparate cast of players. Reference has already been made to certain linkages and overlaps of personnel which aided the British effort, but UTC strategy meetings during the period 1984–6 frequently dealt with issues of coordination and which alignments of interest could best serve UK goals. During 1984, for example, the UTC decided to support OFTII and to encourage member companies to become members of it, despite the fact that it was seen as 'prone to teething troubles' in its operations.[18] The UTC was also instrumental in achieving what one observer referred to as a 'coup' within CUT which had been dominated by Japanese companies, by recruiting more British members. This reflected differences both of interest and over appropriate strategies which are one feature of the unitary tax episode. Whereas the Japanese were by far the most active lobbyists at the state level, particularly in California, their very visible campaign generated quite considerable hostility, especially amongst state legislators. Beyond this, it was clearly felt by the UTC and its lobbyists, that the Japanese would be prepared to settle for less in the way of legislation on unitary taxation than the British considered desirable.

When it came to linkages between the domestics' and foreign MNCs' groupings the picture becomes even more confusing and hazy. Contacts developed as the CBC/UTC experience indicates. But as the OFTII lobbyist, Richard Ratcliff, explained in a note to the OFTII Chairman, Neil Green (senior vice president of Nestlé Holdings), OFTII, CUT and the other foreign industry groups 'have a confusing relationship' with the umbrella group established by COST and the CMA. Depending on their status and relationship to COST and CMA, the US subsidiaries of foreign MNCs might be admitted to the umbrella technical and public affairs groups.[19]

The US Federal Arena

Federal action on the unitary problem had been the original goal of the UTC and was to become so again, in the wake of the Regan Working Group report, with the prospect of federal legislation should the states fail to act. For its part, the White House was anxious to get the issue resolved, bearing in mind the international acrimony that it had created over several years. (It was estimated that by 1989, the US government had received some thirty-five diplomatic notes from governments objecting to the worldwide unitary method.) Yet, at the same time, it was reluctant, both for ideological and practical political reasons, to enter into such a sensitive area involving states' rights. Far more preferable from its point of view was the prospect of a legal solution – a hope dashed by the outcome of the Container case in 1983 – or, failing that, action by the states themselves. Given this situation, the best that UK interests could do was to encourage the British government to apply continuing pressure on Washington through representations by the prime minister to Reagan and by the Chancellor of the exchequer, Nigel Lawson, to his opposite number in the US Treasury.

It was in the US Treasury that the British had their closest allies within the Administration. Donald Regan was keen to see unitary taxation cleared from his desk as quickly as possible. Understandably, therefore, the Treasury was a focus for UTC pressure in the mid 1980s, especially when the White House agreed to sponsor legislation at the end of 1985. Regular meetings took place between officials at the Treasury and representatives of the UTC. The Treasury emphasized the need for British industry to keep up its pressure on the US government and was even supportive of the retaliatory clause as an added weapon in the anti-unitary armoury. (This was not true of the White House which was reported by the British Embassy in Washington as being very unhappy at this turn of events.[20] To business pressure was added parliamentary pressure. Michael Grylls was instrumental in drawing the prospect of the implementation of the retaliatory clause to the attention of bureaucratic, congressional and state-level figures: in such ways were the home and US arenas linked.

The decision by the administration to pursue the legislative option necessitated a refocusing of UTC interest towards Congress. This entailed the employment of the 'access to power' strategy of employing lobbying firms.[21] There are obvious problems in assessing the success or otherwise of this strategy since, in the event, the federal government withdrew the legislation in the wake of the passing of legislation in California. It might well be assumed, therefore, that this was a tactic directed to the goal of state-level action and that federal legislation was unlikely to succeed in the face of the pressures confronting it. Nevertheless, it seems that the UTC's Washington-based lobbying campaign ran into difficulties.

The UTC decided to employ three prominent lobbying firms: A–K Associates (whose California operation represented their interests in Sacramento); Bishop, Liberman, Cook, Purcell and Reynolds; and Patton, Boggs and Blow. A–K Associates were charged with the task of liaising between the lobbyists. Perhaps not unexpectedly, this arrangement appears to have experienced problems of oversight, control and communication. Representatives of IGA were soon reporting to the UTC committee their concern not only with the lack of any obvious return on the considerable financial investment involved (estimated in mid 1986 to stand at some $100 000), but also with the tensions that appeared to exist between the three firms. In the attempt to overcome these problems and to integrate official and non-official pressures in Washington, a pattern of biweekly meetings of the lobbyists at the British Embassy, chaired by the economic counsellor, was established. He, in turn, reported directly to the UTC and liaised with other actors such as OFTII. By June 1986, in the light of these problems and an estimate that there was only a very small likelihood of federal legislation being passed, it was decided to reduce UTC representation in Washington.

It is worth noting here that the British Embassy served a key function in the Washington-based politics of unitary taxation, linking governmental and non-governmental strategies. On the governmental front, regular meetings of interested OECD governments were held at the Embassy to plan future moves. In March 1986, representatives of the Netherlands, Ireland, Switzerland, Canada, Germany, France and Australia attended. It was decided at this meeting that the embassies should contact their major companies to encourage them to put pressure on the Senate and that a joint letter supporting unitary legislation be sent from the OECD countries involved to prominent senators. A standard procedure was developed for use at both the federal and state level, whereby an OECD letter recording objections to the worldwide unitary method would be sent over the signature of the senior OECD ambassador. The EC offered another medium of influence. For example, in March 1986, the chairman of OFTII visited the Dutch ambassador to encourage him to join the lobbying effort. It was noted that this would be particularly useful since the Netherlands currently held the EC presidency.

In terms of their impact on federal legislative action, these activities can hardly be judged successful, given the announcement by the administration in September 1986 that it no longer intended to pursue this course of action. Nevertheless, they cannot be regarded in isolation from state level developments since the adoption of the federal route was always seen, at least in part, as a means of encouraging the state authorities to act.

The State Arenas

It has been noted on several occasions that one of the most demanding aspects of the multitiered lobbying operations in which British and other foreign interests engaged was the central role of the states in the unitary issue. Whether or not specific state governments actually operated the worldwide method, interference in states, rights was a cry which could arouse powerful reactions amongst state politicians. Two of the most potent national voices of the states, the National Governors' Association and the National Conference of State Legislatures, regarded it as such.[22] Moreover, in the 1980s, foreign interest lobbying was becoming a highly-contentious issue. Nevertheless, during 1984 the UTC had concluded that state level operations were essential in the light of Washington's inactivity. The two main weapons available were threat and reward. All the foreign interests seem to have used both techniques in differing measure.

The Japanese were the greatest exponents of the reward principle, making considerable contributions to politicians' campaign funds, especially in California. The main threat – and the one that was most readily understood – was the impact of the worldwide unitary system on foreign MNCs' investment decisions. There were some highly publicized moves by foreign companies intended to demonstrate the point. When Oregon removed its unitary tax, Fujitsu announced that it would build a computer-parts factory there rather than in California.[23] Three major MNCs were reported to have chosen locations other than Colorado because of the state's retention of the worldwide unitary method: the Kyocera Corporation were reported to have chosen Vancouver for this reason. British industry employed a similar tactic in the case of Florida, which adopted the worldwide system in the wake of the Container case. In late 1984, the London Chamber of Commerce had organized a visit, at the invitation of the state, of potential British investors. The LCC cancelled the visit.

The purpose of such tactics went beyond the issuing of threats: they were a key part of the process whereby the unitary tax issue was transformed in the minds of state politicians. From being regarded as another tax-break for big business which would deprive the states of revenue, it became an issue of economic development. In this, the MNCs were assisted by the natural rivalry betweeen the states in attracting investment. Having abandoned unitary tax, the governor of Oregon paid a visit to Silicon Valley in late 1984 with the hope of attracting some of California's high-tech industries should the state fail to end the worldwide system or pass legislation which benefited their foreign competitors.[24] Despite the fact that tax experts and others argued that there were many reasons other than tax regimes which conditioned industrial location policies, pronouncements by industrial giants such as Sony and IBM regarding the impact of unitary tax on their investment decisions undoubtedly played a major part in the evolution of unitary tax politics.

For reasons noted earlier, California, as the most economically powerful state operating the worldwide system, was regarded as a key actor and attracted as much attention from the UTC as did the federal government. Whilst not engaging in the intense lobbying activity employed by the Japanese, the UTC pursued a consistent strategy which combined direct pressures through regular visits from representatives of the UTC and other groupings such as OFTII, parliamentarians and British diplomats from Washington and the consulate-general in San Francisco, with the lobbying activities of A–K Associates. It was also reasonably successful, given the complex tangle of interests involved, in maintaining a working relationship with the US domestics where this was deemed productive. As events transpired, two features of the Californian environment became critical and were instrumental in the failure of the House of Assembly to pass the bill which would have repealed worldwide unitary in 1985: (a) the issue of foreign source dividend relief for the domestics which was strongly opposed in the legislature and by powerful groups such as the unions, who argued that it would result in the export of jobs from California; and (b) the linkage which develped between unitary repeal and other issues.

The most significant of these appeared suddenly and unexpectedly in the form of an amendment which would have disallowed tax relief for corporations with business interests in South Africa. This held up the bill for a year and the governor was not able to sign a bill based on a compomise package until September 1986.[25] Not surprisingly, this failed to give each interest all that it wanted. In particular, the UTC objected to the adoption of an 'election fee' which companies would have to pay if they chose to be assessed on the water's edge system. The struggle continued through the courts with cases brought by foreign parent companies such as Barclays, challenging the worldwide unitary system.

The lobbying campaign pursued by British industry in its battle to end the worldwide unitary tax system casts interesting light on the character of multilayered diplomacy in the highly interdependent world of the advanced industrialized states and, particularly, the relationships between governmental and non-governmental actors. More specifically, in the context of the concerns of this study, it illustrates the diversity of circumstances under which NCGs can become involved in such diplomacy. To take but one state, California did not seek to be drawn into the frenetic politics to which the unitary tax campaign gave rise: clearly, it would have been far happier to have remained outside the controversy. Yet what was originally seen – before the international clouds gathered on the horizon – as an essentially domestic issue, and a technical one at that, was to assume the dimensions of a controversy which focused the attention of numerous governments and some of the world's most powerful companies on California, thereby turning Sacramento for a period into a lobbyist's dream and a politician's nightmare.

The need to operate in this multilevel political environment presented British industry with a formidable set of tasks which involved building coalitions of interests with a remarkably diverse set of official and unofficial actors. Amongst these tasks, as we have seen, was that of operating in a number of local political settings, each of which demanded the acquisition of local knowledge if the key objectives were to be achieved. The key to this complex operation was the development of a sustained multitiered lobbying effort in which the UTC played a crucial part as it attempted to weave the various threads in the picture together.

Estimates of the success or otherwise of the British operation vary, as the author discovered in conversations with participants on the ground. There were obvious successes at the state level, as in Oregon, Colorado and Florida. California could be regarded as a partial success. If the federal theatre is to be judged in terms of the passage of federal legislation to end unitary tax, then it was a failure. But it can also be seen as one dimension of a broader strategy to bring pressure to bear on the states.

Some of those involved criticized the British – and the Europeans in general – for not pursuing the active local lobbying camapaign engaged in by the Japanese, especially Sony. Others tended to feel that the Japanese campaign generated resentment, particularly in California, and had some negative effects on the local politics of the unitary issue. A not infrequently heard comment, especially from the Sacramento-based lobbyists, was that London did not really understand the realities of the US federal system and devoted too much time to Washington in the mistaken assumption that the problem could be resolved there. But then, they have a vested interest in stressing the significance of their own sphere of operations. To one of the central participants, Nancy Ordway, Deputy Director of Finance in California during the crucial stages of the unitary struggle, the British operation appeared well-judged, the UTC and British diplomats seemed adroit at tracking the issue and appearing at the right moments as the issue developed in California.[26] Whatever judgements are made about the British unitary tax effort, however, the episode stands as an illuminating case-study of the intricate linkages that bind together the worlds of domestic and international politics in the conduct of contemporary public policy, and the potential significance of local policies where these affect powerful international interests.

6 The Environmental Agenda: Canada, the United States and Acid Rain

It is not hard to see why environmental issues should be regarded as quintessentially 'international'. After all, by their very nature they deny the logic of accepted territorial divisions both within and between national communities. The actions of one jurisdiction, in the areas of water and air pollution, for example, can have catastrophic consequences for neighbours far and near. Moreover, if solutions are to be found to the problems of global warming, these imply the necessity of international cooperative action. Consequently, the development of the environmental agenda has become closely associated with the growth of international organizations operating in the area.[1] Whether these are intergovernmental bodies such as the United Nations Environment Programme set up in the wake of the 1972 Stockholm Conference on the environment, or nongovernmental – for example, the International Union for the Conservation of Nature and Natural Resources, which has become the most significant non-official organization in the conservation area – their activities reinforce the image of progress in the environmental area residing outside the confines of national borders.

As we saw in Chapter 1, this has led some observers to argue that national political arenas have no part to play in this policy area. Hence Luard's observation:

> effective political activity relating to the environment today can only take place at the global level. Because it is there, not in the relatively insignificant decisions of national states, that the important steps for safeguarding the world's threatened natural heritage must be taken, it is there too that in the future the significant political struggles will occur.[2]

The multilevel political character of much contemporary public policy, demanding the pursuit of multilayered diplomacy is, however, as apparent in the sphere of environmental policy as it is in other issue areas. Robert Boardman has neatly summarized the essential linkages between the domestic and international environmental arenas and the questions which these pose in the evolution of environmental policies:

> To what extent do external pressures, such as developments in international organizations or the lessons provided by other states' experience, influence domestic programmes and policies? What kinds of factors help shape the policies and negotiating strategies of delegations in international conferences? ... ecological processes, and the interactions of these with economies, societies and polities, cannot be contained neatly within the territorial boundaries of states. This is not to say that states lack the power to resist political influences from beyond their borders, however, or that opportunities to shift the burden of environmental adjustment on to others have ceased to be tempting.[3]

The purpose of this chapter is to examine one instance of environmental policy where domestic and international politics have become intermeshed: the long-running dispute between Canada and the US regarding acid rain. Not only has this proved to be a taxing problem for Ottawa to manage within the framework of its most significant foreign policy relationship, it has required the reconciliation of domestic political interests with international objectives in the environmental policy area. In particular, it is an issue in which the US states and Canadian provinces have played a major role.

ENVIRONMENTAL POLITICS AND FEDERAL STATES

Several factors help to reinforce the multilevel character of environmental politics in federal systems and form a crucial dimension of the context in which the acid rain issue in North America has developed. Not the least of these is the fact that federal constitutions frequently endow NCGs with powers over their natural resources and responsibilities for their own economic development which inevitably makes them players in environmental policy processes. Even where central governments might possess, or be able to acquire, the necessary powers to act alone, political prudence demands that they do not ignore subnational interests. As Boardman notes, 'The [Canadian] provinces, like the Australian states, are in many ways the foundation of environment policy. At the same time, the constitutional framework provides for a significant role by the federal government, so that in practice there is considerable jurisdictional overlap in resource and environment areas'.[4] This need for cooperation is underscored by the simple fact that the relevant bureaucratic expertise resides at the local, not the central, level.

To take a specific instance, the Center for Clean Air Policy, established by a group of US state governors in 1985, has pointed to the challenge that global warming poses for all levels of government as well as the private sector. Noting the key role of the federal government, the Center's policy statement goes on to argue that it is at the state level that much of the effort to combat global warming must be directed since the states regulate the charges that their utilities levy on their customers, may control the policies of electric generating facilities, and can adopt a variety of measures (for example, through building code standards) to promote energy-saving and conservation of resources.[5]

Beyond the distribution of powers and functions within a federal system, the fact that subnational authorities are the representatives of diverse economic interests and also constitute a channel through which those interests can project their concerns at the national and international levels means that the sensitive political choices implicit in environmental issues noted earlier will become part of the domestic political debate and help to determine the central government's capacity to pursue environmental policies at the international level. The implications of this domestic–international linkage, moreover, can extend to the balance of powers between levels of government within the federal system itself. As will be shown below, the acid rain issue presented the Canadian government with the difficult problem of managing the provinces whose powers in the environmental field have made them essential actors in the conflict with the US.

In this case, the chosen path was one of cooperation rather than confrontation in the attempt to develop a coherent national position. That this will not always be so is demonstrated clearly in Australia where the internationalization of the environmental agenda has become a means by which, through its responsibility for external affairs assigned to it in the Australian Constitution, the federal government has been able to expand its powers into areas of state government responsibility. Thus the proposal of the Tasmanian government to construct hydroelectric power facilities in southwest Tasmania, thereby flooding a unique wilderness area of the island, was ultimately quashed by Canberra's resort to its obligations under UNESCO's World Heritage convention, justified as a legitimate exercise of its responsibility for external relations.[6]

The federal–state tensions created by such actions has extended into UNESCO itself with the Northern Territory sending a delegation to a World Heritage Committee meeting in Paris in 1987 to oppose the federal government's attempts to have areas of the state listed without the consent of the state authorities.[7] On another environmental issue, the federal minister for the Environment stirred the pot of federal–state relations by suggesting that tackling the problem of global warming might require the transfer of powers from the states to Canberra.[8]

ACID RAIN AND CANADA–US RELATIONS

One of the few achievements of Canada–US acid rain diplomacy in the 1980s was to agree on a common definition of the phenomenon, as set out in the report of the Special Envoys on Acid Rain appointed by President Reagan and Prime Minister Mulroney at their 1985 Summit in Quebec:

> Acid rain is a popular term used to describe a very complex chemical and atmospheric phenomenon that is more properly called acid deposition. It occurs when emissions of sulfur and nitrogen compounds are transported through the atmosphere, transformed by atmospheric chemical processes, and then deposited back again on earth in either a wet or a dry form.[9]

The 'precursors' of acid rain, sulphur dioxide (SO_2) and nitrogen oxides (NO_x) are produced by the burning of coal, oil and other fossil fuels and whilst they may be regarded as an essentially modern problem, warnings of their effects can be found as early as the 1830s when the mayor of Boston, in his inaugural address, warned of the impact of the growing consumption of bituminous coal on the supply of rainwater.[10]

By the middle of the present century, the problem was vastly enhanced with the growing demand for energy which accompanied industrial development. Ever greater consumption of coal and oil meant that in Europe, SO_2 and NOx emissions roughly doubled between 1950 and 1970, whilst in the US, SO_2 emissions grew by 45 per cent in the period 1960–70. By this time, research in Scandinavia had noted a connection between acid rain and the acidification of rivers and lakes with its consequent effects on acquatic life. Public opinion, moreover, was becoming more environmentally conscious as books such as Rachel Carson's *Silent Spring* drew attention to environmental issues – in this case the effects of pesticides on organic life.[11]

Bearing in mind the sensitivity of the political issues to which action in the environmental area gives rise, it was not surprising that governmental responses were cautious. Certainly, governments acted: 1971 saw the creation of Environment Canada (the federal department responsible for environmental matters); in the US, Congress passed the Clean Air Act in 1963. But, not infrequently, official policies and the legislation that enacted them either avoided the core issues of which the management of natural resources and environmental pollution were an expression, or actually enhanced the problems they were intended to solve, or both. In the case of the US, the Clean Air Act encouraged the construction of ever-taller smokestacks (their average height has tripled over the last three decades) with the aim of dispersing emissions from their source. Since this enabled more acid rain precursors to be emitted without exceeding local limits, the consequence was that the problem simply moved to new locations, perhaps several hundred miles away.

In other words, building taller smokestacks became an alternative to tackling the politically far more taxing problem of limiting emissions at their point of source. It is not hard to see, therefore, how a local problem could easily be translated into a national problem and, as pollutants are carried over national boundaries, into a source of international irritation and conflict. Herein lie the origins of acid rain as an example of multilevel politics. To the domestic difficulties of managing the problem, of reconciling the concerns of 'emitter' and 'receptor' regions for example, are added those of international politics since degradation of a state's environment carries with it major implications for its economic well-being, its power as an international actor and ultimately, as suggested above, its national security. Moreover, the transboundary character of the problem poses the difficulties of devising means of resolving international disputes. International environmental law is at present unable to deal satisfactorily with the issues presented by long range transport of air pollution. Thus the Convention on Transboundary Air Pollution signed by the 34 members of the Economic Commission for Europe in 1979 cannot compel signatories to reduce harmful emissions and has no enforcement mechanisms at its disposal.[12] These factors constituted the essence of the Canadian dilemma. Its physical environment was being degraded by emissions occurring in jurisdictions over which it had no control and which were being carried by the prevailing wind patterns over its territory.

Reinforcing these problems is that of the state of scientific knowledge on the whole question of acid rain and its effects. Not surprisingly, this is an area marked by major scientific uncertainties and debates. McCormick cites as one instance the 'linearity' debate: is there a linear relationship between the level of emissions and the level of pollution; consequently, will a specific reduction in emissions produce an equivalent fall in acid rain deposition?[13] The argument that there is no such linear relationship because of climatic variables, for example, has been voiced by those opposed to policies directed towards the reduction of acidic precursors. The nature of the scientific debate has been a major factor in both the domestic and international politics of acid rain. As Regens and Rycroft point out, 'We can use what we already know from the physical and biological sciences to construct a policy rationale for either maintaining existing emissions control programs and expanding R&D or initiating additional control measures'.[14] In other words, science becomes a major input to the political debate, both nationally and internationally, and also a policy instrument. Each of these features of the acid rain issue was to play a part in the Canada–US experience during the 1980s.

CANADA–US RELATIONS AND THE ENVIRONMENTAL AGENDA

Understanding the pattern of diplomacy that developed between the two countries on transboundary air pollution is made easier by an awareness of the general character of bilateral relations in the environmental policy area. As with the broader relationship, this is subject to differing interpretations. On the one hand, cooperation and amity is seen as the norm over the years during which Ottawa and Washington have sought to resolve the problems presented by their close cohabitation on the North American continent, and a substantial history of bilateral agreements (such as the 1909 Boundary Waters Treaty and the 1949 Great Lakes Agreement) lends support to this belief. Hence the testimony of a former associate administrator of the US Environmental Protection Agency: '. . . we have overcome pollution of every sort, in air, water, and soils. This bilateral success shines as a model for all countries grappling with transboundary pollution.'[15] For others, especially in the troubled years of the 1980s when Stephen Clarkson could write of the 'Reagan challenge' to Canada, the environment has been cited not as an example of interdependence and mutuality of interest but the ultimate example of Canada's dependence on her neighbour.[16] So it is seen by Munton who has argued that the bilateral environmental agenda reveals the 'basically conflictual' character of the relationship.[17] Others have used more colourful language: Maurice Strong, a notable Canadian industrialist and environmentalist, reflected the frustrations of many Canadians at Washington's apparent unwillingness to tackle the acid rain issue when he described Canada as the victim of US 'environmental aggression'.

In part, such differences of interpretation reflect the broader fluctuations in the overall pattern of relations and the expectations generated by what has traditionally been regarded as a 'special relationship'. It is probably more realistic and accurate to view the interactions between the two countries in this, as in other areas, as one marked by elements of both conflict and cooperation the balance between which has varied in response to a variety of domestic and international factors. One notable characteristic in the relationship is, however, as relevant to the environmental agenda as it is to other issues; namely, a fundamental asymmetry that assumes several dimensions.[18]

First of all, a general point but one highly relevant to an understanding of Ottawa–Washington relations over acid rain: the asymmetry of interest of one actor in the other. Canada, a middle power whose external relations are dominated by its relations with the US, is continually confronted by the problem of gaining the attention of a superpower with global preoccupations. This intangible factor in the power equation is at least of equal significance to more traditional items on the power inventory. Second, US and Canadian approaches to environmental issues have varied. At root there lie differences in political culture and philosophy, particularly a greater inclination in Canada to accept government intervention in the operation of the economy which are reflected in approaches to environmental issues. John Roberts, Canada's minister for the Environment from 1980 to 1983, expressed the difference in the following terms:

> environmental policy in Canada is increasingly seen as an adjunct to, and as essential to, proper economic planning . . . Rather

> than regarding economic and environmental interests as properly complementary to each other, the US seems to view them as contradictory.[19]

Furthermore, the question of acid rain was linked to different economic priorities in the two countries. Apart from the impact that air pollution might have on highly prized recreational facilities, it was suspected as having a considerable impact on the commercially valuable forest resources of Canada. By the late 1970s and into the 1980s, however, the US administration's concern with air pollution was strongly counterbalanced by a preoccupation with energy self-sufficiency and the possibilities of converting power-generation plants from oil to coal, thereby enhancing the level of harmful emissions.[20]

In turn, this was linked to a fourth factor marking the asymmetry characteristic of the acid rain problem: namely, the imbalance in advantages and disadvantages which it presented to each community. Whilst both countries are responsible for polluting the other's air, approximately 15 per cent of US deposition is estimated to originate in Canada whereas some 50 per cent of Canada's deposition comes from the US. Additionally, Canada is more vulnerable to the effects of acid rain in terms of area affected and because the 'buffering capacity' afforded by Canada's geological formations is generally lower than that enjoyed by the US.

Finally, the various dimensions of asymmetry were reinforced by the simple fact that the solution to Canada's problem lay in the hands of the US; as John Carroll puts it, in the long-running saga, Ottawa was generally cast in the role of complainant and Washington that of defendant.[21] Regrettably, however, from Ottawa's viewpoint, there was no court with the jurisdiction to resolve the dispute.

ACID RAIN DIPLOMACY

These factors constituted a major part of the backcloth against which acid rain diplomacy in North America developed during the 1980s. They help to explain why Canada assumed the role of active partner in the diplomatic dialogue whilst the US administration tended to behave in a reactive fashion, squeezed between Ottawa's concerns and the far more compelling pressures directed to it from domestic constituencies.[22] As the public consciousness of air pollution issues developed during the 1970s and concern with what had hitherto been seen as a problem of local air pollution transformed itself into a far more complex problem of transboundary air pollution (TAP), it appeared that the Carter administration lacked any clear strategy for dealing with such issues, responding in an ad hoc fashion to Canada's concerns. Thus the late 1970s saw several initiatives such as the creation of the Bilateral Research Consultation Group in 1978, a body composed of US and Canadian government scientists. The work of this group facilitated the 1979 Joint Statement on Transboundary Air Quality and the subsequent Memorandum of Intent (MOI) signed in August 1980.[23]

Whilst regarded as more notable for its symbolic value as an indicator that the problem was taken seriously in Washington, the MOI contained some potentially significant provisions, setting up five bilateral working groups consisting of diplomats and scientists who would report to a coordinating committee. It also provided for negotiations on air quality to begin no later than June 1981. Whilst there is little doubt that Carter regarded acid rain as a serious problem (the Acid Precipitation Act of 1980 which authorized the US federal governments's acid rain research programme the National Acid Precipitation Assessment Programme – NAPAP – was the first attempt to deal with the problem in a coherent fashion at the federal level), as indicated above, he was beset with other problems, not the least of which was the need to develop a strategy for energy supply. This preoccupation was reflected in the decision by the White House to support a Department of Energy proposal to convert oil-fired power plants in the northeast and midwest to coal. This policy was opposed by the State Department and the Environmental Protection Agency (EPA), conscious of the effects that it would have on emissions of acid rain precursors and, thereby, on America's international obligations in this area. In the event, the proposal failed to gain Congressional approval, but considerable damage had been done to Canada's confidence in Washington's commitment to reducing acid rain pollution.

THE REAGAN YEARS

With the arrival of the Reagan administration in January 1981, however, Ottawa's problems greatly increased. Whilst some negotiations under the MOI provisions were held in 1981, no agreement was reached; it seemed clear that the new administration's commitment to limiting emissions was notably lacking. Partly, this reflected the commitment of the new president to deregulation, partly the priority given to economic recovery, and the adoption of 'environmental federalism' as part of the 'new federalism' which was intended to devolve policy responsibilities to the state level. The anti-regulation bias of the administration was reflected in its attitude towards the body most concerned with environmental regulation, the EPA. Its staff was reduced by 23 per cent and its budget by 30 per cent.[24]

Rather than engage in serious negotiations, the Reagan administration began to adopt a scientific rationale for inaction. Whereas previously, research was to be used as a means of facilitating action to resolve the acid rain problem, now it was used as an excuse for postponing action in anticipation of the results of further research. This approach indicated a major change in the federal government's entire approach to environmental issues, one in which scientific 'proof' was demanded before regulation of industry was deemed acceptable.[25]

Clearly, any Canadian diplomatic strategy had to take account of this changed environment and, furthermore, of the general deterioration in Canada–US relations that was to characterize the beginning of the Reagan era. Three broad strategies were now, as before, available to Ottawa: unilateral action to reduce Canadian emissions; bilateral action directed to the US; and action through multilateral forums. Bearing in mind the the importance of TAP to Canada's acid rain problem, acting to reduce its own emissions could have only a limited impact on the problem. However, as we shall see below, Canada's own domestic record in emission control was a factor in the bilateral interactions with the US and therefore needed to be considered in this light. Some action had occurred at the multilateral level: Canada for example, criticized US acid rain policy at a UN conference on the global environment in Nairobi in 1982; both the US and Canada were signatories to the Economic Commission for Europe's Convention and Resolution on Long Range Transboundary Air Pollution in 1979. However, the record is hardly substantial and was unlikely to improve given the Reagan administration's policies.

In the Trudeau years of the late 1970s and early 1980s, the most notable feature of Canada's bilateral acid rain diplomacy was the move away from the traditional 'quiet' diplomacy that has traditionally characterized the relationship and the development of a high-profile public diplomacy. On the one hand, this reflected the character of the issue and the fact that acid rain was becoming more prominent in US domestic politics both in Congress and at the level of pressure group activity. This manifested itself in extensive tours by John Roberts, the Canadian environment minister, the sponsorship by Environment Canada of two films on the effects of acid rain, and several testimonies to Congressional committees by Canadian officials. Generally, the aim was to maximize the pressures on the administration from Congress and public opinion in the hope that this would lead to a more accommodating stance on the part of the White House.

With the election of the Mulroney Progressive Conservative government in 1984, the broad thrust of Canadian strategy appeared to shift. The new environment minister, Suzanne Blais-Grenier, announced that the emphasis would now be on bilateral negotiations rather than a multilateral approach to the acid rain problem.[26] This has to be seen within the context of the Mulroney government's general strategy towards the conduct of its relations with Washington, based as it was on the resurrection of the 'special relationship' reinforced by the presence of two like-minded leaders in their respective capitals. At the same time, emphasis was to be placed on cleaning up Canada's own acid rain sources, thereby strengthening its bargaining position. This strategy came under criticism from several quarters on both sides of the border during the next few years as its results appeared to be meagre. Acid rain stood high on the agenda at the annual summit meetings between Mulroney and Reagan but no solution satisfactory to Ottawa was to emerge. Washington adhered firmly to its R&D strategy.

At their 1985 summit meeting, Reagan and Mulroney agreed to the appointment of two 'acid rain envoys' (William Davis, former premier of Ontario, and a former transportation secretary, Drew Lewis). Their report, presented to the two leaders at the 1986 summit and accepted by them, concluded that acid rain was a serious environmental problem for both the US and Canada. However, it stopped short of calling for a programme of emission reductions, relying instead on investment in long-term research into clean coal technology and was not greeted with enthusiasm in Canada. By 1987, in a speech to the Canadian parliament, Reagan made the less-than-compelling announcement that he had 'agreed to consider' Mulroney's proposal for an acid rain agreement. In September of this year, NAPAP produced its interim report in which it argued that the case regarding the effects of acid rain deposition had yet to be established, that technological changes would largely remove what threat to lakes, rivers and forests existed and that no emission controls were needed. Not surprisingly, this was roundly rejected by the Canadian government as it was by environmental groups in both countries. By the time that Reagan had completed his second term, his acid rain policy – or as some saw it, lack of policy – was virtually unchanged. No substantial common ground had been established, no real progress towards an agreement had been made. It was to take a change of administration before a firm commitment to emission reduction by Washington emerged. In his address to Congress in February 1989, the newly elected President Bush spoke of a new attitude to the environment and this was reflected in the more accommodating stance which he adopted at his meeting with Mulroney in the same month.[27] In June 1989, the White House unveiled a major policy proposal on acid rain as part of broader amendments to the Clean Air Act. A key element was the reduction of SO_2 emissions by 50 per cent and NO_x by 10 per cent by the year 2000.[28] By November 1990, the first overhaul of the Clean Air Act for over a decade had passed through Congress, marking a major step towards the accomplishment of the goals that Ottawa had found so elusive during the Reagan presidency.

THE STATES, THE PROVINCES AND ACID RAIN

In the evolution of the acid rain saga, particularly in view of its international dimension, players at the federal level were, obviously, of central significance. In the case of the US, the pattern of events has to take account of the usual complexities of bureaucratic politics in which the Environmental Protection Agency featured large. Given their natural concerns, both the EPA and the State Department were more attuned to the Canadian position on acid rain than was the White House. Similarly, there were reports of differences of approach within the federal bureaucracy, with some officials in the Department of External Affairs expressing caution at the public diplomacy favoured by Environment Canada in case this clouded the broader relationship. However, the very nature of the acid rain problem made it a regional issue and thus a matter of concern for both sets of non-central governments.

Firstly, as mentioned earlier, both states and provinces had a jurisdictional interest in the issue. However, there was a major difference between the two countries in this respect with the provinces possessing far more effective power than the states. In part this was a matter of constitutional powers, but also a question of practical politics given the delicate character of federal–provincial relations in Canada. Consequently, whilst national air quality standards could be set by

Ottawa, it was reliant on them being incorporated into provincial law. One study of acid rain diplomacy describes the situation as follows:

> the federal government can take the lead in international matters, but is severely constrained in its powers in domestic policy development . . . the provinces continue to be the principal actors in most environmental policy matters. We have detected few signs indicating a truly federal approach to acid rain, or, at the least a unified approach by the provinces.[29]

Despite attempts during the Reagan era to enhance the states' role in the environmental area as part of the 'new federalism', far more authority is vested in the federal government than is the case in Canada. Differences derive also from the more general characteristics of the two systems. The provinces are in many senses more influential actors than the states in their respective national settings; they are generally larger and wealthier and possess higher levels of bureaucratic expertise. In particular, the average state official operating in the environmental sphere is less likely to have international experience than is his or her counterpart across the border.[30] Furthermore, as Carroll points out, whereas all the provinces are aware of the acid rain issue there are 'only a few small states with major concern over acid rain, and many states with no awareness'.[31]

The second major factor reinforcing the centrality of the NCGs in each country is the sensitive economic interests that they represent. This is particularly true of the US. Clear differences of interest between the provinces on acid rain do exist depending on their economic interests as emitters or receptors of pollutants. Thus Nova Scotia as a province rich in coal and also depressed when compared with other provincial economies, had adopted a strategy of using its coal resources to lessen its dependence on imported oil. This would be severely undermined by any agreement with the US which required it to install expensive scrubber equipment to reduce emissions of acidic precursors. However, in general terms, the balance between advantages and disadvantages deriving from air pollution were not clearly drawn. So, one of the key provincial actors, Ontario, was both vulnerable to the effects of acid rain and also host to North America's largest single source of SO_2, the International Nickel Company (INCO) smelter at Sudbury.

Such differences of interest were much more evident in the US. Here, low-sulphur coal areas in Alabama, east Kentucky, southern West Virginia and some western states stood to benefit from federal acid rain legislation requiring emission reduction since this would involve a change to low-sulphur coal. For other regions, however, the consequences could be grave: estimates suggested that some twenty to thirty thousand mining jobs in the high-sulphur coal areas of Illinois, Indiana, western Kentucky, Ohio, Pennsylvania and northern West Virginia, could disappear.[32] At the same time eight states (Maine, New Hampshire, Vermont, Massachusetts, New York, Michigan, Wisconsin and Minnesota) were regarded as being seriously affected by acid rain. Added to these differences were those deriving from the costs of emission control programmes and their impact on the varying regional interests. These conflicts of interest lay at the heart of the acid rain problem in the US and, in particular, attempts to deal with the problem in Congress. The inability to gain agreement on the reauthorization of the Clean Air Act reflected the disappearance of the coalition between the midwestern, high-sulphur coal producers and environmental groups which had underpinned the passage of the 1977 CAA amendments. The passage of the 1989 bill was only achieved through the creation of a coalition of 140 members mainly from the northeast and the west sufficiently large to overcome the opposition from midwestern states.[34]

PATTERNS OF INTERACTION

Given this diversity of interests, the potential for a complex multilayered diplomacy across the US–Canada border was obviously very great. Diplomacy between the federal governments would be significant, not because of progress made on resolving the acid rain issue, but because of its international dimension. At another level, it was possible for Canada as the active partner to promote its interests in the state and broader subnational theatres. To do so, of course, carried with it dangers; Ottawa could be accused of interfering in US domestic politics and retaliatory action in Canadian domestic politics might result. A third dimension to the multilayered diplomatic setting lay in the patterns of interaction that could develop between the states on one side and the provinces on the other. The basis for this was well-established in the form of extensive transboundary subfederal links which extended into the environmental field.[35] Thus in 1971 Michigan and Ontario established a committee which developed a programme for the abatement of transboundary air pollution, and in 1974 both governments issued a communique condemning the US federal government for reducing air pollution funding.[36] This was followed by the creation of the Michigan–Ontario Transboundary Air Pollution Commission.

The possibilities for the development of subnational interactions were further enhanced by the the emergence of environmental groups in both countries. On the Canadian side, the main group was the Canadian Coalition on Acid Rain (CCAR), founded in 1981 and representing fifty groups located mainly in Eastern Canada. Listed under the US Foreign Agents Registration Act as a foreign interest engaged in lobbying activities, the CCAR identified its role as primarily one of providing information from an 'independent' stance. In doing so, it found a natural ally in, and developed informal links with, the major US environmental group, the National Clean Air Coalition (NCAC). Groups such as these, together with those representing the interests of coal-producers and utilities producing acid rain precursors, offered a number of possible combinations of interests with an interest in air pollution. In fact, the crucial alignment of interests supportive of action in Congress to reduce emissions was, on the Canadian side, the CCAR, INCO and Ontario Hydro on the industrial front, the Canadian government, and the governments of the eastern provinces, together with, in the US, the states in the northeast affected by acid rain and the NCAC.[37]

CANADA'S DIPLOMATIC TASKS AND STRATEGIES

Given these alignments of forces and the unwillingness of the Reagan administration to act on the transboundary air pollution issue by promoting legislation intended to reduce emissions, domestic factors at home and in the US constituted the central features of Ottawa's diplomatic tasks and strategies in the search for a satisfactory outcome. Within Canada, the emphasis, as noted earlier, was on encouraging the provincial governments to adopt uniform emission standards so as to undermine the frequently heard complaints from US opponents of emission control that Canada should deal with its own acid rain problems. 'Putting its own house in order' became, therefore, a preoccupation of Ottawa's domestic diplomacy during the 1980s. Since, as we have seen, Ottawa's powers, both in constitutional and practical political terms, was limited, this involved engaging in a bout of federal–provincial diplomacy. The basis for this was provided by the

1971 Clean Air Act which required close cooperation between the two levels of government. The main means of achieving this was through regular meetings between provincial and federal environment ministers and the creation of federal-povincial task forces, such as the Federal–provincial Steering Committee on Control Strategies for Long-range Transport of Atmospheric Pollution whose aim was to assess possible abatement programmes. The Ontario–Canada Task Force focused specifically on the reduction of emissions from INCO Ltd and Falconbridge Nickel Mines.[38]

By the early part of 1984, when it was clear that a bilateral US–Canadian agreement was unlikely to be forthcoming, Ottawa and the provincial governments announced that they would be taking unilateral action to reduce industrial emissions by 50 per cent of 1980 levels. It was to be 1987 before formal agreements to implement this goal were put in place. Gaining Ontario's agreement was of central significance and in March 1987, just a few weeks before the scheduled summit meeting between Reagan and Mulroney, Ontario and Ottawa signed a pact whereby the former pledged to cut its acid rain emissions by more than 60 per cent of 1980 levels by 1994 with federal financial support of up to $85 million. New Brunswick and Nova Scotia were the last to formally honour the agreement, arguing that it would be too costly for them to do so. In response, the CCAR launched a major campaign directed towards the two provinces during which it despatched 14 000 letters to its supporters condemning the two provincial governments' lack of action.[39] The House of Commons special committee on acid rain was urged to summon Premier Hatfield of New Brunswick to explain his government's policy.[40]

Turning to the US domestic scene, Canada enjoyed several advantages in promoting its acid rain goals. First, the fact that the northeastern states favoured emission reductions provided an important source of support; second, the US environment lobby was supportive and influential at both state and federal levels; third, the US media were sensitive to the issues and offered an important channel through which Canadian views could be projected. Nevertheless, the possible dangers of an over-active involvement in US domestic politics were always real and the Department of External Affairs was well-attuned to them.[41] Moreover, the Mulroney government had other issues of importance to it on the US agenda, not least the negotiation of the free trade agreement: the possibilities of a destuctive diplomatic linkage emerging on the trade front could not be dismissed. With this in mind Ottawa needed to reconcile the potential advantages of building coalitions with like-minded US interests whilst, at the same time, minimizing the likelihood of incurring costs in doing so. The key strategy here was to rely on the patterns of interaction existing between the states and the provinces, whilst Ottawa continued to pursue its campaign of trying to prod the White House in to action and alert the American public of the justice of its cause.

THE ROLE OF NON-CENTRAL GOVERNMENTS IN ACID RAIN DIPLOMACY

It was suggested in Chapter 2 that it is possible to identify a number of potential roles for NCGs within the framework of multilayered diplomacy depending on several factors, not least the nature of the issues involved. So, in the case of the acid rain issue, it might be that subfederal actors performed the roles of opponents of central diplomatic strategies, agents of that centrally controlled diplomacy or independent 'paradiplomatic' actors pursuing their own interests in the international arena. Clearly, these may not be mutually exclusive categories:

NCGs may act in different ways as a diplomatic dialogue develops and they evaluate its outcomes for their own interests. Additionally, there is quite likely to be a divergence of views amongst the NCGs comprising a federal state as to the acceptable outcome of an international negotiation which encourage them to act in differing ways. In the case of acid rain, this is clearly evident in the case of the US where, as we have seen, regional interests stimulated very different attitudes, and therefore roles, on the part of the state governments. Clearly, states in the northeast as major sufferers from acid deposition were opponents of the Reagan administration's 'hands-off' policy, whereas it was likely to receive greater support from midwestern states as sources of harmful pollutants.

On the Canadian side, however, the picture was different as previous discussion has shown. Despite differences of interest at the provincial level, there was a considerable level of consensus on Canada's interests in this area. This meant that it was possible for Ottawa to, in part, 'devolve' the conduct of its foreign policy in this policy sphere. Indeed, the very domestic sensitivities which acid rain engendered made this a logical strategy. As Andrew Morriss notes, where federal governments are confronted by international conflicts which arouse powerful domestic sensibilities, they will be unwilling to act; however, 'involving the subfederal actors in the policy process restricts the actors' freedom to raise the political stakes with rhetoric from outside the policy process, and forces them to address the problem from a policy perspective rather than from the perspective of attempting short-term political gain'.[42] More than simply coopting the provinces to deflect potential disruption to Ottawa's diplomatic effort, however, they were central to it.

In this light, we can view the importance of the two key provinces involved – Quebec and, in particular, Ontario, as having a twofold importance. On the one hand, they were agenda setters. As an official in the Department of External Affairs told the author, Ontario acted as a continual goad to federal action and was on many occasions critical of what it regarded as Ottawa's failure to pursue the problem with sufficient vigour.[43] In January 1987, Ontario environment minister, Jim Bradley, was reported as having written to his federal counterpart, Tom McMillan, complaining of Ottawa's lack of policy direction.[44] In April 1987, the Quebec legislature voted to demand an increase in the federal government's efforts in tackling Washington on acid rain.

More crucially, however, the provinces – again, particularly Ontario – were central to the implementation of the overall Canadian diplomatic effort. Not only was this true at the domestic level (Ontario and Quebec were key actors in developing the 50 per cent emission-reduction proposal) but also at the bilateral level. Here it becomes hard, and probably not of great significance given the nature of the issue, to distinguish between provincial activities within the US in terms of an independent, paradiplomatic effort and as elements of the federal government's overall diplomatic strategy. The two merged together. The important point was that action across the border was a key part of Ontario and Quebec's strategy on acid rain as it was Ottawa's. Both provinces adopted several techniques in pursuit of their aims.

PROVINCIAL–STATE COOPERATION

The history of transboundary cooperation discussed earlier provided a framework within which Ontario and Quebec could engage in cooperative action with like-minded US states, particularly in the northeastern US. Hence Quebec concluded agreements with New York and Vermont on joint research, exchange of information, and, more sensitively from the political viewpoint, a common strategy for influencing Congress in attempts to build support for an amendment to the Clean Air Act.[45] Cross-border exchange of information proved of value to Ontario when New York informed Ontario of the application by midwestern states to the EPA for a relaxation of emission standards, thus enabling it to intervene.

Cooperative action also came through the regular meetings between state governors and provincial premiers which have become a feature of transboundary relationships in recent years. Thus the 12th annual conference of New England Governors and Eastern Canadian Premiers meeting in June 1984 resolved to convene an international acid rain conference which was held in Quebec in April 1985. The conference, co-chaired by Premier Levesque and Governor Dukakis of Massachusetts, set as its official objectives the exchange of scientific data and the promotion of a dialogue between the states and provinces in developing policies on acid rain. Unofficially, the intention was to bring pressure to bear on the newly-appointed acid rain envoys who had been invited to, but declined to attend, the conference.[46] The issue has appeared regularly at subsequent meetings of the premiers and governors: at the 15th annual conference held in Halifax in 1987, it was agreed that both sets of jurisdictions would notify each other where a project could have an environmental impact on neighbouring areas.

LEGAL ACTIONS AND REGULATORY INTERVENTION

Another tactic, employed particularly by Ontario, is to seek remedies to pollution problems by use of the courts, submissions to regulatory hearings and use of the Clean Air Act's international provisions (Section 115 introduced in the 1977 amendments to the act).[47] In 1981, New York, Pennsylvania and Ontario submitted a suit to the EPA asking it to reject proposals from six US states to reduce their emissions limits. Ontario was allowed to testify before the EPA and the environment minister and officials did so. At the state level, Ontario submitted a petition to the Michigan Air Pollution Control Commission in 1982 in response to Detroit Edison's request for a delay in complying with local emission regulations by one of its power utilities. An important precedent was created in 1987 when Ontario joined with eight eastern US states to submit a petition to the Supreme Court, the first time that a province had gone to the Court. The aim was to obtain an order that would force the EPA to require midwestern utilities to cut their sulphur emissions.[48] The advantages that these routes offered were, first of all, an opportunity to participate in the policy process and to project Canadian interests, whether or not provincial views were accepted. Second, action of this kind generates considerable publicity which, of itself, can be valuable in a high-profile area such as the environment.

LOBBYING AND PUBLIC RELATIONS

Access to the policy process and publicity for the cause could also be secured by the well-tried means of lobbying Congress and general public relations campaigns intended to build on the considerable environmental constituencies in the US. The relevance of action directed towards Congress was obvious for it was here that attempts to amend the Clean Air Act, and therefore hopes for action on transboundary air pollution, were focused. Given the fact that the CAA represented a delicate balance between the competing claims of the environment, energy needs and economic development, it is not surprising that Canadian lobbying efforts, whether sponsored by federal or provincial governments, could have at best only a marginal impact on policy outcomes. Neverthless, Ontario retained a lobbying firm to promote its case for amendments to the CAA and its environment ministry was registered with the Department of Justice as one of five Canadian governmental and non-governmental agencies lobbying on the acid rain issue.[49] The dangers of lobbying are that it will generate resentment within Congress and, unfortunately for Canadian interests, a greater reliance on such techniques was clouded by the case brought against Michael Deaver who was accused of exercising influence on behalf of Canada whilst still in the Reagan White House. Resentment amongst congressional opponents of harsher acid rain regulations would always be to the fore in expressing concerns about Canadian lobbying activities. One of the most prominent of these, John Dingell, a congressman from Michigan, asked the State Department to investigate the legality of Canadian lobbying activities.[50] Apart from this, Ontario officials testified before congressional committees and sponsored on-site briefings for congressional aides in the hope of generating greater sympathy for the Canadian case.

On the broader publicity front, provincial efforts reflected those employed by the federal government. However, it was possible for the provinces to be somewhat more prominent in some of its activities.

Hence, the 'three-day media blitz' organized by Ontario in 1987, during which an information booth on acid rain was set up at the New York National Sportman's Show, a series of media interviews were given by Environment Minister Jim Bradley and a dinner was provided for environmental lobbyists and lawyers.[51] Again, the dangers of such activity were always present. Those opposed to regulatory action to reduce acid rain would always look with a mixture of hostility and suspicion on provincial forays into American domestic politics and question the motives for doing so. A rare instance of this sentiment being voiced at the official level occurred when Donald Hodel, secretary of the interior, accused the Canadian acid rain lobby of a conspiracy to make it more costly and difficult for US power utilities to compete against cheaper electricity imports from Canada.[52]

Taking an overall perspective, it is clear that the provinces were key players as the acid rain saga unfolded during the 1980s. But how do their activities fit into the general pattern of diplomatic interactions that this episode in Canada–US relations created; what light do they shed on the international activities of NCGs and multilayered environmental diplomacy?

First, it would be hard to deny the essentially multilevel character of the problem confronting Canadian policy makers as they sought to pursue solutions through multilateral, bilateral and unilateral means. The domestic dimension impinged on Canadian strategy because the states and provinces could not be ignored for constitutional and political reasons, but also because they assumed a key role in a situation where bilateral negotiations with Washington had reached an impasse. This ensured that domestic diplomacy, managing Ottawa's own domestic constituencies, was supplemented by a need to take a close interest in the patterns of subfederal alignments in the US since, at the end of the day, it would be those interests and their representation in Congress which would determine the possibility of legislative action to curb transboundary air pollution.

Second, the forms that Canadian provincial activity assumed is instructive. To a considerable extent, Ontario and Quebec, as representatives of the provinces in the diplomatic intercourse with US interests, acted in a dual capacity. They can, on the one hand, be regarded as independent players, pursuing their own interests supported by their considerable bureaucratic expertise in the environmental area. At the same time, their activities fitted into the overall strategy pursued by Ottawa; indeed, as we have seen, they were central to it.

There were a number of advantages to be gained from provincial diplomatic involvement from Ottawa's point of view: it created a diplomatic dialogue based on well-established state–provincial links; in so doing, it opened up communication channels with significant and influential US interests which were central to the resolution of the problem in an environment where national negotiations were stalled. Added to this, provincial activities provided modes of action which, for constitutional or political reasons, were not available to the Canadian government. The best example of this is the use made by Ontario and Quebec of the US courts and interventions in regulatory hearings.

An interesting contrast can be made in this respect with the provincial role in the negotiations leading up to the Canada–US Free Trade Agreement where provincial interests were no less central. This presented its own set of problems as Ottawa sought to operate in an equally demanding multilayered diplomatic setting. But whereas considerable efforts were made in pursuing the domestic diplomacy necessary to the successful conclusion of the agreement, Ottawa was far less willing to allow the provinces to engage in their own paradiplomacy. Partly, this reflected the nature of the two issues and the fact that there was a level of consensus within Canada on acid rain that was absent in the case of free trade. It would have been inconceivable for Ontario and Quebec to have acted as provincial representatives in exchanges with US interests on this issue as they did in the case of acid rain. Also, of course, given the fact that the Reagan administration had an interest in the successful outcome, Ottawa was negotiating with a willing partner in Washington which was not true in the case of acid rain. This meant that provincial involvement, rather than furthering the Mulroney government's objectives, would only serve to muddy the diplomatic waters.

A third lesson that can be drawn from the acid rain problem in North America qualifies the previous point. It is that, despite the notable provincial involvement, NCG diplomatic activity could not resolve what was, at base, a fundamental problem of US domestic politics, namely the renewal of the Clean Air Act. Provincial action, particularly directed towards the states, was significant in keeping Canada's concerns at the forefront of public and official consciousness but a solution, in the final analysis demanded action within the US domestic political arena. It required a change of administration before the issue could be resolved. Bearing this in mind, the image of transboundary interactions between subfederal authorities as in some sense constituting alternative structures for problem-solving, perhaps making national power centres irrelevant, seems hard to sustain.[53] More accurately the experience of US–Canadian acid rain diplomacy suggests that in the complex multilevel politics which characterizes the environmental agenda, NCGs and other subnational interests will assume a variety of roles within a diplomatic milieu still dominated by national governments.

7 Managing Multilayered Diplomacy

The emphasis of the foregoing discussion has been on the complexities characteristic of multilayered diplomacy. Rather than existing in different worlds, operating by distinctive rules and insulated from one another by divergent agendas, non-central and central governments are locked together in webs of relationships and patterns of interaction which reinforce the importance of linkage between domestic and international domains of political activity. This is not, of course, to deny the realities of conflict between centre and locality on issues with an external policy dimension. Certainly, conflict there is, as demonstrated by the cases of Quebec in Canada and Queensland in Australia. Furthermore, there are those in the US who see the growing interest of states, regions and localities as illegitimate and dangerous infringements of the federal government's claims to control in the sphere of foreign relations.[1]

This image of conflict has coloured assumptions as to the requirements for policy responses at the centre to growing local international interests and involvement. Hence Spiro's reaction to what he perceives as the threat of 'local activism' is to advocate a policy of containment resting, in the final analysis, on legal sanctions.[2] This emphasis on coercion and constitutional prescription has been the traditional response of the centre to the problems presented by growing subnational involvement in the international milieu. Equally, it is clear that injunctions to strengthened control by foreign policy agencies not only ignore the realities of a vastly more diversified policy making environment, but fail to recognise the underlying forces that have created this phenomenon.

This is not to deny that the management of the multilayered diplomatic environment presents formidable difficulties; rather, it is to point to the fact that it creates challenges that demand practical policy strategies which go beyond simple assertions of the constitutional prerogatives of central government and its agencies in the foreign policy sphere. The essence of the problem is not so much the demarcation of areas of responsibility (particularly where these deny the legitimacy of subnational international interests), but in creating the means by which the increasingly diverse policy interests bearing on the international environment which national communities possess, can be related one to another and integrated into the overall framework of policy. Within the context of federal states, this has involved overcoming the constraints imposed by constitutional norms through processes of intergovernmental negotiation and collaboration, as in the domestic sphere.[3] It is these processes, where they operate at points of interface between the domestic and international environments, with which this chapter is concerned.

The point of departure for this discussion is the recognition that the character of multilayered diplomatic interactions creates mutual needs between levels of political authority within national communities imposed by the changing agenda of international politics and the enhanced points of interface between those communities and the international system. These needs are not, of course, identical. As one Australian state premier has argued, it is quite possible to acknowledge the federal government's primacy in the conduct of foreign policy whilst, at the same time, recognising that 'the states have a legitimate role in the prosecution of their own interests abroad (that is, of their constituent communities and corporations) as well as supporting the national interest'.[4] From this it follows that the tasks confronting the levels of government within national communities will differ; principally in terms of the scope of their concerns. Whereas central governments are required to develop policies reflecting the diversity of interests within a broad agenda, non-central governments' interests will usually be determined by a narrower range of domestic constituencies with more finely targeted objectives.

THE NEED FOR LINKAGES

Nevertheless, the achievement of their respective aims within a policy environment marked by a growing confluence of international and domestic pressures requires the establishment of linkage mechanisms capable of providing for each level of government access to resources over which the other has a relative, if not absolute, advantage. In other words, whilst conflictual relations between national and subnational governments are by no means absent, they are but one point on a spectrum of relationships equally characterized by the need for cooperation.

One area in which this reciprocal need is evident is that of bureaucratic expertise. In specific functional areas with a growing international dimension such as education, human rights and the environmental agenda, key repositories of policy-making skills essential to the conduct of diplomacy, both in terms of policy formulation and implementation, reside at the level of subnational government. In part, this is the reason that NCG specialists are included in international delegations relating to issues within their areas of competence. At the same time, policy-making structures at the centre will be able to command resources which lower levels of government will find it difficult to match. Clearly, this is particularly true of the smaller, less wealthy constituent elements of a federation, but even those capable of devoting considerable resources to the pursuit of their international interests will often require access to skills and information that only the centre can provide. To take but one example, the National Governors' Association in the US, along with individual states including California, have consistently pressed the Department of Commerce to produce more accurate and comprehensive international trade statistics for the states.[5] Most obviously, of course, in spite of the growth of their overseas offices, NCGs lack the international information and communications networks that diplomatic services afford national policy makers. This mutuality of interest in maintaining good and effective working relationships has been stressed by the director general of the US and Foreign Commercial Service in a discussion of a recent US&FCS strategic review. On the one hand, she argues, by 'working together with the "wholesalers" or "multipliers" of our information and services, we increase our export development outreach to regions and companies that might not know about or have ready access to US&FCS's valuable information'. On the other, local 'partners' in the export development drive:

> are a supplement to US&FCS services, not a replacement. Our partners' programs and support vary from region to region. Their funding is inconsistent from year to year. They cannot enjoy the economies of scale necessary to collect and disseminate worldwide market information on a timely and regular basis.[6]

A second motivation for the creation of linkage mechanisms lies in the demands that multilayered diplomacy places on access to the different levels of political activity. As we have seen, one of the crucial dimensions of modern diplomacy lies in the interaction between interests located in a number of arenas, successful outcomes depending on the establishment of adequate communications. Moreover, this is likely to be necessary for the duration of negotiations, not simply the initial or concluding phases. Complex trade negotiations such as the Canada–US Free Trade Negotiations demonstrate how significant the role of NCGs can be as transmitters of information between localities and the centre. Thus the advantage that local bureaucracies can offer to central foreign policy managers is the formers' access to local interests. On the other hand, national governments offer NCGs access to the international system and its networks in pursuit of their regional interests.

This is not to say that non-central governments are entirely dependent on central government for their overseas activities; international offices are set up without the formal permission from the centre. However, the successful operation of these and other international activities rest most frequently on the cooperation of the federal government and its agencies. Furthermore, international legal norms, the operating principles of international organisations and the attitudes of foreign governments, which may see little advantage and some dangers in dealing with a proliferation of subnational entities, all present obstacles to NCGs wishing to develop their international presence. Instances of foreign governments actively courting NCGs (as in the case of France and Quebec) in the face of opposition from the federal authorities appear to be rare.

The creation of cooperative mechanisms is also prompted by the opportunities that the existence of differing levels of political authority offer for the diversion of pressures that flow from the international system. Central policy makers can make effective use of NCGs as part of their overall diplomatic strategies as sensitive political issues are redefined in lower-level, quasi-administrative terms by engaging the services of subnational agencies. Not only will this tend to reduce external pressures on central government, but also lessen the strains that the conduct of evermore complex policy processes impose on national administrations.

Looked at from the perspective of non-central governments, developing close working relationships with central government can be valuable in dealing with growing international forces. Here it has to be recognised that developing an international profile is not a cost-free activity, as the Australian states have discovered in their dealings with Japan, and the Canadian provinces from their proximity to the US. Where the attentions of international actors becomes burdensome, then the constituent governments in a federal system may well find it to their advantage to seek the support of the centre, thereby creating a coalition against external pressures.

THE COORDINATION PROBLEM

This mutuality of interest between central and subnational policy makers which balances conflicts of interest arising in specific policy sectors, creates at both levels the need for modes of cooperation and communication. This is, of course, one dimension of the frequently debated problem of coordination in the foreign policy processes necessitated by their growing bureaucratization.[7] The negative consequences of this trend are seen as growing incoherence in policy as a result of increasing diffusion of information amongst government departments and agencies, the danger of a reduced capacity to respond rapidly to changing events, and the greater opportunities provided for external actors to further their objectives by building alliances with actors in other bureaucratic structures. In turn, these developments reduce the capabilities of governments in their operations within their international environments.

The patterns of intergovernmental relations characteristic of federal systems create an additional dimension to these problems. Usually, foreign policy coordination is seen as an issue for central governmental management, depicted by Underdal, for example, in terms of 'vertical disintegration' as the number of departments in the national bureaucracy possessing external policy interests increases.[8] Here, the role of the foreign ministry, and its capacity to act as a coordinating agency in an increasingly fragmented bureaucratic environment – as we shall see later – is crucial to the debate.

It is more useful to view this phenomenon in terms of a process of 'horizontal' fragmentation between departments at one level of the bureaucratic structure, reserving the term 'vertical disintegration' to refer to the possible consequences of the involvement of subnational levels of bureaucracy in the multilayered diplomatic processes.

In this situation, fragmentation produced by bureaucratic specialization is likely to be reinforced by locally based domestic interests which are clients of NCG bureaucratic structures. The danger is that policies intended to achieve quite general external policy goals can become redefined, not simply in terms of the perspectives and concerns brought to them by domestic agencies of central government, but also through the emergence of regionally based bureaucratic politics.

As the interaction between domestic and international diplomacy has become more pronounced, and as regional and local authorities' international interests have grown, so have the problems associated with coordination. Matching the complexity of multilayered diplomacy, the coordination of policy on which it rests extends across the totality of political systems and is no longer simply an issue concerning the relative status of foreign ministries and domestic departments at the level of central government. Moreover, given the mutuality of interests noted above, each level of government has a vested interest in ensuring, to the extent it can, that the necessary work of coordination is carried out at other levels. In other words, the coordination issue is present both across levels of political authority and within each of those levels. In examining the bureaucratic structures which Ontario has developed to manage its international interests, Dyment points to the range of coordinating tasks that confront NCGs, parallelling – and no less burdensome than – those present at the national level:

- Coordination between provincial ministries and agencies.
- Coordination of local government international activities.
- Liaison with other provincial governments.
- Coordination with the federal authorities.[9]

In one sense, then the coordination problem, long regarded as an issue for national policy makers, has expanded as the international involvement of subnational agencies and interests has grown. Coordination of external policy becomes increasingly essential, yet harder to achieve as policy makers seek to (a) balance domestic and international factors impinging on a decision; (b) link issues which may cut across the responsibilities of several horizontal and vertical layers of bureaucracy; (c) weigh the respective priorities of bilateral relationships and those imposed by membership of international organisations and (d) relate short-term aims to long-term goals.

To a degree, a distinction can be made here in terms of *sectoral* coordination, where the focus is on relatively discrete policy issues, as contrasted with the much broader goal of *strategic* coordination, where the aim is to relate the demands which flow from specific policy sectors within the overall fabric of external policy. Whereas it would be convenient to argue that these two areas remained separate, both in the sense that they involve distinct tasks and that one is the peculiar problem of a particular level of government, it would also be misleading. Firstly, sectoral policy issues can rapidly assume the proportions of a strategic coordination problem for the reasons cited earlier; namely, as a result of pressures exerted by domestic constituencies combined with interbureaucratic conflicts: second, both central and non-central governments confront each type of problem, but to different degrees since the tasks of strategic coordination presented to national policy makers are likely to be broader in scope and more intense reflecting the extent of their responsibilities for the general management of external relations.

LINKAGE MECHANISMS

Given this situation, it is not surprising that federal systems are witnessing the emergence of a variety of 'linkage mechanisms' intended to overcome these policy- fragmentation problems. Despite the mutual interests that have led to the creation of such mechanisms, it should be stressed that the objectives of each level of government in participating in them is likely to be different. They may well be regarded primarily by foreign ministries as a means of containing subnational international activity, whereas NCGs will be inclined to see them as a route to an enhanced role and influence. As a result, the character and operation of the linkage mechanisms themselves can become a source of contention between the levels of government. Taking one example to which we shall return later, namely the inclusion of NCG representatives in international delegations, it is often the case that the terms and objectives of such a practice are the subject of dispute. For the centre, a major goal is to ensure the acquiescence of affected domestic constituencies in any international agreement by establishing immediate channels of contact with their representatives.

Non-central governments, however, may have as their key objective the shaping of policy outcomes and, consequently, be dissatisfied with anything which smacks of tokenism on the part of the national authorities. One senior Californian trade policy official identified the differing perspectives of the US federal government and the states in the following terms:

> We are involved in a push-pull relationship with Washington in the trade area. The federal authorities are anxious to see the states increasingly involved in trade promotion but not in the trade policy area.[10]

SECTORAL POLICY LINKAGES

As one would expect, federal systems utilize the network of consultative and cooperative mechanisms created for the management of domestic policy when dealing with issues of external relations crossing the boundaries of central and regional responsibility. Because subnational international interests normally register a narrower focus than those of the national government, this has been a logical and economical method of dealing with problems resulting from the internationalization of areas of public policy traditionally regarded as domestic. When dealing with such matters, linkages between centre and region have assumed two forms: consultation prior to and during international negotiations and, second, participation by NCG representatives in the negotiations themselves.

Consultation between the levels of bureaucracy in federal states on international issues is well-established, dictated, for example, by the need to ensure regional cooperation in the implementation of International Labour Organisation (ILO) conventions. Here, Australia has developed a three-level machinery of federal–state consultation through which the impact of ILO conventions on labour practices and legislation can be considered, involving meetings of departmental officials, permanent heads, and an annual conference of ministers. The essential task of evaluating the impact of ILO conventions on state practices and the possibilities of adjusting state legislation to allow the ratification of conventions falls to the specialist officers from Canberra and the state departments of labour who, apart from formal twice yearly meetings to monitor both proposed and existing conventions, maintain continuous contact with each other. Similar consultative practices are to be found in a variety of issue areas which have acquired international significance. One of the most sensitive areas, demanding intensive consultations, has been that of human rights. Since the human rights agenda affects many areas of regional competence, it was inevitable that the Australian states should exhibit a great interest in the processes surrounding the ratification of the International Covenant on Civil and Political Rights. Two years of intensive domestic negotiations preceded the final ratification of the ICCPR, negotiations largely conducted through the consultative networks which have developed between Federal and State legal officers.

Similar processes of federal–state/provincial consultations have adapted to the internationalization of the policy agenda, as Boardman has noted in the case of environmental policy in Australia and

Canada.[11] In both cases, subnational governments have established a role for themselves in the framing of international environmental policy issues despite the tensions that have developed on occasions between the two levels of government.

In the Australian case, during the 1970s a federal–state consultative framework evolved, reflected in the establishment of the Australian Environment Council (AEC) and the Council of Nature Conservation Ministers (CONCOM). Such mechanisms have acted as foci for both cooperation and conflict between Canberra and the states as the dramas of federal–state politics came to embrace environmental issues. On the one hand, Canberra was able to take advantage of the international dimensions of environmental policy to expand its powers through creative use of the external affairs power granted to it by the constitution, whilst at the same time recognizing the need for state cooperation if it was to participate in the development of environmental regimes. Boardman has clearly illuminated the interactions between subnational, national and international levels of political activity that have developed over the last two decades:

> State governments varied in the degree of interest they showed in international institutions. Even if they lacked appreciation of how such developments might be relevant to their concerns, however, the federal–state machinery centring on the AEC and CONCOM allowed them access to Australian decision-making in these areas. Some of the more important international programmes to which the Australian government was committed, moreover, required for their effective working some form of active contribution by the states. The MAB [Man and the Biosphere] Programme, for example, had among its objectives the creation of a global network of protected biosphere reserves; Australia could be an active participant in this work only if state authorities were drawn into the process.[12]

The emphasis on an enhanced cooperative relationship between central and subnational governments associated with the assertion of 'new federalism' in various federal systems during the 1970s and 1980s was reflected in the management of external policy. Thus, in the US, the creation of Intergovernmental Affairs sections (IGAs) in federal departments reflected at once the desire of state governments to gain better access to executive agencies at the centre as well as the avowed ambition of the Reagan administration to devolve power within the political system. The degree to which this arrangement touches on the management of external policy depended, obviously, on the functions of a particular department. In the case of the Department of Commerce, the IGA had come, by 1989, to assume a central role, reflecting the desire to establish a closer cooperative framework in the trade promotion area.[13] The aim of IGA programmes such as the Department of Commerce State Initiative, as described to the author, is to coordinate activities at the respective levels of operation, 'to get the right state people and DOC people together'.[14] Apart from working with the states to coordinate export-assistance programmes, the IGA acts as an information point, monitoring the activities of state organisations such as the National Governors' Association and the Southern Governors' Association. Within the department, this information is disseminated to various sections through a series of monthly briefings: 'the aim is to let people know what is going on in the states'.[15]

As the policy agenda spanning the domestic–international divide has expanded, so the impetus to establish more regularized procedures for consultation between levels of government has developed. Characteristically, this is manifested in treaty-consultation procedures of which those in the Federal Republic of Germany are amongst the most well-established.[16] Under the Lindau Convention, the respective roles of the federal government and the *Länder* have been established for policy areas depending on the degree to which they fall under *Land* jurisdiction. So, in the education and cultural spheres, both the responsibility of the *Länder*, the Convention requires that they be involved in the discussions preceding the conclusion of a treaty and that they give their consent if such an agreement requires action at this level of government. Even where the authority of Bonn is undisputed, the combined considerations of political prudence together with the need to consult local expertise, help to ensure that the *Länder* are consulted before a federal stance on a treaty is adopted. Communication between the two levels of government is reinforced by the *Länder* representatives on the Permanent Treaty Commission who 'are part of the Bundesrat machinery and represent their *Länder* in that context, and, as trusted senior officials working at the cutting edge between administration and politics, have ready access to the federal ministries as well as to those in their *Länder* capitals'.[17]

In Australia, under the aegis of the 'new federalism' pursued by the Fraser governments of 1975–83, a regularized system of treaty consultation, monitored by the Department of Prime Minister and Cabinet in Canberra was developed from discussions held during the 1976 and 1977 Premiers' Conferences. This enhanced mode of communication between Canberra and the states was prompted by both ideological and practical considerations, and symbolized a departure from the confrontationist policy of the Whitlam years which threatened to use the external affairs power vested in the federal government to gain access to policy areas under state control. Several considerations, however, were to ensure that whilst a useful opportunity to involve the states in one dimension of Australia's external relations had been created, at the same time the prospect of intrabureaucratic tensions had been enhanced.

In part, these tensions reflected the strains that such consultative processes impose on small bureaucratic machines. The smaller states, such as Tasmania, are ill-equipped to produce responses to proposals from Canberra which involve consultation with a number of state public service departments. Moreover, since the interests of specific states in issues relating to international agreements varies widely, the incentive to devote time to such an activity can frequently be limited. These factors have produced some disillusionment at both federal and state levels. Whilst one official in the Federal Attorney-General's Department questioned the capacity of state officials to engage in consultative processes:

> The States aren't really geared up for the process. . . . Much of the material is above the heads of their officials. We might seek information or opinions and ask for responses within two weeks but often they never arrive. When they do, the response is usually to ask for the insertion of a federal reservation.[18]

An equally frustrated legal officer in Queensland pointed out that since the states had never hitherto been encouraged to express opinions in this area, they lacked the necessary expertise in international law and were having to undergo a rapid process of self-education. Some of these tensions seem to be due to the fact that the process focuses on legal officials at both levels of government. In the view of one former federal public servant, there was 'no meeting of minds' between the state and federal law officers. Each issue was redefined as one of constitutional principle by the state lawyer so that, whilst reasonable discussion might be conducted with officials from state functional departments, nothing but the 'most rabid opposition' was forthcoming from those state officials actually operating the consultative processes.

Despite the election of the Hawke Labor government, committed to an active use of the external affairs power afforded Canberra by the constitution, treaty consultation procedures have survived and developed.[19] However, the suggestion (emerging from the Constitutional Convention in the mid 1980s) that Australia adopt a Treaties Council along the lines of the German system, received little support. The need for a greater degree of cooperation and coordination was nevertheless recognized at the Special Premiers' Conference convened in 1991 to consider the future of the federal system. Apart from reviewing the consultation machinery, it was agreed that a standing committee of senior officers be created 'to provide more timely and coordinated assistance to the Commonwealth on the negotiation and implementation of international treaties.[20]

The precise character and extent of policy linkage mechanisms will depend on a number of factors, such as the interest expressed by NCGs and the attitudes of particular federal government departments. Taking the first point, the problem for national policy managers becomes not so much one of unwelcome interference by subnational governments and the constituencies they represent, but of encouraging an informed interest and involvement in areas of external policy. For one member of the Office of the US Trade Representative (USTR), this was a major constraint in formulating a US position within the context of the Canada–US free trade and Uruguay Round negotiations.

> The states' interest in trade policy is very patchy and depends very much on resources at the local bureaucratic level. It also varies with the character of the issue. The states quickly grasped the issues that affected them in the case of the free trade negotiations; but it is much more difficult to get them involved in the intricacies of the Single European Market or the MTN. We now need the states' cooperation and advice in the context of the GATT talks, on such questions as services and intellectual property rights. USTR has spent two years getting countries to talk about these issues; at the same time we have been trying to bring the states in. In part, our role has become one of educating the states as to the significance of these issues for them.[21]

Differences deriving from styles of federal culture and attitudes of the federal bureaucracy can be seen in the ways in which Australia and Canada have responded to the need for federal–state/provincial consultation in the trade policy area.

In Canada, recognition of the growing provincial concern with trade policy issues during the GATT Tokyo Round, combined with active lobbying by the provinces themselves, led to the creation of the

Canadian Trade and Tariffs Committee (CTTC) as a means of developing communications between the federal government on the one hand and industry and the provinces on the other.[22] In the field of federal–provincial consultation, the CTTC (intended to serve as a conduit for the transmission of information) conducted negotiations with the provinces on non-tariff barrier issues such as government procurement and subsidies, and received briefs from them on provincial attitudes. Demands by the provinces for a greater input into the negotiations was to result later in the creation of an ad hoc federal provincial deputy ministers committee.[23] These processes were greatly expanded, as Chapter 4 has demonstrated, in the context of the Canada–US free trade negotiations.

The fact that similar, regularized mechanisms have not developed in Australia, where consultation has hitherto occurred on a much more spasmodic basis, reflects in part the tendency for domestic economic interests to intercede directly with Canberra rather than use the states as intermediaries when seeking to influence the formulation of foreign economic policy. Additionally, the lack of consultation reflects attitudes on the part of both state and federal officials. One federal trade official recalled touring the states to discuss standards codes and government purchasing policies, a venture which he found was not always welcomed by state officials.[24]

Hence it was impossible for an officer in the British Columbia public service to discover the nature of the Australian states' position on non-tariff barrier issues during the Tokyo Round because there were no regularized consultative mechanisms at the centre through which such information might be obtained.[25] Rather, the Australian pattern assumed the form of irregular contacts on specific issues carried out between Canberra and individual states on a bilateral rather than multilateral basis.[26]

A lack of federal-state consultation was apparent to New Zealand diplomats involved in the negotiations with Australia on closer economic relations. At the suggestion of the federal government, the New Zealand trade minister toured the states to discuss government purchasing policies:

> We received a reasonably good reception but this was because the states hadn't really thought about the issues involved and we left our proposals regarding government purchasing on the table . . . the replies that eventually emerged from the states were strange, linking all kinds of extraneous issues to the government purchasing issue.[27]

The fact that state reaction to CER issues was not very informed and therefore not very helpful was seen by New Zealand negotiators as symptomatic of the style of Australian diplomacy when confronted with the need to engage in consultation with domestic constituencies:

> The New Zealand consensus style of politics involves taking domestic interests into the government's confidence and keeping them informed. But the nature of Australian diplomacy appears to avoid this; in fact one has the impression that there is a contempt for industry in the Department of Trade and that Australian ministers don't want to know what the opinions of industry are.[28]

However, by the early 1990s, stimulated by Australia's declining share of international trade, there were signs that the need for developing linkages was being recognized. In November 1991, the then minister for trade and overseas development, Dr Blewett, struck a very different note from that which had traditionally characterized federal–state relations in the trade area by launching his national trade strategy.[29] The clear intention here is to bring together industry, the states and the federal government within Australia by, for example, cooperating to set up export centres to provide advice for business, and by establishing an annual trade and investment forum for reviewing trade strategy. Overseas, the stated aim is to rationalize federal and state trade promotion activities under the lead of the federal Trade Commission, Austrade.[30]

ACCESS TO NEGOTIATIONS

In the Canadian case, the demand for a greater provincial voice in the shaping of trade policy has, almost inevitably, led to claims for involvement in the negotiating process itself. This has produced pressures for the second kind of sectoral policy linkage, that of participation in international delegations. It is here that the greatest tension between federal and subnational authorities has developed. At one level, demands by NCGs for access to international negotiations may be seen by the centre as a potential threat to the coherence of the national negotiating position and offer negotiating partners the opportunity to exploit domestic differences. At another, bureaucratic, level access for state officials to international forums is likely to be resented by federal public servants who may regard such activity as their own exclusive preserve.

For both reasons, Canadian and Australian federal politicians and public servants have resisted pressures from the regions to include their representatives in negotiating teams. In the case of the Tokyo Round during the 1970s, the Canadian provinces pressed for representation on the negotiating team in Geneva but this was opposed at both the political and bureaucratic levels:

> Federal ministers saw this as a breach of the federal government's constitutional responsibilities, while civil servants emphasised that adding provincial representatives to the small negotiating team (five or six persons) would make the team unworkable and would further introduce a partisan note that would detract from the team's ability to serve the best advantage for Canada as a whole.[31]

Similarly, despite considerable pressure, particularly from the larger provinces, for representation in the Canada–US free trade negotiations, Ottawa refused to concede and by June 1986, shortly after the start of the negotiating sessions, it appeared to be accepted that provincial representatives would not be included in the negotiating team.[32] Nevertheless, in trade negotiations with a narrower focus in which specific provincial interests are involved, then both domestic and international imperatives have suggested the wisdom of a provincial presence at the negotiations themselves. During the Atlantic fisheries negotiations in the mid 1970s, provincial representatives were present on occasions.[33] Again, during the dispute between the European Community and Canada over provincial liquor pricing policies (which had been referred by Brussels to a GATT panel), eight provinces were represented in the negotiating team sent during 1988 in an attempt to resolve the problem.

In this case, provincial representatives attended the initial and closing plenary sessions and were fully briefed as the negotiations proceeded: they were not, however, involved in actual negotiating sessions. According to one Department of External Affairs official, a provincial presence was dictated both by constitutional considerations (the need to obtain provincial cooperation in any agreement concluded) and for strategic reasons; demonstrating to the EC the domestic political difficulties confronting Ottawa, and to the provinces, the international implications of the issue. Consequently, this dual negotiating role created a situation where 'the federal government had to act as a quarterback'.[34]

In the Australian case, as suggested above, there has never been any question of state participation in trade negotiations dealing with broad policy issues. In the words of one official of the federal Department of Trade regarding the CER negotiations, 'no state observers were involved; there is no tradition of this in trade negotiations which are, firmly, a function of the Commonwealth. However, we provided them [the States] with background information and asked for reactions'.

In other areas, however, state representatives have been included in Australian delegations, So, for example, in the case of UNCLOS, a state representative was included in Australian delegations from 1979. Federal public servants whilst admitting the value of the expertise that some State officials have provided, see this largely in terms of political expediency, 'to sell the Law of the Sea to the states' or (in the words of a DFA legal specialist) 'to provide an educative process for the States and to make them aware of international realities and the effective limitations on our actions'. Needless to say, the perspective offered by state officials is somewhat different. One state representative present at several UNCLOS sessions maintained that state representation had made a definite impact on the evolution of Australian policy in this area, 'because of state expertise problems have been identified that the Commonwealth Government did not even see. As new issues have been added to the environmental agenda, so the need for state involvement has been recognized in the composition of Australian delegations. State representatives were included in the delegations to the 1989 World Conference on Preparing for Climate Change[35] and the 1991 third preparatory meeting of the United Nations Conference on Environment and Development, in which an official of the South Australian Department of Environment and Planning acted as an adviser.[36]

The existence of expertise at the regional level is, however, unlikely to provide a sufficient condition for the involvement of the regions in international negotiations. Indeed, as already noted, possession of specialist skills may in itself engender resentment and enhance tensions between the two levels of bureaucracy, as in the management of Australian international fisheries negotiations. One state fisheries officer, suggesting that the federal Department of Primary Industry (DPI) had been forced to create consultative mechanisms with the states because of its own lack of practical experience in the fisheries area, noted the limitations on participation imposed by the DPI where international negotiations are involved:

> We [the states] are able to influence fisheries negotiations where we are consulted, but the Commonwealth is coy about informing the states and try to control the channels of information. The DPI has

taken the view that international issues are its preserve and this reflects the belief of federal bureaucratic empire-builders who believe that they are the only repository of skills.[37]

Not surprisingly, the view from the DPI is somewhat different: 'The problem is that the states don't think in terms of the national interest. They are close to the fishermen, they have a constituency and we don't. But this means that their position reflects purely local interests. They are also trying to maximise their control of fisheries by whatever means available. For both reasons, the States will come into conflict with the DPI.'[38]

PERSONNEL EXCHANGES

A mode of policy linkage with both an internal and external dimension is that of personnel exchanges between central and subnational governmental departments. Obviously, this can be valuable to both levels of government as a means of acquiring information and expertise together with access to the policy-making processes. One factor seen as underpinning California's influence in the trade policy area has been the use of former federal officials with experience in the area. Thus its Washington-based trade policy adviser in the late 1980s and early 1990s had served with the USTR, a factor which was regarded as valuable by both state and federal trade policy officials.[39]

This practice has extended to exchanges between foreign ministries and NCG departments. In addition to the usual familiarization programmes intended to provide serving officers of these departments with a knowledge of the domestic constituencies which external policy is intended to serve, it has become quite common to find either former members of the respective foreign ministries serving in state/provincial bureaucracies, often in premiers' departments, or foreign affairs officers on secondment to particular departments.

In Canada, exchanges seem to have become far more institutionalized than in Australia. Ontario, for example, developed a series of exchanges with the Department of External Affairs in the 1980s. In 1988 a DEA officer from the trade policy branch on secondment to the International Relations Division of the Ministry of Intergovernmental Affairs, had been assigned the task of working on mechanisms for better provincial involvement in the Uruguay Round of GATT negotiations, following the experience of the Canada–US free trade negotiations.[40] Meanwhile, an Ontario official was attached to the DEA working on GATT issues. On the external linkage front, the practice of seconding provincial officials to Canadian embassies has grown in recent years, as has discussion of attaching 'provincial affairs' officers to embassies, either as replacements for, or supplements to, provincial overseas offices.

STRATEGIC POLICY COORDINATION

As suggested earlier, the task of coordinating the overall thrust of external relations will be far greater than in specific policy sectors. In part, as we have seen, this is because it demands the balancing of interests between a number of those sectors each of which may have implications for a particular bilateral or multilateral set of relationships; and partly because the scope for domestic political and bureaucratic tensions are vastly enhanced. Immediately, it poses the vexed issue of who, in modern, complex bureaucratic structures can, and should, act as gatekeeper between the domestic and international political environments and, of course, the continuing claims of foreign ministries to perform this role. The quest for coordination can thus easily become – and be perceived within the torrid milieu of bureaucratic politics – a weapon in the interdepartmental power struggle. Karvonen and Sundelius's study of foreign policy management in Sweden and Finland has illustrated the strategies which foreign ministries can pursue in their attempts to reinforce their central role in the conduct of external policy against the claims of bureaucratic actors.[41] These include, for example, the use of planning meetings, chaired by foreign ministry representatives, for the heads of international sections of domestic ministries and the placement of foreign service officers in key positions in domestic agencies.

One form of response to the particular issues posed by growing international activity on the part of subnational authorities is to create units in the foreign ministry specifically charged with the task of developing linkages between the levels of political authority. Here, it is appropriate to restate the point that this is not a problem for federal states alone. In the case of France, for example, Mény has noted the growing international interests of regions and local government which 'contradicts the central and exclusive function of the Ministry of External Relations, already deeply affected by the intervention of specialized ministries in the international sphere'.[42] This concern led, in

1983, to the appointment of a 'delegate', directly responsible to the secretary-general of the ministry, charged with the task of ensuring that, 'the initiatives of the communes, departments and regions respect the rules of the constitution and the law and do not interfere unfavourably with the foreign policy of France'.[43]

But, of course, the more marked this tendency, the more developed is likely to be the response on the part of a foreign ministry. Taking Belgium as another example, Lejeune has described in some detail the mechanisms of coordination established and intended by the Ministry of External Relations to 'protect its traditional powers and to provide pragmatic responses to the requests of communities and regions'.[44] Amongst these processes of 'concertation' are the Ministerial Coordinating Committee External Relations/Communities/Regions attended by the minister of foreign affairs and his opposite numbers in the communities and regions, and a section within the Ministry of External Relations to oversee relationships between the latter and the ministry. In the case of the well-established federal systems, the Canadian Department of External Affairs appears to have devoted considerable effort to establishing a strategic coordination mechanism in the shape of the Federal Provincial Coordination division (FPCD).

THE ROLE AND OPERATION OF THE FPCD

Created in 1967, partly as a response to the increasing challenge from Quebec, but also with an eye on the growing interests of the provinces in foreign economic policy, the FPCD took over the role of liaising with the provinces from the legal division of the DEA – an indicator of the dominant perspective from which provincial involvement in external policy questions had hitherto been viewed in Ottawa.

Its purpose was to act as a channel of communication between Ottawa and the provinces, as transmitter of information from the DEA to provincial capitals, to monitor provincial activities and as advocate of regional interests within the foreign policy processes. One diplomat beginning his tour of duty within the division in the mid 1980s described his role in the following terms:

> I could be regarded as a 'Mr. Fixit', a troubleshooter. We are trying to keep the door open both ways here. There are legitimate provincial interests in external policy and our job is to see that they are heard. It is also our function to give the provinces the

> information they require. At the same time we are here to see that the national interest is preserved. For example, when we are asked to provide assistance for provincial ministers travelling overseas, we always want to know why they are going and who they are going to see.[45]

This two-way focus was reflected in the way that a desk officer with responsibility for relations with Quebec perceived his role: 'my job is to check that the federal interest is respected in Quebec and that Quebec's interests are respected in Ottawa'. The growing awareness of the potential impact of provincial activities touching on Canada's external relations underscored the significance of the division' operations and by 1984 it had expanded to nine officers under a director who was a senior diplomat. Perhaps not surprisingly, attitudes towards the FPCD's work varied.

Certainly, the common perception within the division was that its role was, at this period, understood and respected. One indicator of this was the fact that it had no problems in attracting experienced officers. Nevertheless, desk officers who had established close working relationships with counterparts in provincial departments, it was recognized, could resent attempts to insert an additional layer of responsibility in the system.

Similarly, attitudes varied at the provincial level. The most positive attitudes came from those responsible for international affairs in ministries of intergovernmental relations. Indeed, in Ontario, officials occupying this position appeared to hold a very high opinion of the FPCD's work, regarding it as meshing in with their own in the pursuit of an overall integrated and coordinated foreign policy machine spanning the levels of governmental interests and activity. The view from provincial line ministries, predictably, was noticeably at variance with this positive attitude. Thus a senior trade development official in Alberta saw the FPCD as 'a filter of information which isn't needed'. Typically, the FPCD was viewed as an obstacle to established channels of communication with Ottawa and the purveyor of outdated and useless information.

Such attitudes help to explain the relative decline of the FPCD by the late 1980s. A senior provincial official in Toronto saw this as a consequence of criticism of the division and the response of the minister of external affairs in the Mulroney government to it. Accordingly, the DEA, at least in theory, had been made a more 'open' system with which communication was far easier than in the days when the FPCD was established. Of equal weight, however, was the changed atmosphere of federal–provincial relations in the mid 1980s and the more relaxed atmosphere that this encouraged towards the issue of the provincial impact on foreign relations. Whatever the reasons, interviews conducted during 1988 revealed that the status of the FPCD had dramatically declined. Not only was this reflected in reduced size and the lower status of officers serving in it, but in its responsibilities and attitudes towards it. Thus one DEA officer no longer regarded the FPCD as possessing the influence that it had in the early 1980s nor as the major route to the provinces within the DEA: 'the days have gone when members of the department would actively seek out membership of the FPCD'.

DETERMINANTS OF STRATEGIC LINKAGE PATTERNS

The experience of the FPCD indicates one factor determining the character and extent of strategic coordinating linkages: namely, perceived need. Not unexpectedly, where the impact of NCG activity is regarded as having potentially serious consequences for the management of external relations, then the greater the likelihood that attention will be paid to devising methods of coping with the problem. A second factor lies in the character and traditions of the federal system and the attitudes that these produce. There is a clear contrast betweeen Canada and Australia here, indicated in the response given to a Canadian diplomat, then serving in Canberra, when he asked an Australian foreign service officer why the Department of Foreign Affairs (as it then was) had not developed a mechanism similar to the FPCD: 'here we barge ahead and try to remedy the damage afterwards'.

A third consideration is the status of the foreign ministry and, therefore, its capacity to assume a key coordinating role in the overall management of external relations and, particularly, in the crucial interface between domestic interests and foreign policy. Although by no means the only factor, the negative images widely held of the US Department of State help to explain the apparently low-key role of its intergovernmental affairs section. The account of its role provided by members of the section to the author emphasized its relative lack of significance compared with the FPCD in Ottawa. Rather than viewing its activities as closely related to policy management, the central functions appear to be of an administrative nature, such as helping to organize state governors' overseas visits.[46] Furthermore, the rationale for its activities seems to relate as much to the need to establish a domestic constituency for the department in the context of intrabureaucratic battles and the struggle to avoid budgetary cuts as any commitment to enhance the states' input into its work.

Questions of status, together with the more general character of the foreign policy process, have affected the extent to which the Australian Department of Foreign Affairs and Trade has developed mechanisms similar to the Canadian FPCD. One factor here lies in the extent to which the conduct of Australian foreign policy has rested on strong links with the national community. It is hard to point to the kind of fundamental evaluation of the relationship between domestic interests and foreign policy that have occurred at regular intervals in Canada. Consequently, the DFAT has not been encouraged to build bridges within the Australian community. Moreover, traditionally the DFAT has not been regarded as a 'strong' department within the Canberra departmental hierarchy, and attempts to establish it as a 'super-department' coordinating Australia's external relations have met with resistence from other departments. Certainly, the 1987 reorganisation which assigned responsibility for multilateral trade negotiations previously held by the Department of Trade to the then Department of External Affairs can only have strengthened its position in Canberra. Nevertheless, other powerful rivals, particularly the Department of Prime Minister and Cabinet which has a significant role in both federal–state relations and foreign policy, are likely to act as constraints on attempts by DFAT to expand its domestic linkages.

Somewhat perversely, the one coordinating mechanism through which state interests in external relations could gain a voice in the policy process – the Japan Secretariat – was abolished in the wake of the DFAT reorganization. Created in the light of criticisms expressed in the Myer Report on Australia–Japan relations to the effect that a lack of coherence in Australia's dealings with Tokyo (partly due to state interests and activities) was disadvantaging Australia, the Secretariat sought to achieve a degree of coordination in this highly significant relationship by establishing a consultative committee comprising representatives of federal public service departments as well as regular consultations with officers from state government departments. Since the secretariat, although responsible to the permanent head of the DFA, was a separate agency, there was a degree of bureaucratic tension regarding its operations.

Following its disappearance, however, the only formal mechanism for maintaining linkages between the states and the DFAT has been the maintenance of Senior Foreign Affairs Representatives in the state capitals, intended to develop contacts with the business community. However, according to those who have served as SFARs, the system has always suffered from scepticism within the department, a lack of resources and, particularly, the absence of any mechanism at the centre for processing information coming in from the state offices.[47]

It has been noted frequently that one feature of the changing context of international relations is the development of transgovernmental relations between national bureaucracies: 'direct contacts between governmental subunits responsible for specific policy sectors are growing in magnitude and intensity' argue Karvonen and Sundelius.[48] In similar vein, Raymond Hopkins suggested several years ago that what he termed 'global management networks' based on linkages between national bureaucracies were of increasing importance.[49] The emergence of linkages between central and non-central bureaucracies within political systems which this chapter has described can be viewed as the reverse side of the coin. Management responses to the changing diplomatic environment require not only international coordination between the central agencies of government involved in the conduct of foreign relations, but also between layers of administration within the state.

In trying to achieve this, each tier of the bureaucracy is confronted by its own problems – not dissimilar in essence – in responding to the internationalization of the environment in which it operates: coordination of external policies is not a problem reserved to central government alone. Quite clearly, governments, federal or unitary in their structure, will respond in different ways as they seek to cope with the more complex policy arenas in which they are constrained to operate. The evidence cited in this chapter suggests, however, that federal systems, experiencing these problems to a marked degree, are able to develop structures and processes capable of responding to them. Such internal bureaucratic adaptation will condition the character of transgovernmental linkages. Thus Hopkins' global management networks are likely to reflect changes in national management structures which are, in turn, responses to the pressures of foreign policy localization.

8 Conclusion

At the beginning of this study, we identified two themes which the subsequent chapters have sought to weave together. The first of these relates to the forces of localization which have accompanied the more frequently observed patterns of globilization marking the character of contemporary international relations. These, it has been argued, result in the interpenetration of what have hitherto been seen as relatively discrete policy arenas with their own cast of players operating to well-defined rules. The second theme focuses on the role of non-central governments in these processes as they come to assume a degree of prominence in the management of foreign relations which constitutional norms appear to deny them.

The link between the two is to be found in the changing character of diplomacy. No longer can this be regarded as an activity in which foreign policy elites interact, divorced from the domestic constituencies on which foreign policy rests; rather, diplomacy has acquired a definite domestic dimension, particularly where social and economic issues are concerned. The emergence of multilayered diplomacy, with its complex patterns of relations, is characterized by the requirements it demands of policy makers. In order to secure the consent of affected domestic interests to the outcome of international negotiations, a simultaneous domestic diplomatic effort has to be conducted. Additionally, policy makers need to be aware of the configurations of forces in other countries likely to determine the attitudes of negotiating partners.

The aim, then, has been to reveal something of the character of contemporary diplomacy in general terms as well as to offer a reevaluation of the ways in which NCGs in federal states impinge upon it.

NCGs IN THE INTERNATIONAL ARENA

The discussion developed from the argument that our images of the nature and significance of NCG international activities have been distorted by, firstly, an assumption that they represent a dramatic shift from traditional patterns of international relations, perhaps even indicative of major movements of political authority away from central to regional centres of power.

Related to this point, a good deal of the literature has tended to focus on the significance of NCGs in terms of their uniqueness as international actors and their separateness from traditional modes of diplomatic intercourse. As a consequence, rather than attempting to locate NCGs within the foreign policy processes alongside their national governments, there has been a strong presumption that each have incompatible interests and stand in opposition to one another. This clearly ignores processes which are rendering the boundaries demarcating state and non-state actors far more permeable than hitherto, thereby creating ambiguities about the status and characteristics of each and the patterns of interaction between them.

The impact of the image of NCG international activity thus created has been to set it apart from the patterns of traditional diplomacy, to seek new terms to describe it (such as 'paradiplomacy' and 'protodiplomacy') which serve to reinforce the distinction, and to emphasize the elements of conflict between national and subnational governments which have accompanied its growth. Furthermore, and somewhat ironically given the desire of some observers to use this phenomenon as a means of rejecting the distortions of state-centric interpretations of world politics, NCGs themselves have tended to be treated as unitary actors, whereas, in reality, they represent quite complex patterns of relationships both inside and outside their national settings, and embrace a diversity of interests.

Indeed, it is the hybrid nature of NCGs which endows them with their qualities as international actors. On the one hand, they lack the attributes of sovereignty that characterize national governments; but, on the other, they demonstrate some of the qualities of statehood and are polities in their own right within their national settings. Nor do they act in a uniform fashion. Generalizations concerning NCG international activities and interests have been shown to be unsustainable. Not only is this because each federal system is unique – which clearly it is – but also because, within federal states, NCGs demonstrate differing characteristics and resources.

Given their economic profile, for example, some may favour free trade policies, others protectionist policies. Some may be endowed with valuable resources whose exploitation requires access to foreign investment; others may not. One of the key determinants of NCG actions in areas of international policy will be the extent to which regional interests accord with those represented by the central government. Regions within the periphery of a federal system are more likely to reflect a basic asymmetry of interest with the centre than are those which are part of the core. In turn, this helps to determine the strategies employed to promote the region's international interests. Two fundamental options exist (although, as we have seen, there are variations based upon them): to gain a voice in the central policy-making processes and to act directly in the international arena. Where NCGs find their interests at variance with those represented at the centre, then there will be a tendency to develop strategies based on the second option.

But however strong the impulsion may be for NCGs to develop an international voice and presence, it has been emphasized that there are a range of factors which will determine their capacity to do so. These include the basic constitutional arrangements of a given political system and the opportunities that they provide for international activities; bureaucratic and political attitudes at the centre, the local resources available to sustain an international strategy and, by no means an inconsiderable factor, the degree of interest possessed by international actors in the affairs of a constituent unit in a federation.

It is not intended here to restate the findings of the various case studies developed above. Nevertheless, it is clear that NCGs can become involved in the policy processes in a variety of ways, in a number of contexts, and with differing results. Furthermore, these roles can change as a given process evolves. Taking one key issue identified above, that of the assumed conflictual nature of NCG–central government relations in the foreign policy area, it is obvious that the two levels of government develop relationships that span the spectrum from high levels of conflict to close cooperation. In the case of the unitary taxation episode, the patterns of interaction became particularly dense and intricate. Here, indeed, there was conflict between the US federal government and the states involved. Whilst it would be a simplification of a complex set of circumstances to view the alignment of forces as consisting of foreign business interests, governments and international bodies, together with key US federal government agencies versus the states, it is not a gross distortion of reality.

The acid rain episode, however, casts a very different light on the role of NCGs in the multilayered diplomatic milieu. In many ways, the Canadian provinces, particularly Ontario and Quebec, took the lead in the evolving dispute between the US and Canada. Far from Ottawa and Toronto conflicting over aims, the provincial environmental bureaucracy became key players in the developing Canadian strategy. This was a clear example of NCGs acting as foreign policy surrogates for the central foreign policy machinery, of the devolution of foreign policy management. The unique features of this case have, of course, to be acknowledged. This was a transboundary issue linking together US states and Canadian provinces. From the US viewpoint, it represented an issue on which the states were clearly divided and thus presented Washington with a difficult instance of multilayered diplomacy. Moreover, it was a case where local expertise was highly relevant and thus underscored a role for NCGs.

The negotiations surrounding the Canada–US Free Trade Agreement offer a more uncertain picture – as do some of the other examples in the trade policy area cited above. One key feature of this experience stands out in clear relief: whatever the constitutional arguments regarding the status of the provinces in the negotiations, from a practical point of view they had to be involved if the agreement was to have legitimacy. In this sense, the federal government had a vested interest in provincial involvement just as did the provinces. At the same time, it was concerned to establish the ground rules for that participation and to control the process. The negotiations also demonstrate the need for negotiating partners – in this case the US – to take a close interest in the domestic diplomacy of negotiating partners. In the Canadian case, the pattern of federal–provincial conflict and cooperation was more confused than in the other cases, with Ontario developing an oppositional role.

THE NATURE OF MULTILAYERED DIPLOMACY

Taking these cases in the more general context of the multilayered diplomatic environment, they reinforce many of the points set out in Chapter 2. It is hardly necessary to stress that contemporary diplomacy has become a far more complex exercise as domestic and international diplomacy are increasingly intertwined. The consequences of this can be summarized in terms of its impact on actors, targets and strategies.

With regard to the actors involved in multilayered diplomacy, the emphasis on NCGs has provided one example and shown the range of roles that they can assume. There are many more equally deserving of examination. Perhaps the most general point worth stressing is, firstly, the diminishing utility of distinctions between domestic and international actors. Increasingly, each of these operate in a variety of political environments, from the subnational to the international, reflecting the growing linkages between domestic and foreign policy. Secondly, it appears to be far harder to make definitive distinctions between state and non-state actors as each interact in a variety of ways and can become allies and agents of the other.

Similar points can be made regarding the targets of diplomacy which are increasingly diverse and focused on domestic interests and political institutions at all levels. Success in diplomacy requires an evaluation of the actors involved and decisions as to which of these need to be targeted at specific points in negotiations. Recognizing that friends and enemies in the diplomatic jungle are not necessarily defined by national boundaries is equally important. It is also significant that, as the discussion of the unitary taxation episode reveals, multilayered diplomacy has elevated the significance of those who are able to interpret the mysteries of diverse domestic environments to those whose interests are affected by them. The age of the international 'political consultant' or lobbyist appears to have arrived. Inasmuch as they are capable of linking policy environments they, rather than national governments, can lay claim to be the new gatekeepers in the era of multilayered diplomacy.

This leads naturally to the development of appropriate strategies. The challenges confronting the policy maker in devising strategies to accomplish goals in the multilayered diplomatic environment are clearly immense. Their implications for the bureaucratic management of foreign relations will be considered below; more general points will be made here. First of all, this more diversified diplomatic environment offers the opportunity to create, as already indicated, a wider range of linkages between actors in differing policy arenas. Establishing these, deciding what is possible and appropriate – and where in the policy cycle – are major challenges confronting the policy maker. One problem is that the old rules of diplomacy still apply to the new multilayered diplomatic milieu. So, for example, there are acknowledged constraints deriving from traditional conceptions of sovereignty on the extent to which foreign domestic interests can be coopted in pursuit of policy goals. As noted in several places in this study, foreign governments are cautious in their dealings with NCGs if only because of the possible alienation of, or retaliatory action from, the relevant central government.

Second, in the home arena a premium has to be placed on the creation of suitable means of consulting affected constituencies. Here, a very real problem emerges in the form of the unexpected. One of the key characteristics of the policy environment described in these pages is the problem it presents to the diplomatic strategist of identifying which are the affected constituencies. In an age of issue-linkage, where pressure groups have become adept at linking often quite diverse and apparently unrelated issues, the task of predicting who will emerge as an actor in a given set of international negotiations is extremely difficult. The reverse side of this coin is the need to alert affected interests to the fact that there are issues at stake which affect their well-being. Interviews with trade officials undertaken in the course of this study often revealed a degree of frustration at the difficulties of getting local officials and constituencies to take an interest in such issues as the Uruguay Round. Yet, as already noted, a failure to do this early on can store up trouble on the domestic front as negotiations progress towards their concluding phases.

FOREIGN POLICY, FEDERALISM AND MULTILAYERED DIPLOMACY

Given the domestic–international character of multilayered diplomacy, the analysis developed in the preceding chapters can be approached at two levels. The first relates to the way in which political systems, particularly but not exclusively federal states, respond as the boundaries between domestic and international policy arenas become hazier. Understanding contemporary federalism increasingly demands that the international environment in which a given system functions be taken into account. Traditional concern with the relationships between central government and the constituent governments of the federation has now to be expanded to embrace the international environment which is capable of redefining the pattern of relationships between them. A two-way process is involved here. On the one side, the expansion of the foreign policy agenda to include issues hitherto seen as essentially domestic has helped to underscore the localization of foreign policy in federal states. Equally, however, it has inserted a new note into the domestic politics of federalism by raising the spectre of enhanced central power as, in the case of Australia, national governments use their foreign policy powers to encroach on areas reserved to the constituent governments.

The second level, and the central focus of this book, concerns the conduct of foreign relations. Whatever else the cases outlined demonstrate, they underscore the fact that the traditional assumption that foreign relations are the exclusive concern of central governments is no longer valid. Certainly, the international interests of NCGs are more limited in scope than are those of national governments and have a pronounced economic orientation. It would, however, be misleading to dismiss them as second-order actors as a result. The global web of world politics ensures that non-central governments have interests and responsibilities which can often, quite unexpectedly and sometimes against their wishes, project them into the international limelight. Increasingly, the various levels of government have legitimate international interests and these have to be accommodated rather than denied.

This is hardly likely to be achieved by recourse on the part of central governments to constitutional claims regarding their exclusive right to deal with international issues or injunctions to strengthened control by foreign policy agencies, such as the State Department. These not only deny the realities of a vastly more diversified policy-making environment, but fail to recognize the underlying forces that have created the problem which they seek to solve. The management of foreign relations demands cooperation between levels of government which take into account the qualities that are demanded in the conduct of contemporary foreign policy.

Traditionally, the quality stressed above all others in the conduct of foreign policy has been, firstly, internal coherence in terms of the pursuit of clearly identified goals reflecting the 'national interest'; second, external coherence whereby national communities speak with one voice in the international arena, thereby preventing others either misunderstanding their intentions or exploiting domestic divisions. Federal systems have usually been viewed as deficient in this regard. Hence one of the most frequently quoted statements on the conduct of foreign relations in federal states is Wheare's observation that a 'spirited foreign policy and federalism go ill together'.[1]

However, quite what characterizes this quality in the context of contemporary multilayered diplomacy is open to question. Where the intricacies of trade and environmental diplomacy are concerned, for example, the often slow and uncertain development of domestic consensus is as fundamental to success as is 'spirit'. Few would deny the significance of coherence in the conduct of external relations; yet it is only one relevant quality. Alongside it stand such factors as flexibility of response to changing circumstances and sustainability of objectives in complex negotiations. It is by no means obvious that federal systems are deficient in these qualities and may indeed enjoy some advantages in a diplomatic milieu which increasingly places a premium on the capacity to manage domestic constituencies. In the context of economic policy-making, Bakvis has made the point that coherence has to be weighed against other considerations: 'National economic policy-making may well be much more coherent in France. But the Canadian political system may be much more responsive when it comes to dealing with local needs than is France'.[2] Bearing in mind the importance of economic issues in the conduct of external relations, this point carries some force.

ADAPTING THE FOREIGN POLICY MACHINERY

Part of the conventional wisdom concerning the conduct of contemporary diplomacy is the relative decline of the foreign ministry as it is confronted by bureaucratic rivals each eager to stake their claim to pursue their interests in the international arena. This investigation has, at least, suggested that a note of caution might be appropriate here. Whilst it has been argued that the foreign policy machinery in federal states is likely to add an element of vertical bureaucratic fragmentation to the more familiar horizontal fragmentation present at the national level, it is also true that federal systems possess traditions of intergovernmental cooperation which are as relevant to the changing context of foreign relations as they are to domestic policy. Indeed, one of the arguments put forward is that the conduct of foreign relations has become more 'intergovernmentalized'. Consequently, federations may well be able to offer useful perspectives on the adaptation of the foreign policy machinery to the changes outlined above.

Here, it is important to note that the processes of globalization and localization of foreign policy pose administrative challenges to both NCGs and central government in administrative terms Each, for example, confront, at their respective levels, the problems of bureaucratic coordination. But beyond this, both have an interest in developing linkage mechanisms and cooperative practices with the other for the reasons set out in Chapter 7. It has been argued that the central foreign machinery has sought to find mechanisms of liaising with NCGs and regional interests and of containing problems in the conduct of foreign policy that the latter may create. These do not reside solely in the foreign ministry; departments dealing with foreign economic relations have a special interest in ensuring that communication with regional economic interests is maintained. Thus the emergence of multilayered diplomacy with its emphasis on the need to relate domestic and international political arenas, is matched by the emergence of multitiered management structures and processes.

This is not, of course to deny the formidable problems that the management of the multilayered diplomatic environment presents. But it does suggest that means exist for dealing with them. What is required is an ability to recognize that the challenges confronting policy makers demand a willingness to move beyond recourse to assertions of the constitutional prerogatives of central governments in the foreign policy sphere. Defending jurisdictional rights in this respect, whilst not unimportant to the functioning of the international system, has to be placed alongside the other considerations set out above.

As has been suggested, the character of contemporary diplomacy adds a new twist to traditional concerns in the pursuit of foreign policy goals; namely, creating the means by which the increasingly diverse policy interests bearing on a national community's foreign relations can be related to one another and brought into the policy process at appropriate points. All the indications are that foreign policy makers of the future will be constrained to operate in ever more diverse arenas as the processes of globalization and regionalization develop alongside those of localization. At the same time that the age of the 'global city' is pronounced, European politicians grapple with the implications of a common European foreign and security policy. Weaving together the disparate strands that these developments represent into coherent and sustainable policies is the challenge of the present and, increasingly, of the future.

Notes and References

1 Localizing Foreign Policy

1. Robert D. Putnam, 'Diplomacy and domestic politics: the logic of two-level games', *International Organization*, 42(3), Summer 1988, p. 459.
2. Bayless Manning, 'The Congress, the executive and intermestic affairs', *Foreign Affairs*, 55, January 1977.
3. See John H. Jackson, Jean-Victor Louis and Mitsuo Matsushita, *Implementing the Tokyo Round: National Constitutions and International Economic Roles* (Ann Arbor University of Michigan Press, 1984). Valuable studies of the interactions between domestic and international politics can also be found in Gilbert R. Winham, *International Trade and the Tokyo Round Negotiation* (Princeton, New Jersey: Princeton University Press, 1986) and Joan E. Twiggs, *The Tokyo Round of Multilateral Trade Negotiations: a Case Study in Building Domestic Support for Diplomacy* (Lanham, University Press of America, 1987).
4. As discussed, for example, in I. M. Destler, *American Trade Politics: System under Stress* (Washington DC: Institute For International Economics, 1986).
5. Evan Luard, *The Globalization of Politics: the Changed Focus of Political Action in the Modern World* (London, Macmillan, 1990) p. 12.
6. Ibid., p. 97.
7. In the context of environmental policy, the relationship between domestic political structures and international regimes is discussed in Robert Boardman, 'Approaching regimes: Australia, Canada, and environmental policy', *Australian Journal of Political Science*, 26(3), November 1991, pp. 446–71.
8. R. O. Keohane and J. S. Nye, *Power and Interdependence: World Politics in Transition* (Boston: Little, Brown, 1977).
9. Amongst the extensive literature pursuing this theme see Seyom Brown, *New Forces, Old Forces and the Future of World Politics* (Glenview, Ill.: Scott Foresman, 1988), Edward L. Morse, *Modernization and the Transformation of International Relations* (New York: Free Press, 1976) and Don C. Piper and Ronald J. Terchek (eds), *Interaction: Foreign Policy and Public Policy* (Washington, DC: American Enterprise Institute for Public Policy Research, 1983).
10. S. Greer, 'Urbanization, parochialism and foreign policy', in J. N. Rosenau *Domestic Sources of Foreign Policy* (New York: Free Press, 1967, p. 253).
11. Brown, *New Forces, Old Forces*, p. 237.
12. M. H. Shuman 'Dateline Main Street: local foreign policies', *Foreign Policy*, 65, Winter 1986/7, p. 170.
13. See Gerhard Pohl, 'Trade policy making in China', in Henry R. Nau (ed.), *Domestic Trade Politics and the Uruguay Round* (New York:

Columbia University Press, 1989) pp. 51–68. Also the survey on growing provincial autonomy in China in the *Far Eastern Economic Review*, 4 April 1991, pp. 21–30.

14. D. L. Sheth, 'Grass roots stirrings and the future of politics', *Alternatives*, 9, Summer 1983, p. 13.
15. Chadwick F. Alger 'Perceiving, analysing and coping with the local-global nexus', *International Social Science Journal*, 117, August 1988, pp. 321–40.
16. James N. Rosenau, *Turbulence in World Politics: a Theory of Change and Continuity* (London: Harvester Wheatsheaf, 1990) p. 125.
17. Shuman, op. cit., p. 157.
18. Chadwick F. Alger and Saul H. Mendlovitz, 'Grass roots initiatives and the challenge of linkages', in Saul. H. Mendlovitz and R. B. J. Walker (eds), *Towards a Just World Peace: Perspectives from Social Movements* (London: Butterworth, 1987; pp. 333–62.
19. Alger, 'Perceiving, analysing and coping with the local-global nexus', p. 332.
20. R. B. J. Walker and Saul H. Mendlovitz, 'Peace, politics and contemporary social movements', in Mendlovitz and Walker, *Towards a Just World Peace*, p. 10.
21. Sheth, ibid.
22. Janice Love, *The U.S. Anti-Apartheid Movement: Local Activism in Global Politics* (New York: Praegar, 1985).
23. R. Simeon *Federal-Provincial Diplomacy: the Making of Recent Policy in Canada* (University of Toronto Press, 1972) p. 4.
24. Daniel J. Elazar, 'States as Polities in the Federal System', *National Civic Review*, 70(2), 1981, pp. 77–82.
25. Luigi Di Marzo, *Component Units of Federal States and International Agreements* (Netherlands: Sijthoff and Noordhoff, 1980) pp. 21ff.
26. John M. Kline, *State Government Influence in US International Economic Foreign Policy* (Lexington, Mass: D. C. Heath) 1983: p. 15.
27. Ivo D. Duchacek, *The Territorial Dimension of Politics: Within, Among and Across Nations* (Boulder: Westview Press, 1986) pp. 118–24.
28. Daniel J. Elazar, 'Federalism, intergovernmental relations and changing models of the polity', in L. A. Picard and R. Zeriski *Subnational politics in the 1980s* (New York: Praegar, 1986) p. 12.
29. Geoffrey Sawer, *Australian Federal Politics and Law 1901–1929* (Melbourne: Melbourne University Press, 1956) pp. 31–2. See also P. G. Edwards, *Prime Ministers and Diplomats: The Making of Australian Foreign Policy 1901–1949* (Melbourne: Oxford University Press, 1983) pp. 4–6.
30. See Elazar, 'Federalism, intergovernmental relations and changing models of the polity'.
31. Kline, op. cit., Chapter 4.
32. David A. Caputo, 'Political, social, and economic aspects of the "old" and the "new" new federalism', in L. A. Picard and R. Zeriski, *Subnational politics*, pp. 21–34.
33. For a perspective from Alberta on this, see Wayne Clifford, 'The western provinces of Canada: the importance and orientation of their

international relations' (Edmonton, Alberta: Department of Federal and Intergovernmental Affairs, October 1981).

34. Daniel E. Pilcher and Lanny Proffer, *The States and International Trade: New Roles in Export Development – A Legislator's Guide* (Denver, Col.: National Conference of State Legislatures, 1985) pp. 4–6; also Kline, *State Government Influence*, p. 42.
35. Brown, *New Forces, Old Forces*, part three.
36. Barry B. Hughes *et al.*, *Energy in the Global Arena:Actors,Values, Policies and Futures* (Durham, NC: Duke University Press, 1985) p. 53.
37. See, for example, Andrew Fenton Cooper, 'Subnational activity and foreign economic policy-making in Canada and the United States: perspectives on agriculture', *International Journal*, vol. 41(3) Summer 1986, pp. 655–73.
38. Elazar, 'Federalism, intergovernmental relations', pp. 13–15.
39. J.L. Granatstein and Robert Bothwell, *Pirouette: Pierre Trudeau and Canadian Foreign Policy* (Toronto: University of Toronto Press, 1990) chapter four. Also, G.Bruce Doern and Glen Toner, *The Politics of Energy: The Development and Implementation of the NEP* (Toronto: Methuen, 1985).
40. See Deil S. Wright, *Understanding Intergovernmental Relations* (second edition) (Monterey, Cal: Brooks/Cole, 1982).
41. M.J.C. Vile, *The Structure of American Federalism* (Oxford University Press, 1961) pp. 194–5.
42. Richard J. Samuels, *The Politics of Regional Policy in Japan: Localities Incorporated?* (Princeton, NJ: Princeton University Press, 1983) p. 8.
43. This is discussed in Chapter 2 below. See Gary A. Rumble, 'Federalism,external affairs and treaties: recent developments in Australia', *Case Western Reserve Journal of International Law*, 17(1) 1984, pp. 1–42; Robert Boardman, *Global Regimes and Nation States: Environmental Issues in Australian Politics* (Ottawa: Carleton University Press, 1990), particularly Chapter 7.
44. Simon Bulmer and William Paterson, *The Federal Republic of Germany and the European Community* (London: Allen and Unwin, 1988) Chapter 8.
45. *Report of the Ad Hoc Working Committee on Australia–Japan Relations* (Canberra: Australian Government Publishing Service, 1975) pp. 156–7.
46. On this see, for example, James N. Rosenau, 'Patterned chaos in global life: structure and process in the two worlds of world politics', *International Political Science Review*, 9(4) 1988, pp. 327–64.
47. This view is clearly taken by Chadwick Alger in his various pieces on the subject. See, for example, his comments on the need to draw together democratic theory and international relations in Chadwick F. Alger, 'Local, national and global politics in the world: a challenge to international studies', *International Studies Notes of the International Studies Association*, 5(1), 1978, pp. 2–4.
48. Lauri Karvonen and Bengt Sundelius, *Internationalization and Foreign Policy Management* (Aldershot: Gower, 1987) pp. 1–16.
49. These arguments are rehearsed in Steve Smith, 'Foreign policy analysis and interdependence', in R.J. Barry Jones and P. Willetts, *Interdepen-*

dence on Trial: Studies in the Theory and Reality of Contemporary Interdependence (London: Pinter, 1984) pp. 64–82.
50. On the need to challenge what he terms 'the tenacious hold of state system ideology', see Chadwick F.Alger, 'Bridging the micro and the macro in international relations research', *Alternatives*, 10(3) 1984–5, pp. 320–2.
51. Joe D. Hagan, 'Regimes, political oppositions and comparative analysis of foreign policy', in Charles. F. Hermann, Charles W. Kegley Jr and James N. Rosenau (eds), *New Directions in the Study of Foreign Policy* (Boston: Allen and Unwin, 1987) pp. 339–65.
52. Simeon, *Federal–Provincial Diplomacy.*

2 Non-central Governments and Multilayered Diplomacy

1. Daniel Latouche, 'State building and foreign policy at the subnational level', in Ivo D. Duchacek, Daniel Latouche and Garth Stevenson (eds), *Perforated Sovereignties and International Relations*, (New York: Greenwood Press, 1988) p. 30.
2. Much of this descriptive material does, of course, provide valuable data. See, for example, Earl H. Fry, 'Trans-sovereign relations of the American states' in Duchacek *et al.*, *Perforated Sovereignties.*
3. Ivo D. Duchacek, 'Multicommunal and bicommunal politics and their international relations, in Duchacek *et al.*, *Perforated Sovereignties.*
4. Joel Garreau, *The Nine Nations of North America* (New York: Avon Books, 1981).
5. Gerard F. Rutan 'Micro-diplomatic relations in the Pacific Northwest: Washington State–British Columbia interactions, in Duchacek *et al.*, *Perforated Sovereignties*, p. 1987.
6. Martin Lubin, 'New England, New York and their Francophone neighbourhood', in Duchacek *et al.*, *Perforated Sovereignties*, p. 158.
7. James N. Rosenau, 'Patterned chaos in global life: structure and process in the two worlds of world politics', *International Political Science Review*, 9(4), October 1988.
8. Wolfram F. Hanrieder, 'Dissolving international politics: reflections on the nation-state', *American Political Science Review*, 72, December 1978.
9. Ernst-Otto Czempiel, 'Internationalizing politics: some answers to the questions of who does what to whom', in Ernst-Otto Czempiel and James N.Rosenau (eds), *Global Changes and Theoretical Challenges: Approaches to World Politics for the 1990s* (Lexington, Mass: Lexington Books, 1989).
10. Loc. cit.
11. Bayless Manning, 'The Congress, the executive and intermestic affairs', *Foreign Affairs*, 55, January 1977.
12. Helen M. Ingram and Suzanne L. Fiederlein, 'Traversing boundaries: a public policy approach to the analysis of foreign policy', *Western Political Quarterly*, 41(4), 1988.
13. Robert D. Putnam, 'Diplomacy and domestic politics: the logic of two-level games', *International Organization*, 42(3) 1988, p. 434.

14. On domestic coalition building see Steve Smith and Michael Clarke (eds), *Foreign Policy Implementation* (London: George Allen and Unwin, 1985).
15. Putnam, 'Diplomacy and domestic politics', p. 449.
16. Stephen P. Mumme, 'State influence in foreign policy-making: water related environmental disputes along the United States–Mexican border', *Political Quarterly*, 38(4), December 1985.
17. Stephen Greene and Thomas Keating, 'Domestic factors and Canada–United States fisheries relations', *Canadian Journal of Political Science*, 13(4), December 1980.
18. Gilbert R. Winham, 'International negotiation in an age of transition', *International Journal*, 35(1), Winter 1979–80.
19. I. William Zartman, 'Prenegotiation: phases and functions', *International Journal*, 44(2), Spring 1989, p. 245.
20. Hans J. Michelmann, 'The Federal Republic of Germany', in Hans J. Michelmann and Panayotis Soldatos (eds), *Federalism and International Relations: the Role of Subnational Units*, (Oxford: Clarendon Press, 1990) pp. 224–8. See also David Goodheart, 'For Lander, Brussels poses both threat and opportunity', *Financial Times*, 30 May 1989.
21. Charles F. Doran and Joel J. Sokolsky, *Canada and Congress:Lobbying in Washington* (Halifax: Centre for Foreign Policy Studies, Dalhousie University, 1985) pp. 1–15.
22. Bernard Simon, 'Foresters on the defensive', *Financial Times*, 10 January 1991.
23. Michael Keating, 'Introduction', in Michael Keating and Barry Jones (eds), *Regions in the European Community* (Oxford: Clarendon Press, 1985) p. 10.
24. The categories employed here are taken from Brian Hocking and Michael Smith, *World Politics: an Introduction to International Relations* (London: Harvester Wheatsheaf, 1990) pp. 72–6.
25. Ivo D. Duchacek, 'Perforated sovereignties: towards a typology of new actors in international relations', in Michelmann and Soldatos, *Federalism and International Relations*, p. 4.
26. Ibid., p. 5.
27. Harold W. Stoke, *The Foreign Relations of the Federal State* (Baltimore: Johns Hopkins Press, 1931).
28. Luzius Wildhaber, 'Switzerland', in Michelmann and Soldatos, *Federalism and International Relations*, p. 250.
29. Howard A. Leeson, *External Affairs and Canadian Federalism: the History of a Dilemma* (Toronto: Holt, Rinehart and Winston, 1973) pp. 61–3.
30. Michael Shuman, 'What the framers really said about foreign policy powers', *Intergovernmental Perspective*, vol. 16(2), Spring 1990; p. 30.
31. Loc. cit.
32. Peter J. Spiro, 'The limits of federalism in foreign policymaking', *Intergovernmental Perspective*, 16(2), Spring 1990, p. 34.
33. Michelmann, 'The Federal Republic of Germany', pp. 216–7.
34. Jean Holmes and Campbell Sharman, *The Australian Federal System* (Sydney: George Allen & Unwin, 1977) p. 114.

35. William M. Chandler, 'Challenges to federalism: comparative themes', in William M. Chandler and Christian W. Zollner (eds), *Challenges to Federalism: Policy-Making in Canada and the Federal Republic of Germany* (Kingston, Ontario: Institute of Intergovernmental Relations, Queen's University, 1986) p. 9.
36. Garth Stevenson, 'Western alienation in Australia and Canada', in Larry Pratt and Garth Stevenson (eds), *Western Separatism: the Myths, Realities and Dangers* (Edmonton: Hurtig, 1981) pp. 119–133.
37. Garth Stevenson, *Mineral Resources and Australian Federalism* (Canberra: Centre for Research on Federal Financial Relations, Australian National University, 1976) p. 10.
38. Brian Head, 'Economic development in state and federal politics', in Brian Head (ed.), *The Politics of Development in Australia* (Sydney: Allen and Unwin, 1986) pp. 22–4.
39. Hans Michelmann, 'Conclusion', in Michelmann and Soldatos, *Federalism and International Relations*, p. 307.
40. See the *Financial Times* article by Goodheart cited in note 20.
41. 'Basle and the Upper Rhine', *Financial Times Survey*, 21 November 1991.
42. Yves Lejeune, 'Belgium', in Michelmann and Soldatos, *Federalism and International Relations*, pp. 152–5.
43. Daniel Latouche, 'State building and foreign policy at the subnational level', in Duchacek, Latouche and Stevenson, *Perforated Sovereignties*, p. 34.
44. Loc. cit.
45. Kim Richard Nossal, '"Micro-diplomacy": the case of Ontario and economic sanctions against South Africa', in William M.Chandler and Christian W.Zollner (eds), *Challenges to Federalism: Policy-Making in Canada and the Federal Republic of Germany* (Kingston, Ontario: Institute of Intergovernmental Relations, Queen's University, 1986) pp. 235–7.
46. On this, see Hugh Tinker, *Race, Conflict and the International Order: from Empire to United Nations* (London: Macmillan, 1977).
47. Colin Tatz, *Race Politics in Australia: Aborigines, Politics and Law* (Armidale: University of New England Publishing Unit, 1979) pp. 100–101.
48. *Sydney Morning Herald*, 13 August 1980.
49. *Courier Mail* (Brisbane), 3 November 1981.
50. Hugh Collins, 'Aborigines and Australian foreign policy: some underlying issues', in Coral Bell *et al.*, *Ethnic Minorities and Australian Foreign Policy*, Canberra Studies in World Affairs No. 11 (Canberra, Department of International Relations, Australian National University, 1983) p. 56.
51. *The Age* (Melbourne), 25 April 1975.
52. *Sydney Morning Herald*, 29 September 1981.
53. *National Times*, 23 May 1982.
54. Interview on ABC radio news programme, A.M., 26 February 1980.
55. *Canberra Times*, 29 June 1980.
56. Collins, 'Aborigines and Australian foreign policy', p. 64.

57. *Canberra Times*, 9 September 1976.
58. *The Bulletin*, 11 May 1982.
59. *The Age* (Melbourne), 15 June 1982.
60. *Canberra Times*, 12 June 1982.
61. *The Age* (Melbourne), 22 June 1982.
62. ANZUS Council communique.
63. Jacob Bercovitch (ed.), *ANZUS in Crisis: Alliance Management in International Affairs* (London: Macmillan, 1988) pp. 1–2.
64. Ibid., p. 2.
65. Murray Goot and Peter King, 'ANZUS reconsidered: the domestic politics of an alliance', in Bercovitch, op. cit., pp. 110–13.
66. *The Sydney Morning Herald*, 28 January 1985, p. 1.
67. Loc. cit.
68. *The Australian*, 29 January 1985, p. 4.
69. *The Courier-Mail* (Brisbane), 30 January 1985, p. 1.
70. Interviews with Australian diplomats conducted by the author in the mid-1980s suggested that considerable effort had been devoted to dealing with this issue.

3 The Trade Agenda

1. California State World Trade Commission, 'Federal and State Cooperation in Promoting United States Exports: a View From California' (a special memorandum to the transition team of the forty-first President of the United States of America) (Sacramento, 9 November 1988).
2. Quoted in Joan E. Twiggs, *The Tokyo Round of Multilateral Trade Negotiations: a Case Study in Building Domestic Support for Diplomacy* (Lanham, MD: University Press of America, 1987) p. vii.
3. Joan Edelman Spero, *The Politics of International Economic Relations* (fourth edition) (London: Unwin Hyman, 1990) p. 67.
4. See John H. Jackson, Jean-Victor Louis and Mitsuo Matsushita, *Implementing the Tokyo Round: National Constitutions and International Economic Roles* (Ann Arbor: University of Michigan Press, 1984) pp. 206–7.
5. Robert B. Reich, *The Work of Nations: Preparing Ourselves for 21st-Century Capitalism* (New York: Knopf, 1991).
6. On the Australian submarine contract, see John Warhurst, Jenny Stewart and Brian Head, 'The promotion of industry', in Brian Galligan (ed.), *Comparative State Policies* (Melbourne: Longman Cheshire, 1988) pp. 211–13. The Canadian case is examined in Brian Hocking, 'Bringing the "outside" in: the role and nature of foreign interest lobbying', *Corruption and Reform*, 5, 1990, pp. 228–30.
7. See note 74 below.
8. 'Mulroney makes pitch for Japanese investment', *Globe and Mail*, 28 May 1991.
9. Peter Drysdale and Hirofumi Shibata, 'Perspectives', in, Peter Drysdale and Hirofumi Shibata (eds), *Federalism and Resource Development: the*

Australian Case (Sydney: Allen & Unwin in association with The Australia–Japan Research Centre, Australian National University, 1985) p. 15.

10. This has to be seen as part of the growing concern with economic development demonstrated by the US states in recent years. Analyses of this can be found in Peter Eisinger, *The Rise of the Entrepreneurial State: State and Local Economic Development Policy in the United States* (University of Wisconsin Press, 1988) and R. Scott Fosler, *The New Economic Role of American States: Strategies in a Competitive World Economy* (New York: Oxford University Press, 1988).
11. National Governors' Association, *America in Transition: the International Frontier; Report of the Task Force on Foreign Markets* (Washington, DC: 1989) p. iv.
12. Martin and Susan Tolchin, *Buying in to America: How Foreign Money is Changing the Face of Our Nation* (New York: Berkeley, 1989) p. 30.
13. California Economic Development Corporation, *Vision: California 2010, A Special Report to the Governor* (Sacramento, CA, March 1988) p. 11. The figures for Georgia are taken from Georgia, *Financial Times Survey*, 7 November 1988.
14. Government of Victoria, *Victoria: Trading on Achievement* (Melbourne: August 1988) p. 65; Ontario, Ministry of Industry, Trade and Technology, *The Competitive Advantage* (Toronto: 1989) p. 30.
15. National Association of State Development Agencies, *State Export Program Database, Fiscal Year 1987–1988* (Washington, DC) pp. 5–6.
16. Ontario Ministry of Industry Trade and Technology, *How to Export* (Toronto, 1985) p. 22.
17. NASDA, op. cit., p. 8.
18. California World Trade Commission, *Building Exports: a Six Year Track Record* (Sacramento: January 1989) p. 4
19. Ontario Ministry of Industry Trade and Technology, *How to Export* (Toronto, 1985) pp. 22–3.
20. Ibid., and Ontario Ministry of Industry, Trade and Technology, *Annual Report 1986–7* (Ontario, 1987).
21. Government of Victoria, *Victoria: Trading on Achievement* (Melbourne: August 1988) p. 60.
22. Loc. cit., p. 63.
23. Loc. cit., p. 62.
24. NASDA, op. cit., pp. 15–16.
25. A useful survey of provincial overseas representation is to be found in Alberta Federal and Intergovernmental Affairs, *Alberta International Offices: Report to the Alberta Legislature* (Edmonton: April 1991).
26. Paul V. Oliva, *State Overseas Operations: August 1988* (Sacramento, California State World Trade Commission, 1988) p. 2.
27. These functions are listed in a leaflet produced by British Columbia House entitled 'Canada's Opportunity Province'.
28. Ibid., p. 3.
29. Ontario Ministry of Industry, Trade and Technology, *Annual Report 1986–1987* (Toronto, 1987) p. 15.
30. Information provided by Victoria House, London, 1989.

31. Oliva, *State Overseas Operations*, p. 1.
32. John Lancaster, 'Assembly wage tug of war on governance', *Washington Post*, 14 January 1989, pp. B1, B5.
33. Blaine Liner, States and Localities in the Global Marketplace, *Intergovernmental Perspective*, 16(2), Spring 1990, p. 12.
34. Rose A. Horowitz, 'States face hurdles in united trade effort', *Journal of Commerce*, 26 July 1989.
35. Lee Walker, *Economic Development in the States, vol.2, The Changing Arena: State Strategic Economic Development* (Council of State Governments, 1989) p. 3.
36. E. Chaples, H. Nelson and K. Turner (eds), *The Wran Model* (Melbourne: Oxford University Press, 1985) p. 246; quoted in J. Warhurst, J. Stewart and B.Head 'The promotion of industry', in B. Galligan (ed.) *Comparative State Policies* (Melbourne: Longman Cheshire, 1988) p. 208.
37. This point is made by Hugh O'Neill, 'The role of the states in trade development', *Proceedings of the Academy of Political Science*, 37(4), 1990, p. 187.
38. Jonathan Kandell, 'US governors wooing foreign investors', *Wall Street Journal*, 15 December 1988, p. A14.
39. Chris Sherwell, 'Worldly Australian heads a mission to Europe', *Financial Times*, 6 October 1988, p. 3, and Rex Jory, 'SA may open up EC office', *The Advertiser* (Adelaide), 21 October 1988.
40. Committee for Review of Export Market Development Assistance, *Australian Exports: Performance, Obstacles and Issues of Assistance* (Canberra: Australian Government Publishing Service, July 1989) p. 53.
41. Susan C. Schwab, 'Building a national export development alliance', *Intergovernmental Perspective*, 16(2), Spring 1990, p. 20.
42. Interview, State of New York Department of Economic Development, London office, 25 April 1989.
43. Schwab, op. cit., p. 19.
44. National Governors' Association, *America in Transition: the International Frontier Report of the Task Force on Foreign Markets*, op. cit., p. 32.
45. Office of State Services, National Governors' Association, *Program Brief: International Trade* (Washington, DC: November 1986) p. 23.
46. Jerry Levine, *Going Global: a Strategy for Regional Cooperation* (Denver,Col.: Western Governors' Association, July 1989).
47. Quoted in Katherine Barrett and Richard Greene, 'Over there over there', *FW*, 17 April 1990, p. 44.
48. John Warhurst, Jenny Stewart and Brian Head, 'The promotion of industry', in Brian Galligan (ed.), *Comparative State Policies* (Melbourne: Longman Cheshire, 1988) p. 200.
49. Robert B. Reich, *The Work of Nations: Preparing Ourselves for 21st Century Capitalism* (New York: Knopf, 1991) pp. 295–6.
50. Norman J. Glickman and Douglas P. Woodward, *The New Competitors: How Foreign Investors are Changing the US Economy* (New York: Basic Books, 1989) Chapter 8.

51. See, for example, Brian Head, 'Economic development in state and federal politics', in Brian Head (ed.), *The Politics of Development in Australia* (Sydney: Allen and Unwin) pp. 38–43.
52. On this, see Dennis J. Encarnation and Louis T. Wells Jr, 'Sovereignty en garde: negotiating with foreign investors', *International Organization*, vol. 39(1), Winter 1985, pp. 47–78.
53. *Buying into America*, op. cit., pp. 40–1.
54. Head, 'Economic development in state and federal politics', op. cit., p. 40.
55. Greg Crough and Ted Wheelwright, *Australia: a Client State* (Ringwood, Vic.: Penguin, 1982).
56. Garth Stevenson, 'The control of foreign direct investment in a federation: Canadian and Australian experience', in R. M. Burns *et al.*, *Political and Administrative Federalism* (Research Monograph 14) (Canberra: Centre for Research on Federal Financial Relations, Australian National University, 1976) p. 40.
57. Ibid., pp. 54–6.
58. Hugh O'Neill, 'The role of the states in trade development', *Proceedings of the Academy of Political Science*, vol. 37(4), 1990, p. 188.
59. *Western Trade Objectives: Report of the Western Ministers Responsible for Multilateral Trade Negotiations to the Premiers of British Columbia, Alberta, Saskatchewan, Manitoba*, Western Premiers' Conference, Camrose, Alberta, June 27–8, 1989, p. 1.
60. Office of State Services, National Governors' Association, *Program Brief*, op. cit.; p. 4.
61. John Warhurst, *State Governments and Australian Tariff Policy* (Research Monograph No. 33) (Canberra: Centre for Research on Federal Financial Relations, Australian National University, 1980) pp. 78–81.
62. These structures are discussed in Chapters 4 and 7.
63. Interview, Department of Trade, Canberra, March 1987.
64. Interview, Multilateral Trade Division, Department of Trade, Canberra, April 1987.
65. However, Glezer's study of tariff politics assigns a far less significant role to the states than does Warhurst. See Leon Glezer, *Tariff Politics: Australian Policy Making 1960–1980* (Melbourne: Melbourne University Press, 1982) pp. 256–8; and Warhurst, op. cit., pp. 67–73.
66. Burlington & Associates Consulting Ltd in conjunction with officials of the Ministry of International Business and Immigration, *The Uruguay Round of Multilateral Trade Negotiations: British Columbia Consultations with the Private Sector: Executive Summary*, December 1988, p. 1.
67. See, for example, *The GATT and the Uruguay Round of Multilateral Trade Negotiations: a Guide for California Business* (Sacramento: California State World Trade Commission/California Council for International Trade, 1987).
68. California World Trade Commission, 'Key California industry voices trade concerns', *Newsletter*, Spring 1990, p. 1.

69. Information gathered from CACIT brochure and California World Trade Commission, *Report to the Legislature* (Sacramento: January 1988) p. 26.
70. Interview, Fisheries Division, Department of Primary Industry, Canberra, July 1984.
71. G. W. P. George, 'Linkage diplomacy and bilateral economic interdependence' (PhD thesis) (Canberra: Australian National University, 1981) pp. 188, 263.
72. Robert A. Rosenblatt, 'How "swat team" of Toshiba lobbyists took on Congress and won', *Washington Post*, 1 May 1988.
73. See I. M. Destler, *American Trade Politics: System under Stress* (Washington, DC: Institute for International Economics; New York: Twentieth Century Fund, 1986) particularly Chapter 10.
74. Roger Hill, 'An Ontario perspective on trade issues between Canada and the United States', in Deborah Fretz, Robert Stern and John Whalley, *Canada/United States Trade and Investment Issues* (Toronto: Ontario Economic Council, 1985) p. 486.
75. This – and other – incidents involving the Australian states and the conduct of foreign policy in the Whitlam period are discussed in Henry S. Albinski, 'Australian external policy, federalism and the states', *Political Science*, 28(1), July 1976, pp. 4–5.
76. Hill, 'An Ontario perspective', op. cit., p. 478.
77. Monica Langley, 'West Virginia senators hold divergent views of US trade problem', *Wall Street Journal*, 23 March 1987, pp. 1, 15.
78. Spero, op. cit., pp. 85–6.
79. Jon R. Johnson and Joel S. Schachter, *The Free Trade Agreement: a Comprehensive Guide* (Aurora, Ont.: Canada Law Book Inc., 1988) p. 85.
80. Warhurst, Stewart and Head, 'The promotion of industry', op. cit., p. 214. (See note 46.)
81. John M. Kline, *State Government Influence in U.S. International Economic Policy* (Lexington, Mass: Lexington Books, 1983) p. 88.
82. John H. Jackson, Jean-Victor Louis and Mitsuo Matsushita, *Implementing the Tokyo Round: National Constitutions and International Economic Rules* (Ann Arbor: University of Michigan Press, 1984) p. 144.
83. Interview, Department of Trade, Canberra, July 1984.
84. Penelope Lemov, 'Europe and the States: free trade but no free lunch', *Governing*, January 1991, p. 51. See also Brandon Roberts, 'EC 1992: opportunities and challenges for state and local governments', *Government Finance Review*, December 1990.
85. The background is set out in the report of the GATT panel which considered the case brought by the EC against Canada. See The Contracting Parties to the General Agreement on Tariffs and Trade, 'Canada – Import, Distribution and Sale of Alcoholic Drinks by Canadian Provincial Marketing Agencies', *Report of the Panel adopted on 22 March 1988 (L/6304)*, in GATT, *Basic Instruments and Selected Documents, Thirty-fifth Supplement, Protocols, Decisions, Reports 1987–1988* (Geneva, June 1989) pp. 37–41.

86. Christopher Waddell, 'GATT finds provincial liquor policies violate trade rules', *Globe and Mail*, 6 November 1987, pp. A1, A2.
87. GATT, 'Disputes taken up in the Council', *GATT Activities 1988* (Geneva: June 1989) pp. 61–2.
88. John Kohut, 'Deal is reached on beer, wine by Canada, EC', *Globe and Mail*, 21 December 1988.
89. Philip DeMont, 'There's trouble brewing on the American Front', *Financial Times* (Canada), 21 March 1988.
90. Peter Hadekel, 'Trade negotiators have staggering task ahead', *The Gazette* (Montreal), 5 March 1988, p. C1.
91. 'Peterson derides negotiators in EC talks', *Globe and Mail*, 17 December 1991.
92. Christopher Waddell, 'Ottawa and provinces to plot strategy for next EC round on wine, beer sales', *Globe and Mail*, 18 February 1988, p. B12.
93. Interview, Trade Policy Group, Department of External Affairs, Ottawa, November 1988.
94. Alan Story, 'Wine deal may not suit everyone's palate', *Toronto Star*, 19 March 1989.
95. This classification of local sanctions was developed by the American Legislative Exchange Council. See 'The divestiture debates: American states and South Africa', *State Policy Reports*, 3(16) August 1985, p. 3.
96. This is discussed in Janice Love, *The U.S. Anti-Apartheid Movement: Local Activism in Global Politics* (New York: Praegar, 1985) and Peter J. Spiro, 'Taking foreign policy away from the Feds', *Washington Quarterly*, Winter 1988. The constitutional aspects of divestment policies are discussed in Kevin P. Lewis, 'Dealing with South Africa: the constitutionality of state and local divestment legislation', *Tulane Law Review*, 61(3), February 1987.
97. Richard B. Bilder, 'The role of states and cities in foreign relations', *American Journal of International Law*, 83, 1989, p. 822.
98. Janet Bush, 'Pressure over jobs in Ulster', *Financial Times*, 24 February 1989.
99. The issues are reviewed in 'The divestiture debates', *State Policy Reports*, op. cit., pp. 5–6. (See note 87.)
100. Peter J. Spiro, 'State and local anti-South Africa action', *Virginia Law Review*, 72, May 1986, p. 825.
101. Ibid., p. 827.
102. Interview, British Embassy, Washington, September 1989.
103. *The Economist*, 'Fear of foreigners', 10 August 1991, p. 23.

4 Multilayered Diplomacy and Free Trade

1. Gilbert R. Winham, *Trading with Canada: the Canada–US Free Trade Agreement* (New York: Priority Press, 1988).
2. Brian W. Tomlin, 'The stages of prenegotiation: the decision to negotiate North American Free Trade', *International Journal*, 44(2), Spring 1989.
3. F. Harrison, 'US expected to take tough stand with Canada on talk of free trade', *Financial Post*, 9 March 1985.

4. Winham, *Trading with Canada*, op. cit., p. 27.
5. See Ronald A. Shearer, 'Regionalism and international trade policy', in John Whalley, *Canada–United States Free Trade* (Toronto: University of Toronto Press, 1985) pp. 326–35.
6. On this see David Conklin, 'Options for new international agreements: an overview', in David W. Conklin and Thomas J. Courchene, *Canadian Trade at a Crossroads: Options for New International Agreements*, (Toronto: Ontario Economic Council, 1985) pp. 6–9; also references in note 67 below.
7. I. M. Destler, 'United States trade policy making in the Uruguay Round', in Nau, op. cit., pp. 191–207.
8. Information on this is provided in Pilcher and Proffer, op. cit; see note 5.
9. The CWTC has produced a good deal of impressive documentation on trade policy issues. Amongst these are California World Trade Commission and California Council for International Trade, *The GATT and the Uruguay Round of Multilateral Trade Negotiations: A Guide for California Business* (Sacramento: 1987).
10. Interview at the office of the United States Trade Representative, Washington DC, September 1989.
11. Interview at the Ministry of Business and Immigration, Victoria, BC, September 1989.
12. John F. Ontko, 'Canada–US trade: Economic revolution is brewing', *State Government News*, June 1987, p. 13.
13. Charles F. Doran, *Forgotten Partnership: US–Canada Relations Today* (Toronto: Fitzhenry & Whiteside, 1984) p. 141.
14. I. William Zartman, 'Prenegotiation: phases and functions', *International Journal*, 44(2), Spring 1989.
15. Tomlin, op. cit.
16. C. Goar, 'Glossing over the costs and benefits of free trade', *Toronto Star*, 31 January 1985.
17. D. Martin, 'Canada's great trade debate', *New York Times*, 23 January 1985.
18. F. Harrison, 'Unease over US trade relations as Brock goes', *Financial Post*, 30 March 1985.
19. Ross Laver *et al.*, 'Free talk', *Maclean's*, 98(37), 16 September 1985.
20. 'Free trade without debate', editorial, *Toronto Star*, 27 September 1985.
21. C. D. Howe Institute, 'Closing a trade deal: the provinces' role', *Commentary*, 11 August 1986, p. 5.
22. D. Stewart-Patterson, 'Manitoba wants exclusions on trade talks with US', *Globe and Mail*, 28 October 1985.
23. D. Crane, 'How free trade has the West thinking twice', *Toronto Star*, 3 August 1985.
24. M. Cohen, 'Some important lessons for Canadian, US negotiators', *The Citizen*, Ottawa, 16 January 1986.
25. Changes to the trade policy machinery are discussed in W. R. Hines, *Trade Policy Making in Canada: Are We Doing it Right?* (Montreal: Institute for Research on Public Policy, 1985).
26. R. Howard, 'Barriers between provinces obstacles in free trade talks', *Globe and Mail*, 17 February 1986.

27. See M. Clark, 'The softwood factor', *Maclean's*, 99(18), 5 May 1986, and F. Harrison, 'US senator tough on timber issues', *Financial Post*, 9 November 1985. A brief survey of Canada and US trade frictions can be found in E. A. Carmichael, 'High stakes: a Canadian–US trade agreement', *Reorientating the Canadian Economy* (Toronto: C. D. Howe Institute, 1985).
28. During interviews conducted in April 1986, officials in the Trade Negotiations Office claimed that events had unfolded as expected; representatives of the Canadian Chamber of Commerce suggested, however, that Ottawa had put too much faith in Yeutter and had not adequately consulted congressional opinion.
29. Interview, Ministry of Business and Immigration, Victoria, September 1989.
30. Gordon Ritchie, 'The negotiating process', in John Crispo (ed.), *Free Trade: the Real Story* (Toronto: Gage, 1988) p. 18.
31. Interview, Trade Negotiation Office, Ottawa, November 1988.
32. Interview, Ministry of Industry Technology and Trade, Ontario, November 1988.
33. On the relationships within the Canadian federal bureaucracy during the negotiations see Bruce H. Fisher, 'The federal bureaucracy and free trade', *International Insights*, A(1), Spring 1988.
34. A typical example of the kind of discussion that occurred can be seen when Clayton Yeutter testified before the Senate Finance Committee in April 1986. See *Negotiation of United States–Canada Free Trade Agreement* hearings before the Committee on Finance, United States Senate, Ninety-ninth Congress, 11 April 1986 (Washington DC: US Government Printing Office) pp. 44–56.
35. On the softwood lumber issue see David Leyton-Brown, 'The political economy of Canada–US relations', in Brian W. Tomlin and Maureen Appel Molot, *Canada Among Nations 1986: Talking Trade* (Toronto: Lorimer, 1987) pp. 158–61.
36. David Leyton-Brown, 'The softwood lumber dispute', paper prepared for the 1988 Pearson-Dickey Conference on *Federalism and Regional Politics: Challenges to American Canadian Diplomacy*, Dartmouth College, Hanover New Hampshire, 10–12 November 1988.
37. Leyton-Brown, 'The political economy of Canada–US relations', op. cit., p. 160.
38. Amongst the many discussions of the constitutional position see R. E. Sullivan, 'Jurisdiction to negotiate and implement free trade agreements in Canada: calling the provincial bluff', *University of Western Ontario Law Review*, vol. 24(z), 1987 and Marilyn L. Pilkington, 'Free trade and constitutional jurisdiction' in Mark Gold and David Leyton Brown, *Trade-Offs on Free Trade: the Canada–US Free Trade Agreement* (Toronto: Carswell 1988) pp. 92–9.
39. Mary Janigan *et al.*, 'Going public on trade', *Maclean's*, 23 March 1987.
40. Christopher Waddell, 'First ministers' talks to open critical week for free trade', *Globe and Mail*, 11 March 1987.
41. Alan Christie, 'Ontario ready to stand alone on free trade, Peterson says', *Toronto Star*, 14 September 1987.

42. Ian Austen, 'Dealing with Congress' *Maclean's*, 6 April 1987.
43. Mary Janigan *et al.*, 'The big red wave', *Maclean's*, 21 September 1987.
44. 'Free trade key to economic salvation, Bourassa says', *Toronto Star*, 14 September 1987.
45. Alan Christie *et al.*, 'Premiers split over whether talks are dead', *Toronto Star*, 24 September 1987.
46. Martin Cohn, 'Mulroney briefs premiers on state of trade talks', *Toronto Star*, 2 October 1987.
47. Derek Ferguson, 'Provinces could scuttle free trade, expert says', *Toronto Star*, 28 October 1987.
48. Bertrand Marotte, 'Bourassa wiling to help PM sell agreement to Canadians', *Globe and Mail*, 8 October 1987.
49. Rosemary Speirs, 'Trade pact has Peterson in tight spot', *Toronto Star*, 10 October 1987.
50. Mark Kennedy, 'Peterson plans hearings to our trade-deal flaws', *Ottawa Citizen*, 9 October 1987.
51. Deborah Dowling, 'Premiers horse trading on free trade', *Ottawa Citizen* 28 November 1987.
52. Lauren S. McKinsey, 'Federalism and regional politics: challenges to American–Canadian Diplomacy', Paper prepared for the 1988 Pearson-Dickey Conference on *Federalism and Regional Politics: Challenges to American–Canadian Diplomacy*, Dartmouth College, Hanover, New Hampshire, 10–12 November 1988, p. 9.
53. 49th Parallel Institute for Canadian–American Relations, *US–Canada Free Trade: a Western Regional Perspective* (Bozeman: Montana State University, 1988).
54. Ibid., p. 127.
55. Interview, Trade Negotiations Office, Ottawa, November 1988.
56. John F. Burns, 'Ontario Defiance threatens Canada–US pact on trade', *New York Times*, 18 May 1988.
57. Interview, Office of the Western Governors' Association, Washington, DC, September 1989.
58. Elliot J. Feldman and Nels Ackerson 'The Auto pact is a mountain that must move', *Globe and Mail*, 18 June 1987.
59. Clyde H. Farnsworth, 'House backs accord with Canada', *New York Times*, 10 August 1988.
60. Interview, Ministry of Business and Immigration, Victoria, BC, September 1989.
61. Interview Office of the United States Trade Representative, Washington, DC, September 1989.
62. Interview, California World Trade Commission, Sacramento, August 1989.
63. Interview, Office of the United States Trade Representative, Washington, DC, September 1989.
64. Robert Fife and Gord McIntosh, 'B.C.'s behind-the-back meddling hurt softwood strategy, officials say', *Toronto Star*, 9 January 1987.
65. 49th Parallel Institute, op. cit., p. 127.
66. William Walker, 'US protectionists distorting trade figures, Peterson says', *Toronto Star*, 29 July 1988.

67. 49th Parallel Institute, loc. cit.
68. Ibid.
69. Ritchie, op. cit., pp. 19–20.
70. C. Michael Aho, 'A US perspective', in Crispo, op. cit., p. 182.
71. *Negotiations of United States–Canada Free Trade Agreement* hearings before the Committee on Finance, United States Senate, op. cit., p. 140.

5 British Industry versus US State Governments

1. John M. Kline, *State Government Influence in US International Economic Policy* (Lexington, Mass: Lexington Books) Chapter 8.
2. Kline, loc. cit.
3. John Symons, 'An unjust tax exposed', *BAT Industries Outlook*, 2, December 1984, p. 6.
4. Chung-In Moon, 'Complex interdependence and transnational lobbying: South Korea in the United States', *International Studies Quarterly*, 32(1) 1988, pp. 68–73.
5. Interview with Peter Welch, London, 1989.
6. Interview, British Embassy,Washington DC, 1989.
7. UTC files.
8. UTC files.
9. UTC files.
10. Interview with Peter Welch
11. Memo of meeting between Peter Welch and Keidanren representative, 19 March 1985, UTC files.
12. Minutes of a UTC strategy meeting in October 1984 record the decision to liaise more closely with UNICE.
13. Telephone interview, EC Delegation, Washington DC, 1989.
14. UTC files.
15. UTC files, letter from General Tax Counsel, Esso to Peter Welch, September 1985.
16. Revell Communications, *Agency Resume*, p. 3 (Sacramento, undated).
17. A helpful overview of these operations in the Californian theatre can be found in Cris Oppenheimer, 'The battle over the unitary tax', *San José Mercury News*, 2 September 1985, pp. 1, 4D.
18. UTC files, Steering Group meetings, 24 May 1984 and 4 October 1984.
19. UTC files, UNICE; letter from Richard E. Ratcliff, Applied Strategies, to Neil H. Green, Nestlé Holdings, chairman of OFTII.
20. UTC files, letter from Economic Counsellor, British Embassy.
21. The information in the following section is based on various UTC files and interviews conducted with UTC representatives and lobbyists in Washington and Sacramento.
22. Interview, National Governors' Association, Washington, DC, September 1989.
23. Martin and Susan Tolchin, *Buying into America: How Foreign Money is Changing the Face of Our Nation* (New York: Berkeley Books, 1989) p. 100.

24. California Business Council/Revell Communications, *Unitary Tax Primer* (Sacramento: February 1985) p. 25.
25. Tolchin, op. cit., pp. 112–14.
26. Interview, Washington DC, May 1989.

6 The Environmental Agenda

1. On the environmental dimension of environmental politics see Jim MacNeill, 'The greening of world politics', *International Journal*, 45(1), Winter 1989–90.
2. Evan Luard, *The Globalization of Politics: the Changed Focus of Political Action in the Modern World* (London: Macmillan, 1990) p. 12.
3. Robert Boardman, *Global Regimes and Nation States: Environmental Issues in Australian Politics* (Ottawa: Carleton University Press, 1990) p. 2.
4. Ibid., p. 200.
5. Bruce Driver and Elizabeth Nixon, *Healing the Environment: State Options for Addressing Global Warming* (Washington: Center for Clean Air Policy, 1989).
6. Boardman, *Global Regimes*, pp. 51–5, 141–5.
7. M. Seccombe, 'States torpedoing federal heritage plans in Unesco', *Sydney Morning Herald*, 23 December 1987.
8. 'Pollution now threatens states' rights', *Australian Financial Review*, 24 May 1989.
9. Fitzhugh Green, 'Acid rain and US–Canadian relations', *Washington Quarterly*, 9(3) Summer 1986, p. 103.
10. Roy Gould, *Going Sour: Science and Politics of Acid Rain* (Boston: Birkhauser, 1985) p. 10.
11. Rachel Carson, *Silent Spring* (London: Hamish Hamilton, 1963).
12. On the international legal aspects of acid rain, see Jeffrey Maclure, 'North American acid rain and international law', *Fletcher Forum*, 7, Winter 1983.
13. John McCormick, *Acid Earth: The Global threat of Acid Pollution* (2nd edn) (London: Earthscan, 1989) pp. 23–4.
14. James L. Regens and Robert W. Rycroft, *The Acid Rain Controversy* (University of Pittsburgh Press, 1988) p. 51.
15. Green, 'Acid rain', loc. cit.
16. Stephen Clarkson, *Canada and the Reagan Challenge: Crisis and Adjustment 1981–85* (Toronto: Lorimer 1985) Chapter 8.
17. Don Munton, 'Conflict over common property: Canada–US environmental issues', in M.A. Molot and B.W. Tomlin, *Canada Among Nations, 1987: A World of Conflict* (Toronto: Lorimer, 1985).
18. On this see Charles F. Doran, *Forgotten Partnership: US–Canada Relations Today* (Toronto: Fitzhenry and Whiteside, 1984).
19. John Roberts 'The diplomacy of acid rain: the North American experience in global perspective', in A.K. Henrikson (ed.), *Negotiating World Order: the Artisanship and Architecture of Global Diplomacy* (Wilmington, Del: Scholarly Resources, 1986) p. 22.
20. Doran, *Forgotten Partnership*, p. 188.

21. John E. Carroll, *Acid Rain: an Issue in Canadian–American Relations* (Toronto: C. D. Howe Institute, Washington: National Planning Association, 1982) p. 21.
22. In addition to the sources cited above, the ensuing discussion is based on interviews conducted by the author in 1988 and 1989 and on the the following sources: John E. Carroll, *Environmental Diplomacy* (Ann Arbor, University of Michigan Press, 1983); Helen M. Ingram and R. Kenneth Godwin (eds), *Public Policy and the Natural Environment* (Greenwich, Conn: JAI Press, 1985); Chris C. Park, *Acid Rain: Rhetoric and Reality* (London: Methuen, 1987); Jurgen Schmandt and Hilliard Roderick (eds), *Acid Rain and Friendly Neighbours: the Policy Dispute Between Canada and the US* (Durham, NC: Duke University Press, 1985).
23. Carroll, *Acid Rain*, (1982), pp. 38 ff.
24. McCormick, *Acid Earth*, p. 149
25. Gould, *Going Sour*, pp. 119–20.
26. Peter L. McKenna, 'Where has the acid rain gone?', *International Insights*, 1(1) Spring 1985, p. 136.
27. Ross Howard and Jennifer Lewington, 'US says it must end own acid rain first', *Globe and Mail*, 8 February 1989.
28. Ross Howard, 'Acid rain plan hailed as "major breakthrough"', *Globe and Mail*, 13 June 1989.
29. Schmandt and Roderick, *Acid Rain*, p. 94.
30. Carroll, *Acid Rain*, p. 17.
31. Carroll, *Environmental Diplomacy*, p. 29.
32. Nancy M. Davis, 'Acid Rain: no truce is in sight in the eight-year war between the states', *Governing*, 2(3), December 1988.
33. James L. Regens, 'The political economy of acid rain', *Publius*, vol. 15, Summer 1985, p. 59.
34. Jennifer Lewington and Susan Delacourt, 'Acid rain bill introduced by political coalition in US', *Globe and Mail*, 17 March 1989.
35. On state–provincial interactions, see Roger F. Swanson, *Intergovernmental Perspectives on the Canada–US Relationship* (New York: New York University Press, 1978).
36. Andrew Morris, 'Supporting structures for resolving environmental disputes among friendly neighbours' in Schmandt and Roderick (eds), *Acid Rain*, pp. 236–7.
37. Tom Albin and Steve Paulson, 'Environmental and economic interests in Canada and the US', in Schmandt and Roderick (eds), *Acid Rain*, p. 165.
38. Robert Egal, 'Canada's acid rain policy: federal and provincial roles', Schmandt and Roderick (eds), *Acid Rain*, pp. 102–3.
39. David Israelson, 'Ontario, Ottowa to sign acid rain cleanup pact', *Toronto Star*, 7 March 1987.
40. 'Signing of provincial pacts first break in acid rain battle', *Globe and Mail*, 10 March 1987.
41. Interview, US Transboundary Division, Department of External Affairs, Ottowa, November 1988.
42. Morris, 'Supporting structures', pp. 241–2.
43. Interview, Department of External Affairs, Ottawa 1989.

44. David Israelson, 'Ontario takes acid rain message to US', *Toronto Star*, 28 January 1987.
45. Egel, 'Canada's acid rain policy', p. 113.
46. 'US–Canada to meet on acid rain issues', *Boston Globe*, 11 April 1985, and Graham Fraser, 'Plan to fight acid rain ready for June', *Globe and Mail*, 13 April 1985.
47. Morris, 'Supporting structures', pp. 213–23.
48. Christie McLaren, 'Ontario joins states in court fight on acid rain', *Globe and Mail*, 24 February 1987.
49. Charles F. Doran and Joel J. Sokolsky, *Canada and Congress: Lobbying in Washington* (Halifax, NS: Centre for Foreign Policy Studies, Dalhousie University, 1985), p. 165.
50. 'Congressman attacks lobbying over acid rain', *Globe and Mail*, 7 October 1987.
51. David Israelson, 'Ontario takes acid rain message to US', *Toronto Star*, 28 January 1987.
52. Jennifer Lewington, 'Canadian acid rain lobby accused of aiming to boost power exports', *Globe and Mail*, 16 February 1987.
53. At least one observer of the 1985 Quebec provincial–state acid rain conference seems to have regarded it as an example of this trend. See the comments of Elliot Feldman as reported by Grahame Fraser, 'New approval greets provincial foreign links', *Globe and Mail*, 6 April 1985.

7 Managing Multilayered Diplomacy

1. An instance of this line of argument can be found in Peter J. Spiro, 'The limits of federalism in foreign policymaking', *Intergovernmental Perspective*, 16(2), Spring 1990.
2. Spiro, op. cit., p. 34.
3. See, for example, Ronald L. Watts, *Administration in Federal Systems* (London: Hutchinson, 1970).
4. Wayne Goss, 'Advancing the international interests of the states', *World Review*, 30(2), June 1991, p. 40.
5. National Governors' Association, *Infoletter*, 1 May 1989.
6. Susan C. Schwab, 'Building a national export development alliance', *Intergovernmental Perspective*, 16(2), Spring 1990, p. 19.
7. For a summary of the arguments relating to bureaucratization of the foreign policy process, see Lloyd Jensen, *Explaining Foreign Policy* (Englewood Cliffs, NJ: Prentice-Hall, 1982) pp. 121–9.
8. Arild Underdal, 'What's left for the MFA? Foreign policy and the management of external relations in Norway', *Cooperation and Conflict*, 22(3), 1987, p. 188.
9. David Dyment, 'Substate para-diplomacy: the international activities of non-sovereign governments: the case of Ontario', Conference of the Canadian Political Science Association, University of Victoria, British Columbia, May 1990; p. 14.
10. Interview, California Trade and Investment Office, London, September 1989.

11. Robert Boardman, *Global Regimes and Nation-States: Environmental Issues in Australian Politics* (Ottawa: Carleton University Press, 1990) and Robert Boardman, 'Approaching regimes: Australia, Canada, and environmental policy', *Australian Journal of Political Science*, 26(3), 1991, pp. 446-71.
12. Boardman, *Global Regimes*, pp. 128–9.
13. Schwab, 'Building a national export development alliance', pp. 19–20.
14. Interview, Department of Commerce, Washington, DC, September 1989.
15. Ibid.
16. The following discussion is based on the survey by Hans J. Michelmann, 'The Federal Republic of Germany', in Hans J. Michelmann and Panayotis Soldatos (eds), *Federalism and International Relations: the Role of Subnational Units* (Oxford: Clarendon Press, 1990) pp. 219–21.
17. Ibid., p. 221.
18. Interview, Attorney-General's Department, Canberra, July 1984.
19. See Henry Burmester, 'Federalism, the states and international affairs: a legal perspective', in Brian Galligan (ed.), *Australian Federalism* (Melbourne: Longman Cheshire, 1989) pp. 208–9.
20. Communique, Special Premiers' Conference, Sydney, 30–31 July 1991, p. 37.
21. Interview, Office of the US Special Trade Representative, Washington, DC, September 1989.
22. G. R. Winham, 'Bureaucratic politics and Canadian negotiation', *International Journal* 34(1) Winter 1978–9, p. 73
23. Ibid., p. 76.
24. Interview, Department of Trade, Canberra, March 1987.
25. Interview, International Economic Relations Branch, British Columbia, July 1984.
26. Information provided during interviews in Department of Trade and Resources, and Department of Industry and Commerce, July 1983.
27. Interview, New Zealand High Commission, Canberra, August 1983.
28. Ibid.
29. David Lague, 'Government, industry join in export booster', *Australian Financial Review*, 29 November 1991; 'Tiers of government unite on trade', *Canberra Times*, 29 November 1991.
30. Guy McKanna, 'Governments trial new trade strategy', *Australian Financial Review*, 1 November 1991.
31. Winham, 'Bureaucratic politics', op. cit., p. 78.
32. See Chapter 4 on the consultative processes.
33. M. Cohen, 'Some important lessons for Canadian, US negotiators', *The Citizen*, Ottawa, 16 January 1986.
34. Interview, Trade Policy Group, Department of External Affairs, Ottawa, November 1988.
35. Department of Foreign Affairs and Trade, *News Release*, D51, Canberra, 7 December 1989.
36. Department of Foreign Affairs and Trade, *News Release*, D62, Canberra, 13 August 1991.
37. Interview, Department of Fisheries, Hobart, July 1983.

38. Interview, Fisheries Division of Department of Primary Industry, Canberra, July 1983.
39. Interviews; California State World Trade Commission, Governor's Office, Washington DC, and Office of the US Trade Representative, Washington, DC, September 1989.
40. Interview, International Relations Division, Ministry of Intergovernmental Affairs, Toronto, November 1988.
41. Lauri Karvonen and Bengt Sundelius, 'Interdependence and foreign policy management in Sweden and Finland', *International Studies Quarterly*, 34, 1990, pp. 222–3.
42. Yves Mény, 'French regions in the European Community', in Michael Keating and Barry Jones (eds), *Regions in the European Community* (Oxford: Clarendon Press, 1985) p. 202.
43. Loc. cit.
44. Yves Lejeune, 'Belgium', in Michelmann and Soldatos (eds), *Federalism and International Relations*, pp. 148, 162–7.
45. Interview, Department of External Affairs, Ottawa, May 1984.
46. Interview, Intergovernmental Affairs section, Department of State, Washington, DC, May 1990.
47. Information gathered from interviews held with SFARs in Melbourne, Sydney, Brisbane and Perth between 1983 and 1986.
48. Lauri Karvonen and Bengt Sundelius, *Internationalization and Foreign Policy Management* (Aldershot: Gower, 1987) p. 11.
49. Raymond F. Hopkins, 'The international role of 'domestic' bureaucracy', *International Organization*, 30, 1976.

8 Conclusion

1. K.C. Wheare, *Federal Government* (Oxford University Press, 1963) p. 186.
2. Herman Bakvis, *Federalism and the Organization of Political Life: Canada in Comparative Perspective* (Kingston, Ontario: Institute of Intergovernmental Relations, Queen's University, 1981) p. 10.

Bibliography

INTRODUCTION

This bibliography comprises the main sources used in preparing the book. As noted in the Introduction, much of the information has been gathered through interviews and these are cited in the notes to each chapter. In the case of Chapter 5, dealing with the unitary taxation case, the discussion relies very heavily on interviews supplemented by the files of the Unitary Tax Campaign in London. In all the case studies, newspaper and periodical articles formed an important element in the investigation; again these are referred to in the chapter notes are and not listed here.

As suggested in Chapters 1 and 2, there is a growing literature on the international activities of subnational governments. These are listed below, but it will be helpful to readers to indicate briefly the main contributions to the discussion. Firstly, there is a very useful annotated bibliography covering the mutual interactions between the US states, Canadian provinces and the international economy: Dwight Herperger, *States and Provinces in the International Economy: a Bibliographic Review* (Kingston, Ontario: Institute of Intergovernmental Relations, Queen's University, 1989).

One of the few full-length studies of the involvement of non-central governments in foreign economic policy is to be found in John E. Kline, *State Government Influence in US International Economic Policy* (Lexington, Mass: Lexington Books, 1983). In addition, there are a number of collections of papers on various aspects of the theme. Taking them in order of publication, they include a collection of articles published in the American journal devoted to federalism, *Publius*, vol. 14(4), Fall 1984. Two years later, the journal of the Canadian Institute of International Affairs, *International Journal*, vol. 41(3), Summer 1986, focused on the theme 'Foreign Policy in Federal States'. The latter has a broader geographical focus and a more issue-oriented approach. As its title suggests, the next collection to appear was concerned with the contacts between NCGs in different nation-states: Ivo. D.Duchacek, Daniel Latouche and Garth Stevenson (eds), *Perforated Sovereignties: Trans-Sovereign Contacts of Subnational Governments* (New York: Greenwood Press, 1988). As with much of the literature, there is a strong North American emphasis here, but it is supplemented by some European material.

A much broader survey is to be found in Hans J. Michelmann and Panayotis Soldatos (eds), *Federalism and International Relations* (Clarendon Press: Oxford, 1990). Alongside some useful analytical articles, the volume covers the major federal systems with contributors varying in their approach but frequently adopting a legal–constitutional perspective. Finally, there is a collection of papers given at a conference in Australia House, London in March 1992, to be published by Leicester University Press in 1993: Brian Hocking (ed.), *Managing Foreign Relations in Federal States* (Leicester University Press, forthcoming). Here, the aim is to focus more on the policy processes and to look at the impact of NCG international activity on the management of foreign relations.

AHO, C. MICHAEL (1988) 'A U.S. perspective', in John Crispo (ed.) *Free Trade: the Real Story*, Toronto: Gage.

ALBERTA, FEDERAL AND INTERGOVERNMENTAL AFFAIRS (1991) *Alberta International Offices: Report to the Alberta Legislature*, Edmonton, April.

ALBINSKI, HENRY S. (1976) 'Australian external policy, federalism and the states', *Political Science*, 28(1), July.

ALBINSKI, HENRY S. (1977) *Australian External Policy Under Labor: Content, Process and the National Debate,* St.Lucia: University of Queensland Press.

ALGER, CHADWICK F. (1978) 'Local, national and global politics in the world: a challenge to international studies', *International Studies Notes of the International Studies Association*, 5(1).

ALGER, CHADWICK F. (1984–5) 'Bridging the micro and the macro in international relations research', *Alternatives* 10(3).

ALGER, CHADWICK F. (1988) 'Perceiving, analysing and coping with the local-global nexus' *International Social Science Journal*, 117, August.

ALGER, CHADWICK F. and MENDLOVITZ, SAUL H. (1987) 'Grass roots initiatives and the challenge of linkages', in Saul. H. Mendlovitz, and R. B. J. Walker, (eds), *Towards a Just World Peace: Perspectives from Social Movements*, London: Butterworths.

ATKEY, RONALD G. (1970–71) 'The role of the provinces in international affairs', *International Journal*, 26.

BARROWS, DAVID and BOUDREAU, MARK (1987) 'The evolving role of the provinces in international trade negotiations', in Allan M. Maslove and Stanley M. Winer, *Knocking on the Back Door: Canadian Perspectives on the Political Economy of Freer Trade with the United States*, Halifax, Nova Scotia: Institute for Research on Public policy.

BERCOVITCH, JACOB (ed.) (1988) *ANZUS in Crisis: Alliance Management in International Affairs*, London: Macmillan.

BERNIER, IVAN (1973) *International Legal Aspects of Federalism*, London: Longman.

BILDER, RICHARD B. (1989) 'The role of states and cities in foreign relations', *American Journal of International Law*, 83.

BOARDMAN, ROBERT (1990) *Global Regimes and Nation States: Environmental Issues in Australian Politics*, Ottawa: Carleton University Press.

BOARDMAN, ROBERT (1990) 'Approaching regimes: Australia, Canada, and environmental policy', *Australian Journal of Political Science* 26(3), November.

BROWN, DOUGLAS M. (1989) 'Canadian federalism and trade policy: the Uruguay Round agenda', in Ronald L.Watts and Douglas M.Brown (eds), *Canada: the State of the Federation 1989*, Kingston, Ontario: Institute of Intergovernmental Relations, Queen's University.

BROWN, SEYOM (1988) *New Forces, Old Forces and the Future of World Politics*, Glenview, Ill.: Scott Foresman.

BULMER, SIMON and PATERSON, WILLIAM (1988) *The Federal Republic of Germany and the European Community*, London: Allen and Unwin.

BURLINGTON & ASSOCIATES CONSULTING LTD (1988) in conjunction with officials of the Ministry of International Business and Immigration, *The Uruguay Round of Multilateral Trade Negotiations: British Columbia Consultations with the Private Sector: Executive Summary*, December.

BURMESTER, HENRY (1989) 'Federalism, the states and international affairs: a legal perspective', in Brian Galligan (ed.) *Australian Federalism*, Melbourne: Longman Cheshire.

CALIFORNIA BUSINESS COUNCIL/REVELL COMMUNICATIONS (1985) *Unitary Tax Primer*, Sacramento: February.

CALIFORNIA ECONOMIC DEVELOPMENT CORPORATION (1988) *Vision: California 2010, A Special Report to the Governor*, Sacramento: Cal.: March.

CALIFORNIA STATE WORLD TRADE COMMISSION (1988) *'Federal and State Cooperation in Promoting United States Exports: a View From California' (a special memorandum to the transition team of the forty-first president of the United States of America)*, Sacramento: 9 November.

CALIFORNIA WORLD TRADE COMMISSION and CALIFORNIA COUNCIL FOR INTERNATIONAL TRADE (1987) *The GATT and the Uruguay Round of Multilateral Trade Negotiations: A Guide for California Business*, Sacramento.

CALIFORNIA WORLD TRADE COMMISSION (1988) *Report to the Legislature*, Sacramento: January.

CALIFORNIA WORLD TRADE COMMISSION (1989) *Building Exports: a Six Year Track Record*, Sacramento: January.

CAPUTO, DAVID A. (1986) 'Political, social, and economic aspects of the "old" and the "new" new federalism', in L.A. Picard and R. Zeriski, *Subnational politics in the 1980s*, New York: Praegar.

CARROLL, JOHN E. (1982) *Acid Rain: an Issue in Canadian–American Relations*, Toronto: C.D. Howe Institute; Washington: National Planning Association.

CARROLL, JOHN E. (1983) *Environmental Diplomacy*, Ann Arbor: University of Michigan Press.

CARSON, RACHEL (1963) *Silent Spring*, London: Hamish Hamilton.

CHANDLER, WILLIAM M. (1986) 'Challenges to federalism: comparative themes', in William M. Chandler and Christian W. Zollner (eds), *Challenges to Federalism: Policy-Making in Canada and the Federal Republic of Germany*, Kingston, Ontario: Institute of Intergovernmental Relations, Queen's University.

CHOATE, PAT (1990) *Agents of Influence: How Japan's Lobbyists in the United States Manipulate America's Political and Economic System*, New York: Knopf.

CLARKSON, STEPHEN (1985) *Canada and the Reagan Challenge: Crisis and Adjustment 1981–85*, Toronto: Lorimer.

CLIFFORD, WAYNE (1981) 'The western provinces of Canada: the importance and orientation of their international relations', Edmonton, Alberta: Department of Federal and Intergovernmental Affairs, October.

COLLINS, HUGH (1983) 'Aborigines and Australian foreign policy: some underlying issues', in Coral Bell *et al.*, *Ethnic Minorities and Australian Foreign Policy*, Canberra Studies in World Affairs No 11, Canberra: Department of International Relations, Australian National University.

COMMITTEE FOR REVIEW OF EXPORT MARKET DEVELOPMENT ASSISTANCE (1989) *Australian Exports: Performance, Obstacles and Issues of Assistance*, Canberra: Australian Government Publishing Service, July.

CONKLIN, DAVID (1985) 'Options for new international agreements: an overview', in David W. Conklin and Thomas J. Courchene, *Canadian Trade at a Crossroads: Options for New International Agreements*, Toronto: Ontario Economic Council.

COOPER, ANDREW FENTON (1986) 'Subnational activity and foreign economic policy-making in Canada and the United States: perspectives on agriculture', *International Journal*, 41(3), Summer.

CROUGH, GREG and WHEELWRIGHT, TED (1982) *Australia: a Client State*, Ringwood, Vic: Penguin.

CZEMPIEL, ERNST-OTTO (1989) 'Internationalizing politics: some answers to the questions of who does what to whom', in Ernst-Otto Czempiel and James N. Rosenau (eds), *Global Changes and Theoretical Challenges: Approaches to World Politics for the 1990s*, Lexington, Mass: D.C. Heath.

DAVIS, NANCY M. (1988) 'Acid rain: no truce is in sight in the eight-year war between the states', *Governing*, 2(3), December.

DESTLER, I.M. (1986) *American Trade Politics: System Under Stress*, Washington, DC: Institute for International Economics; New York: Twentieth Century Fund.

DESTLER, I.M. (1989) 'United States trade policy making in the Uruguay Round', in Henry R. Nau, *Domestic Politics and the Uruguay Round*, New York: Columbia University Press.

DOERN, G. BRUCE and TONER, GLEN (1985) *The Politics of Energy: The Development and Implementation of the NEP*, Toronto: Methuen.

DORAN, CHARLES F. (1984) *Forgotten Partnership: US–Canada Relations Today*, Toronto: Fitzhenry & Whiteside.

DORAN, CHARLES F. and SOKOLSKY, JOEL J. (1985) *Canada and Congress: Lobbying in Washington*, Halifax: Centre for Foreign Policy Studies, Dalhousie University.

DRIVER, BRUCE and NIXON, ELIZABETH (1989) *Healing the Environment: State Options for Addressing Global Warming*, Washington: Center for Clean Air Policy.

DRUCKMAN, DANIEL (ed.) (1977) *Negotiations: Social-Psychological Perspectives*, Beverly Hill/London: Sage.

DRYSDALE, PETER and SHIBATA, HIROFUMI (1985) 'Perspectives', in Peter Drysdale and Hirofumi Shibata (eds), *Federalism and Resource Development: the Australian Case*, Sydney: Allen & Unwin in association with the Australia–Japan Research Centre, Australian National University.

DUCHACEK, IVO D. (1986) *The Territorial Dimension of Politics: Within, Among and Across Nations*, Boulder: Westview Press.
DUCHACEK, IVO D. (1988) 'Multicommunal and bicommunal politics and their international relations', in Ivo D. Duchacek, Daniel Latouche and Garth Stevenson (eds), *Perforated Sovereignties and International Relations*, New York: Greenwood Press.
DUCHACEK, IVO D. (1990) 'Perforated sovereignties: towards a typology of new actors in international relations', in Hans Michelmann and Panayotis Soldatos, *Federalism and International Relations*, Oxford: Clarendon Press.
DYMENT, DAVID (1990) 'Substate para-diplomacy: the international activities of non-sovereign governments: the case of Ontario', *Conference of the Canadian Political Science Association*, University of Victoria, British Columbia; May.
EDWARDS, P. G. (1983) *Prime Ministers and Diplomats: The Making of Australian Foreign Policy 1901–1949*, Melbourne: Oxford University Press.
EGAL, ROBERT (1985) 'Canada's acid rain policy: federal and provincial roles', in Schmandt, Jurgen and Roderick, Hilliard (eds), *Acid Rain and Friendly Neighbours: the Policy Dispute Between Canada and the United States*, Durham, NC: Duke University Press.
EISINGER, PETER (1988) *The Rise of the Entrepreneurial State: State and Local Economic Development Policy in the United States*, University of Wisconsin Press.
ELAZAR, DANIEL J. (1981) 'States as polities in the federal system', *National Civic Review*, 70(2).
ELAZAR, DANIEL J. (1986) 'Federalism, intergovernmental relations and changing models of the polity', in L. A. Picard and R. Zeriski, *Subnational politics in the 1980s*, New York: Praegar.
ENCARNATION, DENNIS J. and WELLS JR, LOUIS T. (1985) 'Sovereignty en garde: negotiating with foreign investors', *International Organization* 39(1), Winter.
FELDMAN, ELLIOTT J. and BATTIS, PRISCILLA (eds) (1987) *New North American Horizons*, Cambridge, Mass: University Consortium for Research on North America.
49TH PARALLEL INSTITUTE FOR CANADIAN–AMERICAN RELATIONS (1988) *US–Canada Free Trade: a Western Regional Perspective*, Bozeman: Montana State University.
FISHER, BRUCE H. (1988) 'The federal bureaucracy and free trade' *International Insights*, 4(1), Spring.
FOSLER, R. SCOTT (1988) *The New Economic Role of American States: Strategies in a Competitive World Economy*, New York: Oxford University Press.
FRY, EARL H. (1988) 'Trans-sovereign relations of the American states', in Ivo D. Duchacek, Daniel Latouche and Garth Stevenson (eds) *Perforated Sovereignties and International Relations*, New York: Greenwood Press, pp. 53–67.
FRY, EARL H. (1989) 'The impact of federalism on the development of international economic relations: lessons from the United States and Canada', *Australian Outlook*, 43(1), April.

GARREAU, JOEL (1981) *The Nine Nations of North America*, New York: Avon Books.

GATT SECRETARIAT (1989) The Contracting Parties to the General Agreement on Tariffs and Trade, 'Canada – Import, Distribution and Sale of Alcoholic Drinks by Canadian Provincial Marketing Agencies', *Report of the Panel*, adopted on 22 March 1988 (L/6304), in GATT, *Basic Instruments and Selected Documents, Thirty-fifth Supplement, Protocols, Decisions, Reports 1987–1988*, Geneva, June.

GATT SECRETARIAT (1989) 'Disputes taken up in the Council', *GATT Activities 1988*, Geneva: June.

GEORGE, G. W. P. (1981) 'Linkage Diplomacy and Bilateral Economic Interdependence', PhD thesis, Canberra: Australian National University.

GLEZER, LEON (1982) *Tariff Politics: Australian Policy Making 1960–1980*, Melbourne University Press.

GLICKMAN, NORMAN J. and WOODWARD, DOUGLAS P. (1988) *The New Competitors: How Foreign Investors are Changing the US Economy*, New York: Basic Books.

GOLD, MARC and LEYTON-BROWN, DAVID (eds) (1988) *Trade-offs on Free Trade: the Canada-US Free Trade Agreement*, Toronto: Carswell.

GOSS, WAYNE (1991) 'Advancing the international interests of the states', *World Review*, 30(2), June.

GOULD, ROY (1985) *Going Sour: Science and Politics of Acid Rain*, Boston: Birkhauser.

GOVERNMENT OF VICTORIA (1988) *Victoria: Trading on Achievement*, Melbourne: August 8.

GRANATSTEIN, J. L. and BOTHWELL, ROBERT (1990) *Pirouette: Pierre Trudeau and Canadian Foreign Policy*, University of Toronto Press.

GREEN, FITZHUGH (1986) 'Acid rain and US–Canadian relations', *Washington Quarterly*, 9(3), Summer.

GREENE, STEPHEN and KEATING, THOMAS (1980) 'Domestic factors and Canada–United States fisheries relations', *Canadian Journal of Political Science* 13(4), December.

GREER, SCOTT (1967) 'Urbanization, parochialism and foreign policy', in James. N. Rosenau, *Domestic Sources of Foreign Policy*, New York: Free Press.

HAGAN, JOE D. (1987) 'Regimes, political oppositions and comparative analysis of foreign policy', in Charles. F., Hermann, Charles W. Kegley Jr and James N. Rosenau (eds), *New Directions in the Study of Foreign Policy*, Boston: Allen and Unwin.

HANRIEDER WOLFRAM F. (1978) 'Dissolving international politics: reflections on the nation-state', *American Political Science Review*, 72, December.

HEAD, BRIAN (1986) 'Economic development in state and federal politics', in Brian Head (ed.), *The Politics of Development in Australia*, Sydney, Allen and Unwin.

HILL, ROGER (1985) 'An Ontario perspective on trade issues between Canada and the United States', in Deborah Fretz, Robert Stern and John Whalley, *Canada/United States Trade and Investment Issues*, Toronto: Ontario Economic Council.

HINES, W. R. (1985) *Trade Policy Making in Canada: Are We Doing it Right?*, Montreal: Institute for Research on Public Policy.

HOCKING, BRIAN (1984) 'Pluralism and foreign policy: the states and the management of Australia's external relations', *The Year Book of World Affairs.*

HOCKING, BRIAN (1986) 'Regional governments and international affairs: foreign policy problem or deviant behaviour?', *International Journal*, 41(3) Summer.

HOCKING, BRIAN (1990) 'Bringing the "outside" in: the role and nature of foreign interest lobbying', *Corruption and Reform*, 50.

HOLMES, JEAN and SHARMAN, CAMPBELL (1977) *The Australian Federal System*, Sydney: George Allen & Unwin.

HOPKINS, RAYMOND F. (1976) 'The international role of "domestic" bureaucracy', *International Organization*, 30.

HUGHES, BARRY B. *et al.* (1985) *Energy in the Global Arena: Actors, Values, Policies and Futures*, Durham, NC: Duke University Press.

INGRAM, HELEN M. and FIEDERLEIN, SUZANNE L. (1988) 'Traversing boundaries: a public policy approach to the analysis of foreign policy', *Western Political Quarterly*, 41(4), September.

INGRAM, HELEN M. and GODWIN, R. KENNETH (eds), (1985) *Public Policy and the Natural Environment*, Greenwich, Conn: JAI Press.

JACKSON, JOHN H., LOUIS, JEAN-VICTOR and MATSUSHITA, MITSUO (1984) *Implementing the Tokyo Round: National Constitutions and International Economic Roles*, Ann Arbor: University of Michigan Press.

JENSEN, LLOYD (1982) *Explaining Foreign Policy*, Englewood Cliffs, NJ: Prentice-Hall.

JOHANNSON, P. R. (1977–8) 'Provincial international activities', *International Journal*, 33.

JOHNSON, JON R. and SCHACHTER, JOEL S. (1988) *The Free Trade Agreement: a Comprehensive Guide*, Aurora, Ont.: Canada Law Book Inc.

KARVONEN, LAURI and SUNDELIUS, BENGT (1987) *Internationalization and Foreign Policy Management*, Aldershot: Gower.

KARVONEN, LAURI and SUNDELIUS, BENGT (1990) 'Interdependence and foreign policy management in Sweden and Finland', *International Studies Quarterly*, 34.

KEATING, MICHAEL and JONES, BARRY (eds) (1985) *Regions in the European Community*, Oxford: Clarendon Press.

KEATING, TOM and MUNTON, DON (eds) (1985) *The Provinces and Canadian Foreign Policy*, Toronto: Canadian Institute of International Affairs. (proceedings of a conference held at the University of Alberta, 28–30 March 1985.)

KEOHANE, ROBERT O., and NYE, JOSEPH S. (1972) *Transnational Relations and World Politics*, Cambridge, Mass: Harvard University Press.

KEOHANE, ROBERT O. and NYE, JOSEPH S. (1977) *Power and Interdependence: World Politics in Transition*, Boston: Little, Brown.

KETTNER, BONNI RAINES (1980) 'Canadian Federalism and the International Activities of Three Provinces: Alberta, Ontario and Quebec', MA thesis, Simon Fraser University.

KINCAID, JOHN (1984) 'The American governors in international affairs', *Publius* 14(4)4.
KINCAID, JOHN (1990) 'State and local governments go international', *Intergovernmental Perspective*, 16(2).
KLINE, JOHN M. (1983) *State Government Influence in US International Economic Policy*, Lexington, Mass: Lexington Books.
LATOUCHE, DANIEL (1988) 'State building and foreign policy at the subnational level', in Ivo D. Duchacek, Daniel Latouche and Garth Stevenson (eds) *Perforated Sovereignties and International Relations*, New York: Greenwood Press.
LEESON, HOWARD A. (1973) *External Affairs and Canadian Federalism: the History of a Dilemma*, Toronto: Holt, Rinehart and Winston.
LEJEUNE, YVES (1990) 'Belgium', in Hans J. Michelmann, and Panayotis Soldatos, (eds), *Federalism and International Relations*, Oxford: Clarendon Press.
LEMOV, PENELOPE (1991) 'Europe and the States: free trade but no free lunch', *Governing*, January.
LEVINE, JERRY (1989) *Going Global: a Strategy for Regional Cooperation*, Denver, Col: Western Governors' Association, July.
LEVY, THOMAS A. (1974) 'Some Aspects of the Role of the Canadian Provinces in International Affairs', Ph.D thesis, Duke University.
LEVY, THOMAS A. (1975) 'The international economic interests and activities of the Atlantic provinces', *American Review of Canadian Studies* 5(1).
LEWIS, KEVIN P. (1987) 'Dealing with South Africa: the constitutionality of state and local divestment legislation', *Tulane Law Review*, 61(3), February.
LEYTON-BROWN, DAVID (1987) 'The political economy of Canada–US relations' in Brian W. Tomlin and Maureen Appel Molot, *Canada Among Nations 1986: Talking Trade*, Toronto: Lorimer.
LEYTON-BROWN, DAVID (1988) 'The softwood lumber dispute', paper prepared for the 1988 Pearson-Dickey Conference on *Federalism and Regional Politics: Challenges to American–Canadian Diplomacy*, Dartmouth College, Hanover New Hampshire, 10–12 November.
LINER, BLAINE (1990) 'States and Localities in the Global Marketplace', *Intergovernmental Perspective*, 16(2), Spring.
LOVE, JANICE (1985) *The US Anti-Apartheid Movement: Local Activism in Global Politics*, New York: Praegar.
LUARD, EVAN (1990) *The Globalization of Politics: the Changed Focus of Political Action in the Modern World*, London: Macmillan.
LUBIN, MARTIN (1988) 'New England, New York and their Francophone neighbourhood', in Ivo D. Duchacek, Daniel Latouche and Garth Stevenson (eds), *Perforated Sovereignties and International Relations*, New York: Greenwood Press.
MACLURE, JEFFREY (1983) 'North American Acid Rain and International Law', *Fletcher Forum*, 7, Winter.
MACNEILL, JIM (1989–90) 'The greening of world politics', *International Journal* 45(1), Winter.
MANNING, BAYLESS (1977) 'The Congress, the executive and intermestic affairs', *Foreign Affairs*, 55, January.

MARTIN, PAUL (1968) *Federalism and International Relations*, Ottawa: Queen's Printer.

MARZO, LUIGI DI (1980) *Component Units of Federal States and International Agreements*, Netherlands: Sijthoff and Noordhoff.

MCCORMICK, JOHN (1989) *Acid Earth: The Global threat of Acid Pollution* (2nd edn), London: Earthscan.

MCKENNA, PETER L. (1985) 'Where has the acid rain gone?', *International Insights*, 1(1) Spring.

MCKINSEY, LAUREN S. (1988) 'Federalism and regional politics: Challenges to American–Canadian Diplomacy', paper prepared for the 1988 Pearson-Dickey Conference on *Federalism and Regional Politics: Challenges to American–Canadian Diplomacy*, Dartmouth College, Hanover, New Hampshire, November 10–12.

MéNY, YVES (1985) 'French regions in the European Community', in Michael Keating and Barry Jones (eds), *Regions in the European Community*, Oxford: Clarendon Press.

MICHELMANN, HANS J. (1986) 'Federalism and international relations in Canada and the Federal Republic of Germany', *International Journal*, 41(3), Summer.

MICHELMANN, HANS J. (1990) 'The Federal Republic of Germany', in Hans J. Michelmann and Panayotis Soldatos (eds), *Federalism and International Relations: the Role of Subnational Units*, Oxford: Clarendon Press.

MICHELMANN, HANS J. and SOLDATOS, PANAYOTIS (eds), (1990) *Federalism and International Relations: the Role of Subnational Units*, Oxford: Clarendon Press.

MOON, CHUNG-IN (1988) 'Complex interdependence and transnational lobbying: South Korea in the United States', *International Studies Quarterly*, 32(1), March.

MORRISS, ANDREW (1985) 'Supporting structures for resolving environmental disputes among friendly neighbours', in Jurgen Schmandt and Hilliard Roderick, (eds), *Acid Rain and Friendly Neighbours: the Policy Dispute Between Canada and the United States*, Durham, NC: Duke University Press.

MORSE, EDWARD L. (1976) *Modernization and the Transformation of International Relations*, New York: Free Press.

MUMME, STEPHEN P. (1985) 'State influence in foreign policy making: water related environmental disputes along the United States–Mexican border', *Political Quarterly*, 38(4), December.

MUNTON, DON (1985) 'Conflict over common property: Canada–US environmental issues', in M. A. Molot and B. W. Tomlin, *Canada Among Nations, 1987: A World of Conflict*, Toronto: Lorimer.

NASS, KLAUS OTTO (1989) 'The foreign and European policy of the German Lander', *Publius*, 19(4) Fall.

NATIONAL ASSOCIATION OF STATE DEVELOPMENT AGENCIES (1988) *State Export Program Database, Fiscal Year 1987–1988*, Washington, DC.

NATIONAL GOVERNORS' ASSOCIATION (1989) *America in Transition: the International Frontier; Report of the Task Force on Foreign Markets*, Washington, DC.

NOSSAL, KIM RICHARD (1986) '"Micro-diplomacy": the case of Ontario and economic sanctions against South Africa', in William M.Chandler and Christian W.Zollner (eds), *Challenges to Federalism: Policy-Making in Canada and the Federal Republic of Germany*, Kingston, Ontario: Institute of Intergovernmental Relations, Queen's University.

OFFICE OF STATE SERVICES (1986) National Governors' Association, *Program Brief: International Trade*, Washington, DC: November.

OLIVA, PAUL V. (1988) *State Overseas Operations: August 1988*, Sacramento: California State World Trade Commission.

O'NEILL, HUGH (1990) 'The role of the states in trade development', *Proceedings of the Academy of Political Science*, 37(4).

ONTARIO MINISTRY OF INDUSTRY TRADE AND TECHNOLOGY (1985) *How to Export*, Toronto.

ONTARIO MINISTRY OF INDUSTRY, TRADE AND TECHNOLOGY (1987) *Annual Report 1986–1987*, Toronto.

ONTARIO, MINISTRY OF INDUSTRY, TRADE AND TECHNOLOGY (1989) *The Competitive Advantage*, Toronto.

PARK, CHRIS C., (1987) *Acid Rain: Rhetoric and Reality*, London: Methuen.

PILCHER, DANIEL E. and PROFFER, LANNY (1985) *The States and International Trade: New Roles in Export Development – A Legislator's Guide*, Denver, Col.: National Conference of State Legislatures.

PILKINGTON, MARILYN L. (1988) 'Free trade and constitutional jurisdiction', in Mark Gold and David Leyton Brown, *Trade-Offs on Free Trade: the Canada–US Free Trade Agreement*, Toronto: Carswell.

PIPER, DON C. and TERCHEK, RONALD J. (eds) (1983) *Interaction: Foreign Policy and Public Policy*, Washington DC: American Enterprise Institute for Public Policy Research.

PIRAGES, DENNIS (1978) *Global Ecopolitics: the New Context for International Relations*, North Scituate, Mass: Duxbury.

POHL, GERHARD (1989) 'Trade policy making in China', in Henry R. Nau, (ed.), *Domestic Trade Politics and the Uruguay Round*, New York: Columbia University Press.

PUTNAM, ROBERT D. (1988) 'Diplomacy and domestic politics: the logic of two-level games', *International Organization* 42(3), Summer.

QUINN, JOHN (1985) 'Federalism and foreign economic relations', *Canada–United States Law Journal*, 10.

RAIFFA, HOWARD (1982) *The Art and Science of Negotiation*, Cambridge, Mass: Harvard University Press.

REGENS, JAMES L. (1985) 'The political economy of acid rain', *Publius*, 15, Summer.

REGENS, JAMES L. and RYCROFT, ROBERT W. (1988) *The Acid Rain Controversy*, University of Pittsburgh Press.

REICH, ROBERT B. (1991) *The Work of Nations: Preparing Ourselves for 21st-Century Capitalism*, New York: Knopf.

REPORT OF THE AD HOC WORKING COMMITTEE ON AUSTRALIA–JAPAN RELATIONS (1975) (Myer Report), Canberra: Australian Government Publishing Service.

RITCHIE, GORDON (1988) 'The negotiating process' in John Crispo (ed.) *Free Trade: the Real Story*, Toronto: Gage.

RIX, ALAN (1987) 'Japan's comprehensive security and Australia', *Australian Outlook*, 41(2), August.

ROBERTS, JOHN (1986) 'The diplomacy of acid rain: the North American experience in global perspective', in A. K. Henrikson (ed.), *Negotiating World Order: the Artisanship and Architecture of Global Diplomacy*, Wilmington, Del.: Scholarly Resources.

ROBERTSON, GORDON (1987) 'Federalism, the provinces and foreign policy', *International Perspectives*, September/October.

ROSENAU, JAMES N. (1988) 'Patterned chaos in global life: structure and process in the two worlds of world politics', *International Political Science Review*, 9(4) October.

ROSENAU, JAMES N. (1990) *Turbulence in World Politics: a Theory of Change and Continuity*, London: Harvester Wheatsheaf.

RUMBLE, GARY A. (1984) 'Federalism, external affairs and treaties: recent developments in Australia', *Case Western Reserve Journal of International Law*, 17(1).

RUTAN, GERARD F. (1988) 'Micro-diplomatic relations in the Pacific Northwest: Washington State–British Columbia interactions', in Ivo D. Duchacek, Daniel Latouche and Garth Stevenson (eds), *Perforated Sovereignties and International Relations*, New York: Greenwood Press.

SAMUELS, RICHARD J. (1983) *The Politics of Regional Policy in Japan: Localities Incorporated?*, Princeton University Press.

SAWER, GEOFFREY (1956) *Australian Federal Politics and Law 1901–1929*, Melbourne University Press.

SCHMANDT, JURGEN and RODERICK, HILLIARD (eds) (1985) *Acid Rain and Friendly Neighbours: the Policy Dispute Between Canada and the United States*, Durham, NC: Duke University Press.

SCHWAB, SUSAN C. (1990) 'Building a national export development alliance', *Intergovernmental Perspective*, 16(2), Spring.

SHEARER, RONALD A. (1985) 'Regionalism and international trade policy', in John Whalley, *Canada–United States Free Trade*, University of Toronto Press.

SHETH, D. L. (1983) 'Grass roots stirrings and the future of politics', *Alternatives*, 9, Summer.

SHUMAN, MICHAEL H. (1986–7) 'Dateline Main Street: local foreign policies', *Foreign Policy*, 65, Winter.

SHUMAN, MICHAEL (1990) 'What the framers really said about foreign policy powers', *Intergovernmental Perspective*, 16(2), Spring.

SIMEON, RICHARD (1972) *Federal–Provincial Diplomacy: the Making of Recent Policy in Canada*, University of Toronto Press.

SMITH, MURRAY G. (1986) 'Closing a trade deal: the provinces' role', C. D. Howe Institute, *Commentary*, 11.

SMITH, STEVE (1984) 'Foreign policy analysis and interdependence', in R. J. Jones, Barry Jones and P. Willetts, *Interdependence on Trial: Studies in the Theory and Reality of Contemporary Interdependence*, London: Pinter.

SMITH, STEVE and CLARKE, MICHAEL (eds) (1985) *Foreign Policy Implementation*, London: George Allen and Unwin.

SPERO, JOAN EDELMAN (1990) *The Politics of International Economic Relations* (fourth edition), London: Unwin Hyman.

SPIRO, PETER J. (1986) 'State and local anti-South Africa action', *Virginia Law Review*, 72, May.

SPIRO, PETER J. (1988) 'Taking foreign policy away from the Feds', *Washington Quarterly*, Winter.

SPIRO, PETER J. (1990) 'The limits of federalism in foreign policymaking', *Intergovernmental Perspective*, 16(2), Spring.

STAIRS, DENIS and WINHAM, GILBERT R. (1985) *The Politics of Canada's Economic Relationship with the United States*, University of Toronto Press.

STEVENSON, GARTH (1976) *Mineral Resources and Australian Federalism*, Canberra: Centre for Research on Federal Financial Relations, Australian National University.

STEVENSON, GARTH (1976) 'The control of foreign direct investment in a federation: Canadian and Australian experience', in R. M. Burns *et al.*, *Political and Administrative Federalism* (Research Monograph 14), Canberra: Centre for Research on Federal Financial Relations, Australian National University.

STEVENSON, GARTH (1981) 'Western alienation in Australia and Canada', in Larry Pratt and Garth Stevenson (eds), *Western Separatism: the Myths, Realities and Dangers*, Edmonton: Hurtig.

STOKE, HAROLD W. (1931) *The Foreign Relations of the Federal State*, Baltimore: Johns Hopkins Press.

SULLIVAN, R. E. (1987) 'Jurisdiction to negotiate and implement free trade agreements in Canada: calling the provincial bluff', *University of Western Ontario Law Review*, 24.

SWANSON, ROGER F. (1978) *Intergovernmental Perspectives on the Canada–US Relationship*, New York University Press.

SYMONS, JOHN (1984) 'An unjust tax exposed', *BAT Industries Outlook*, 2, December.

TATZ, COLIN (1979) *Race Politics in Australia: Aborigines, Politics and Law*, Armidale: University of New England Publishing Unit.

TINKER, HUGH (1977) *Race, Conflict and the International Order: from Empire to United Nations*, London: Macmillan.

TOLCHIN, MARTIN and TOLCHIN, SUSAN (1989) *Buying into America: How Foreign Money is Changing the Face of Our Nation*, New York: Berkeley.

TOMLIN, BRIAN W. (1989) 'The stages of prenegotiation: the decision to negotiate North American Free Trade', *International Journal*, 44(2), Spring.

TWIGGS, JOAN E. (1987) *The Tokyo Round of Multilateral Trade Negotiations: a Case Study in Building Domestic Support for Diplomacy*, Lanham: University Press of America.

ULLMAN, R. H. (1987) 'Redefining security', *International Security*, 8(1), August.

UNDERDAL, ARILD (1987) 'What's left for the MFA? Foreign policy and the management of external relations in Norway', *Cooperation and Conflict*, 22(3).

UNITED STATES SENATE (1986) *Negotiation of United States–Canada Free Trade Agreement: Hearings before the Committee on Finance*, United States Senate, Ninety-ninth Congress, 11 April 1986, Washington DC: US Government Printing Office.

VILE, M. J. C. (1961) *The Structure of American Federalism*, Oxford University Press.

WALKER, LEE (1989) *Economic Development in the States, vol.2, The Changing Arena: State Strategic Economic Development*, Council of State Governments.

WALKER, R. B. J. and MENDLOVITZ, SAUL H. (1984) 'Peace, politics and contemporary social movements', in Saul H. Mendlovitz, and R. B. J. Walker, (eds), *Towards a Just World Peace*: Perspectives from Social Movements, London: Butterworths.

WARHURST, JOHN (1980) *State Governments and Australian Tariff Policy* (Research Monograph No. 33), Canberra: Centre for Research on Federal Financial Relations, Australian National University.

WARHURST, JOHN, STEWART, JENNY and HEAD, BRIAN (1988) 'The promotion of industry', in Brian Galligan (ed.), *Comparative State Policies*, Melbourne: Longman Cheshire.

WATTS, RONALD L. (1970) *Administration in Federal Systems*, London: Hutchinson.

WESTERN PREMIERS' CONFERENCE (1989) *Western Trade Objectives: Report of the Western Ministers Responsible for Multilateral Trade Negotiations to the Premiers of British Columbia, Alberta, Saskatchewan, Manitoba*, Western Premiers' Conference, Camrose, Alberta, June 27–28.

WINHAM, GILBERT R. (1978–9) 'Bureaucratic politics and Canadian negotiation', *International Journal*, 34(1), Winter.

WINHAM, GILBERT R. (1979–80) 'International negotiation in an age of transition', *International Journal*, 35(1), Winter.

WINHAM, GILBERT R. (1980) 'Robert Strauss, the MTN and the control of faction', *Journal of World Trade Law* 14(5).

WINHAM, GILBERT R. (1986) *International Trade and the Tokyo Round Negotiation*, Princeton University Press.

WINHAM, GILBERT R. (1988) *Trading with Canada: the Canada–US Free Trade Agreement*, New York: Priority Press.

WRIGHT, DEIL S. (1982) *Understanding Intergovernmental Relations* (second edition), Monterey, Cal.: Brooks/Cole.

ZARTMAN, I. WILLIAM (1978) (ed.) *The Negotiation Process: Theories and Applications*, Beverly Hills/London: Sage.

ZARTMAN, I.WILLIAM (1989) 'Prenegotiation: phases and functions', *International Journal*, 44(2), Spring.

ZARTMAN, I. WILLIAM and BERMAN, MAUREEN R. (1982) *The Practical Negotiator*, New Haven: Yale University Press.

Index

Lightning Source UK Ltd.
Milton Keynes UK
UKOW02f0921300316

271167UK00001B/6/P

9 781349 229659